CW00435329

Hillwalking in Wales

Vol. 1

Front cover: The Mermaid's Pool, Cwm Rhiwnant

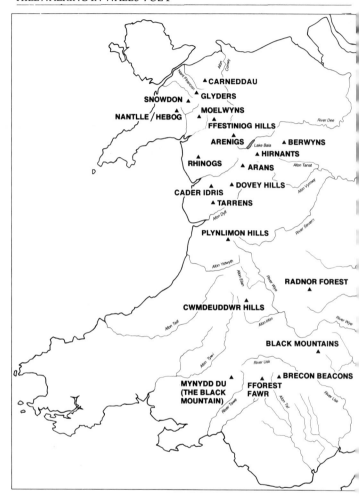

Hillwalking in Wales

ARRANGED ALPHABETICALLY IN MOUNTAIN GROUPS

Vol. 1
(Arans - Dovey Hills)

by

Peter Hermon

CICERONE PRESS
MILNTHORPE, CUMBRIA

© Peter Hermon 1991
ISBN 1 85284 081 1
First published 1991
Reprinted1996

To David
my first companion on the hills

"The hills are beautiful. They are beautiful in
line and form and colour; they are beautiful in
purity, in their simplicity and in their freedom;
they bring repose, contentment and good health."

F.S.Smythe

Acknowledgements
I would like to thank Pam Boswell for preparing some early
drafts before I had learned to use a word processor myself;
Juliet Ryde for checking the whole draft and Don Sargeant for
drawing the maps. Most of the photographs are my own, but I
am also indebted to the following for permission to use some of
their pictures: Celtic Picture Agency; Hamish Brown; Douglas
Milner; Roger Redfern; Maurice and Marion Teal; Peter Wild.

CONTENTS

Craig Cywarch

PREFACE

These two volumes are for all those who derive happiness, challenge, excitement or peace of mind from walking in the hills. Indeed if you are as lucky as I am, you will enjoy all those emotions at the same time. What I have tried to do is to provide a comprehensive guide to walkers' routes up all the 2000ft mountains in Wales, at the same time indicating ways to view the mountain lakes they nurture. While it would be foolish to claim to have covered all the routes, I am not conscious of having omitted any of note.

Some of the routes are easy, others more strenuous. All tastes are catered for, from those seeking to capture something of the spirit of the hills in short half-day walks, to real 'tigers' whose aims are to stride the long ridge walks or to bag as many summits as possible. Most of the routes cover the high ground over 2000ft, but there are lower-level expeditions as well. All are suitable for the hillwalker and no climbing skills are required. However, proper precautions are necessary in winter, as they are for any excursion into wild and remote places.

People visit the hills for many reasons. Some come to pursue an interest in rocks or plantlife. Others are attracted by legends and traces of past civilisations, or wish to practise the arts of photography or rock climbing. While I do not cater specifically for any one of these tastes, I hope that by describing ways over, across and through the hills I shall have something of value for all of them, as well as for the many who love the hills for themselves - 'because they are there'.

As someone who has walked the English and Welsh hills for upwards of 25 years I am often asked which I like best - Lakeland, the Pennines, Wales? To this question I always give the same simple answer: 'I like them all best'. Having said that, less has been written about the Welsh hills - this is an attempt to redress the balance.

There is another balance I would like to correct. The Welsh hills cover a vast area from the Nantlle ridge in the west to the Radnor Forest in the east, from the Carneddau in the north to the Brecon Beacons in the south. Yet it is probably true to say that 90% of all the hill-miles walked in Wales are within a five-mile radius of the top of Snowdon. There is thus a whole universe of new peaks waiting to be discovered, more days in the hills to be enjoyed. So whilst denying nothing to the peaks of Snowdonia, my aim is to cover all the Welsh hills equally thoroughly.

One final point on access; please remember that all the land in Wales belongs to someone and that the legal situation is complex. Put simply, the only legal right of a hillwalker is to be on a public footpath. Many of the routes in this book extend well beyond the range of public footpaths, and though no problems on access usually arise with well behaved parties, it is as well to remember that such access is a privilege and not a right. It should not be taken for granted. Therefore if you are ever in doubt as to whether a right of way exists or not, always seek permission from the local farmer first and then, if he agrees, please adhere to the Country Code.

Good luck and happy rambling

Peter Hermon, 1991

INTRODUCTION

For ease of description I have divided the mountains into 21 groups arranged alphabetically in two volumes. Each is the subject of a separate chapter. Each chapter starts with a list of the 2000ft peaks and mountain lakes in its area. Rather than invent yet another definition of what constitutes a 2000ft peak, I have relied instead on existing lists between which there are, in any case, only minor variations.

In doing this I have included every peak that a hillwalker would recognise as a genuine 2000 footer in its own right. Also included are a few peaks that just miss the magical 2000ft barrier but which are obviously real mountains and fun to climb. On the other hand I have sometimes omitted mere tops that might qualify technically by the quirk of some contour line, but which on the ground clearly lack the presence one expects from a separate mountain. When all is said and done, I do not think my lists will cause many surprises. (I use the terms 'peaks' and 'top' more or less interchangeably in this book and without any technical significance.)

The lakes present a more difficult problem. What exactly is a mountain lake? Clearly there is no simple answer. Some of the prettiest tarns and lakes are too small for inclusion on the map; others come and go with the weather, or even with successive revisions of the OS maps! I have therefore had to rely heavily on judgement in my treatment of lakes. In any event I have restricted myself to lakes in the immediate vicinity of each mountain group that have an altitude of at least 1000ft. It would be pedantic in these circumstance to aim for consistency, but I hope that any anomalies which may have crept in are not serious ones.

With the field of endeavour thus set out, I next give a brief overview of the group before getting to the heart of the matter with descriptions of (hopefully) all the routes up each peak that are likely to be of interest to hillwalkers. An interesting route in this context can mean several things: it may be a route with fine views or good scrambling; a route that is useful as a link in planning a longer multi-peak expedition; or simply a route that gives a quick way home at the end of a long day.

Most of the routes I describe are direct ones, i.e. ways to the top which do not cross any other summit en route. Non-direct routes, such as those along connecting ridges, are usually included as part of the high-level walks. However, there are a few cases where the lie of the land would make it artificial to follow this guideline exclusively. Most routes are described as ascents, but as every hillwalker knows there are some routes which intuitively seem more natural as a way down. Where this is so they are described as descents.

Once the routes for individual peaks have been given, the way is clear to introduce more varied expeditions. First come high-level walks, by which I normally mean routes taking in more than one of the 2000ft peaks. Many of these are ridge walks of the sort that give the very best days in the hills. Sometimes, however, the high ground is too broad for the term 'ridge' to be appropriate; in other cases there may be a pass to be crossed. To keep this section within reasonable bounds my suggestions are restricted to combinations falling wholly within one of my defined mountain groups. Thus I do not cover more ambitious walks such as expeditions stretching over both the Berwyns and Arans, or straddling the four South Wales groups, or serious challenges like climbing all 14 of the Welsh 3000 footers in a single day.

Next come the lower-level walks. These are generally easier than the high-level walks. However, a few of them are quite exacting as my definition of lower-level is simply any walk that does not cross one of the recognised 2000 footers! This still leaves some pretty stiff, but at the same time excellent expeditions, especially in the foothills surrounding the main ranges.

Not even the hardiest walkers always feel like tramping the tops, so I also give some suggestions for easier days. (In many chapters, where it is difficult to draw a distinction, the lower-level and easier day sections are combined.) These generally keep to lower ground and are suitable for days when the weather causes a late start or when the height of ambition is for a lazy day lying in the heather or picnicking by a mountain stream. They may also appeal to the more elderly hillwalker. Shortened versions of some of the other walks can, of course, also be used to give easier days.

My suggestions for lower-level walks and easier days are little more than the tip of the iceberg. They are almost incidental to my main purpose of covering the high ground as fully as I can, and to have gone further would have meant extending the scope and size of these volumes beyond all reasonable bounds. In any case the reader will have no difficulty, and hopefully a lot of fun, in constructing many other walks from the 'building bricks' provided by my suggested routes which between them include visits to the shores of all the lakes; or, in a few instances, to nearby vantage points.

As few walkers are likely to have a chauffeur, paid or otherwise, most of the walks return the climber to his starting point at the end of the day. However a few point-to-point traverses are classics, too good to be missed, and so they too are included, transportation difficulties notwithstanding. All of the walks are intended for completion in a day, although clearly this will depend on the dedication and fitness of the party.

To avoid repetition as far as possible, common sections of different routes are usually only described once and then cross referenced to one other. This is particularly the case with the high-level walks as these are often based on combinations of routes up the different peaks. I realise that it can be frustrating when reading a description to have to refer elsewhere but, with the way routes in mountains tend to interleave, anything else would soon lead to tiresome repetition. Nevertheless I have tried to strike a balance between extremes.

In describing the routes I have tried to avoid too much of the 'follow the hedge, take the second gate R, cross a field, turn L at the stile' sort of description. In my experience this soon becomes confusing and ambiguous, however careful the instructions. I have therefore tended, more than some writers, to quote directions (N, SW etc), map references and the occasional grid bearing (do not forget to allow for the magnetic variation when setting your compass!). Bearings should only be regarded as approximate. Mountain paths usually twist and turn and so it is not always possible to give more than a broad indication and you should always check directly with the map yourself. (Incidentally, where I use (say) N this is an abbreviation for any of north, northern or northerly, according to context.)

It goes without saying that my descriptions are not meant to be complete in themselves but should be read in conjunction with, and as a supplement to, careful study of the map. No one should venture on serious hillwalking unless he/she is fully adept at map reading and the use of a compass. In this respect the 1:25,000 series of OS maps, on which I have relied heavily for the areas for which it exists, is much to be preferred to the older 1:50,000 series.

As I am primarily concerned with the uplands I have generally started my routes from a convenient point on the nearest road on which a family car can sensibly be driven and parked. Parking may not always be easy, and late risers may sometimes have a slightly longer walk, but with this proviso parking is usually possible near my suggested starting points. Obviously this leaves open a multiplicity of approaches in the lower reaches. These I leave to readers' own ingenuity.

All of the walks are within the competence of a normally fit and active person provided the weather is kind. However, in wintry conditions it is a different story and serious problems may arise. Walks that are simple enough in summer may turn out to be surprisingly hazardous when snow or ice is about. No one should venture out on the high ground in winter without being properly equipped and knowing how to handle the extreme conditions that may arise.

No climbing technique is called for. When I refer to 'scrambling' it only means the occasional use of hands to steady oneself on loose boulders or, very rarely, getting into a sitting position to ease oneself over a particularly awkward rock. Rather than being anything to worry about, elementary scrambling of this kind can often add zest to a day's outing. Having said that, most of my routes could be undertaken with hands in pockets all the way!

I have not given timing estimates. In my experience these depend on so many factors - weather, fitness, experience, size of party, morale, footwear, route-finding ability, use of camera etc - that they are virtually meaningless when quoted in isolation. Most people soon learn from their own practical experience what they are comfortable with and how to judge a walk from the map. The only point I would make is the obvious one: until you know what you are capable of always err on the side of caution; hillwalking is more exacting than it seems.

Now, let me return to the field of endeavour. To many of their admirers the Welsh hills mean, if not just Snowdon, then at most Snowdonia (that popular area to the N of Porthmadoc and to the W of Betws-y-Coed). This is both natural and understandable, for therein lies all the very highest ground, including all 14 of the 3000 footers. Nowhere else in Wales is there such a concentration of raw rugged splendour, the feeling of latent power, as when one bestrides Snowdon itself, Tryfan, the Glyders, the broad rolling uplands of the Carneddau and their lower acolytes.

Yet there is much more in Wales: not another Snowdonia, not something better, not a lesser creation, but hills with their own unique charms. The Black Mountains with their expansive, whale-backed, grassy ridges; the precipitous escarpments of the Brecon Beacons; the strange uplands of the Cwmdeuddwr hills; Plynlimon and its unknown valleys; the heather-clad Berwyns.

Further N the hills start to shed some of their softness and assume the rockier profiles one associates with Snowdonia. The grassy tops of the Dovey and Tarren hills face the corries and cwms of Cader Idris; the E cliffs of the Arans yield nothing in severity to the Glyders. The Arenigs offer the walker the widest choice of all from the vast solitudes of the Migneint, through Arenig Fawr and the rolling moors of the Lliw Valley to the shapely top of Dduallt. Then there are the Rhinogs and the wildest land in Wales.

The point is not that these hills and the others in S and Central Wales are in any sense 'better' than the mountains in the N, but that they are 'there', each with their own special attractions and each offering more grand days in the hills. It is for this reason and in the spirit of more worlds for the walker to 'conquer' that I cover these lesser known hills as comprehensively as the better known heights of Snowdonia.

*   *   *

It is useful to summarise the structure of each of the chapters covering the 21 mountain groups. It is as follows:

A list of the peaks and lakes in the group.

A diagrammatic map of the group.

A general overview of the group.

13

The main ways up each of the peaks.
High-level walks.
Lower-level walks.
Walks for easier days.

All routes are numbered. Each number begins with a two-letter prefix to identify the mountain group concerned (eg RG stands for the Rhinogs). The main routes are then numbered sequentially (eg RG1, RG2, etc). Localised variations within routes are distinguished by numeric suffixes (eg RG2,1). High-level, lower-level, and easy day walks are given H, L, and E designators respectively after the mountain group code (eg in the case of the Rhinogs high-level walks are numbered RG H1, RG H2 etc).

The maps are diagrammatic only and should in no way be regarded as a substitute for the proper OS map. Their purpose is to show the relationships between the various routes in the simplest and most uncluttered way. Details of towns, roads, streams etc are therefore only shown to the extent needed to give a general sense of whereabouts and are not necessarily consistent between one map and another. To avoid congestion only the main ways up each peak are shown on these maps. The other walks are not marked; nor are the local variations indicated by numeric suffixes to their route numbers.

Each peak is considered in turn (the order in which they are treated has been chosen to minimise cross-referencing and is not alphabetic or according to height). Brief introductory notes on the peak itself come first, followed by descriptions of the routes on that peak. It is advisable to gain at least a general impression of each group as a whole before concentrating on any particular peak or route.

Taken together the walks include visits to all the lakes. Except in a few cases, where it would mean a rather artificial expedition of little interest to the majority of ramblers, this means routes to the very shoreline. Otherwise it is to a nearby vantage point from where the really dedicated can make their own way. A glance at my diagrammatic maps will usually show which sections of the text to read to obtain the routes to a given lake. However, please bear in mind that these maps do not include the high-level, lower-level and easier day walks, nor the suffixed variations. (Alternatively the index gives the page numbers where directions for each peak may be found.)

Finally, there is always a difficulty over the spelling of Welsh place names - even the Ordnance Survey is not fully consistent! What I have done, therefore, is to adopt spellings from the latest available OS maps at the time of writing and standardise on those. However complete success in this would probably be too much to hope for, and I therefore apologise for any residual errors or inconsistencies.

LIST OF PEAKS

The abbreviations for the 21 groups shown in the following list are:

AG	Arenigs	FF	Fforest Fawr
AN	Arans	FG	Ffestiniog hills
BB	Brecon Beacons	GL	Glyders
BM	Mynydd Ddu	HN	Hirnants
	(Black Mountain)	NH	Nantlle/Hebog hills
BN	Berwyns	PN	Plynlimon
BS	Black Mountains	RF	Radnor forest
CA	Carneddau	SM	Siabod/Moelwyns
CI	Cader Idris	SN	Snowdon
CR	Cwmdeuddwr hills	RG	Rhinogs
DY	Dovey hills	TN	Tarrens

2000ft Peaks in Descending Order

Peak	Group	Height (ft)	Map Ref
Snowdon	SN	3560	609544
Crib y Ddysgl	SN	3493	611552
Carnedd Llewelyn	CA	3490	684644
Carnedd Dafydd	CA	3425	663631
Glyder Fawr	GL	3279	642579
Glyder Fach	GL	3262	656583
Pen yr Ole Wen	CA	3211	656619
Foel Grach	CA	3196	689659
Yr Elen	CA	3152	673651
Y Garn	GL	3104	631596
Foel Fras	CA	3092	696682
Elidir Fawr	GL	3030	612613
Crib Goch	SN	3026	624552
Tryfan	GL	3010	664594
Aran Fawddwy	AN	2969	863224
Y Lliwedd	SN	2947	622533
Penygadair	CI	2928	711131

Peak	Group	Height (ft)	Map Ref
Pen y Fan	BB	2906	012215
Aran Benllyn	AN	2901	867243
Corn Du	BB	2863	007213
Erw y Ddafad-ddu	AN	2860	865234
Moel Siabod	SM	2860	705546
Mynydd Moel	CI	2804	727137
Arenig Fawr	AG	2802	827369
Llwytmor	CA	2785	689692
Penyrhelgi-du	CA	2733	698630
Foel Goch	GL	2727	628612
Cadair Berwyn (S top)	BN	2723	072324
Moel Sych	BN	2713	066319
Craig Gwaun-taf	BB	2704	005206
Carnedd y Filiast	GL	2695	621628
Mynydd Perfedd	GL	2665	623619
Waun Fach	BS	2660	215300
Bera Bach	CA	2647	672678
Cyfrwy	CI	2646	703133
Nameless	GL	2636	678582
Bannau Brycheiniog	BM	2631	825217
Pen y Gadair Fawr	BS	2624	229287
Pen Llithrig-y-wrach	CA	2622	716623
Cribin	BB	2608	023213
Bera Mawr	CA	2604	675683
Craig y Cau	CI	2595	710122
Cadair Bronwen	BN	2572	077347
Moel Hebog	NH	2565	564469
Glasgwm	AN	2557	837195
Drum	CA	2529	708696
Moelwyn Mawr	SM	2527	658449
Waun-rydd	BB	2522	061208
Gallt yr Ogof	GL	2499	685586
Drosgl	CA	2484	664680
Y Llethr	RG	2475	661258
Plynlimon Fawr	PN	2467	789869
Moel Llyfnant	AG	2464	808352

Peak	Group	Height (ft)	Map Ref
Diffwys	RG	2462	661234
Bannau Sir Gaer	BM	2460	812218
Yr Aran	SN	2451	604515
Gwaen Cerrig-llwydion	BB	2450	055203
Tomle	BN	2431	085336
Plynlimon Arwystli	PN	2428	815877
Fan Fawr	FF	2409	970193
Craig Cwm Silyn	NH	2408	525502
Rhobell Fawr	AG	2408	787257
Fan Hir	BM	2400	830210
Craig Cwareli	BB	2393	042197
Craig Eigiau	CA	2390	714656
Moel Eilio	SN	2382	556577
Fan Gihirych	FF	2379	881191
Rhinog Fawr	RG	2362	657290
Pen Allt-mawr	BS	2360	207243
Fan y Big	BB	2358	036207
Pen Rhos Dirion	BS	2338	212334
Moelwyn Bach	SM	2334	660437
Rhinog Fach	RG	2333	665270
Trum y Ddysgl	NH	2329	544516
Black Mountain	BS	2306	255350
Twyn Tal-y-cefn	BS	2303	222324
Pen Cerrig-calch	BS	2300	217223
Garnedd Goch	NH	2296	511495
Mynydd Mawr	NH	2291	539547
Allt Fawr	SM	2287	682475
Mynydd Drws-y-coed	NH	2280	548518
Cnicht	SM	2265	645466
Foel Wen	BN	2263	100334
Twmpa	BS	2263	225350
Arenig Fach	AG	2260	821416
Foel Hafod-fynydd	AN	2260	878227
Gwaun y Llwyni	AN	2248	857205
Y Garn	PN	2244	775851
Mynydd Tawr	BN	2234	113324
Gau Craig	CI	2230	745142
Pen y Bryn-fforchog	AN	2230	818179
Chwarel y Fan	BS	2228	258294

Peak	Group	Height (ft)	Map Ref
Godor	BN	2224	095307
Creigiau Gleision	CA	2224	729615
Pen y Beacon	BS	2219	244366
Moel Druman	SM	2218	671477
Maesglasau	DY	2213	823152
Moel Cynghorion	SN	2211	586564
Ysgafell Wen	SM	2204	667481
Esgeiriau Gwynion	AN	2201	889236
Pencerrigtewion	PN	2201	798882
Waun-oer	DY	2197	785148
Carnedd y Filiast	AG	2195	871446
Plynlimon Fach	PN	2192	787875
Tarren y Gesail	TN	2186	710059
Cyrniau Nod	HN	2185	988279
Fan Nedd	FF	2176	913184
Mynydd Llysiau	BS	2173	207279
Dduallt	AG	2172	811274
Craig Las	CI	2168	676136
Manod Mawr	FG	2168	724446
Great Rhos	RF	2166	182639
Post Gwyn	BN	2165	049294
Nameless	FG	2159	727458
Pen-twyn-mawr	BS	2153	242267
Moel yr Ogof	NH	2149	556478
Mynydd Tal-y-mignedd	NH	2148	535514
Allt-lwyd	BB	2143	079189
Black Mixen	RF	2132	196644
Cribin	DY	2132	794153
Foel Cwm Sian Llwyd	HN	2125	996314
Moel yr Hydd	SM	2124	672454
Pen y Boncyn Trefeilw	HN	2119	963283
Pentwynglas	BS	2115	213257
Carnedd Llechwedd Llyfn	AG	2110	857446
Gyrn Wigau	CA	2109	654676
Drygarn Fawr	CR	2103	863584
Black Hill	BS	2102	275348
Great Creigniau	RF	2102	198636
Moel Lefn	NH	2093	553485
Y Garn	NH	2077	551526

Peak	Group	Height (ft)	Map Ref
Garreg Las	BM	2076	777202
Tarrenhendre	TN	2076	683042
Fan Llia	FF	2071	938186
Moel Fferna	BN	2066	116398
Stac Rhos	HN	2066	969278
Fan Frynych	FF	2063	957228
Foel Gron	SN	2063	560568
Y Garn	RG	2063	702230
Craig Cerrig-gleisiad	FF	2060	961218
Foel y Geifr	HN	2053	937275
Moel y Cerrig Duon	HN	2050	923241
Moel Penamnen	FG	2044	716483
Moel Ysgyfarnogod	RG	2044	658346
Pen y Castell	CA	2043	721688
Carnfachbugeilyn	PN	2041	827904
Craig-y-llyn	CI	2040	665120
Nameless	BN	2037	089369
Waen Camddwr	AN	2035	848207
Pen yr Allt-uchaf	AN	2034	871196
Gallt yr Wenallt	SN	2032	642532
Foel Boeth	AG	2031	778345
Cefn yr Ystrad	BB	2025	087137
Garreg-lwyd	BM	2020	740179
Cefn Gwyntog	HN	2017	976266
Llechwedd Du	AN	2014	894224
Gorllwyn	CR	2011	918591
Y Gyrn	BB	2010	989216
Trum y Gwrgedd	HN	2008	942284
Plynlimon Cwmbiga	PN	2008	831899
Bryn Garw	CR	2005	798771
Foel Goch	AG	2005	953423
Red Daren	BS	2003	281308
Foel Goch	HN	2001	943292
Bache Hill	RF	2001	214636
Tal-y-fan	CA	2001	729727

THE ARANS
OS maps 1:25,000 - Sheet 23   1:50,000 - Sheets 124/125

Peaks	Height (ft)	Map Ref	Page
Aran Fawddwy	2969	863224	30
Aran Benllyn	2901	867243	27
Erw y Ddafad-ddu	2860	865234	34
Glasgwm	2557	837195	39
Foel Hafod-fynydd*	2260	878227	36
Gwaun y Llwyni	2248	857205	35
Pen y Bryn-fforchog	2230	818179	41
Esgeiriau Gwynion	2201	889236	36
Waen Camddwr	2035	848207	34
Pen yr Allt-uchaf	2034	871196	35
Llechwedd Du	2014	894224	36

sometimes known as Craig Cwm-du

Mountain Lakes

Bach	2500	837196
Creiglyn Dyfi	1900	868226
Lliwbran	1475	876255
Nameless (2)	2820	866243
Nameless (2)	2820	865241
Nameless (2)	2460	860215
Nameless	2390	873213
Pen-aran (2)	2750	868247
Y Fign	2500	837194

THE ARANS

Few peaks dominate their surroundings as completely as Aran Benllyn, the lofty sentinel that stands guard over Lake Bala. This is just as well, for otherwise the Arans are self-effacing to a fault, hiding their nobility and virility from the casual passer-by behind a shield of wooded slopes and flowing green foothills. Drive down

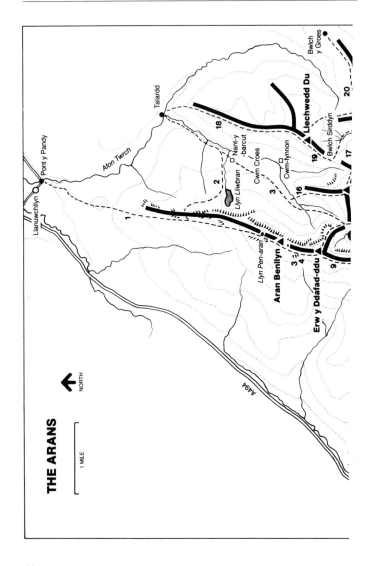

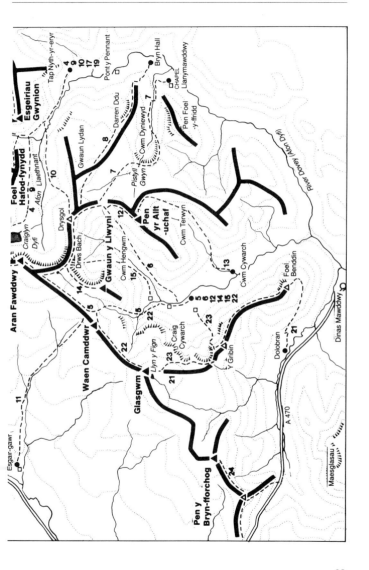

the old Roman road from Bala to Dolgellau and you will be charmed by pretty pastures, tangled woodland and tumbling streams. Charmed but not inspired. Cross Bwlch Oerddrws from Dolgellau to Dinas Mawddwy and you are more likely to admire the Dovey cwms and hills than the Arans' S fringe.

Matters only improve when you travel the third side of the Aran triangle on the narrow road that snakes through the hills from Dinas Mawddwy, over Bwlch y Groes and back to Lake Bala. Now at last you begin to be stirred rather than charmed. Fearsome hills hover ominously, even threateningly, over the pretty little village of Llanymawddwy. Farther N, where the road curls round Cwm Croes, black cliffs fleetingly arc the sky.

But enough of road work! Boots must be donned if the Arans' heartland is to be probed, and there is no better entrée than the peat-hagged ridge that forms the E flank of Cwm Croes and culminates in the two swampy outliers of Esgeiriau Gwynion and Llechwedd Du. Now for the first time the long furrowed precipice of the Arans' E face is revealed in all its splendour. Dark, menacing, unyielding, riddled with gullies, it carries the twin citadels of Aran Benllyn and Aran Fawddwy with consummate ease. No mean feat, for Aran Fawddwy is the highest point in Wales S of a line joining Tremadoc and Llanwrst, and nowhere between the two peaks does the land drop below 2700ft. Nestling beneath the cliffs are two lonely lakes: Lliwbran, sun-starved and desolate, hemmed in by barren screes and rivers of boulders; Dyfi, windswept, open to the world, birthplace of the Dovey.

So compelling is the aura of impregnability that it comes as quite a surprise to find that the emperor has feet of clay - two breaches in the ramparts give hope to the humble walker! A grassy nose sweeps down to Creiglyn Dyfi, smooth and inviting, before carrying on (albeit with diminished vigour) to the rounded grassy top of Foel Hafod-fynydd. The second line of attack hinges on Drysgol, a grassy spur overlooking the sodden moors above Llanymawddwy.

S of Drysgol the cliffs temporarily abate. The severity, however, does not as now Gwaun y Llwyni throws green slopes a stupendous 1400ft down into the depths of Hengwm. In any case the change is short-lived. The cirque at the head of Cwm Cywarch, beneath the

The Arans from Lake Bala

placid moorland tops of Glasgwm and Pen y Bryn-fforchog, restores the magic and undiminished grandeur with a massive rock face over a mile long. It is a fitting epitaph to the mountains of N Wales.

I say 'epitaph' because as you wander further S in Wales, never again will you experience such power and desolation, such wild, cold beauty. This is the moment of truth, the Rubicon; from now on softer climes prevail and thoughts centre on hills rather than mountains, on rambling rather than scrambling or climbing. Gazing N from the Aran spine the eye feasts on the impressive serrated skyline of Snowdonia. As you turn S the skylines mellow to rounded hills, the greys of crag and rock give way to the greens of turf and bracken and the higher ground becomes less thrusting, less intense, rising from meadows and pastures as often as from moorland heath. Wild Wales lives on, to be sure; but wildest Wales has gone. (Cader Idris does not fit into this neat division. Great mountain that it is, why should it? No, Cader is Wales in transition, offering the best of both worlds - the rocky grandeur of the N and the more feminine charms of the S.)

There are two cwms that thrust deeply into the heart of the Arans. In the N Cwm Croes provides ready access to Creiglyn Dyfi where a simple but tiring plod up the grassy nose gives you the main ridge, midway between Benllyn and Fawddwy on the bare plateau of Erw y Ddafad-ddu. Personally I would save that for a quick way home. Far better to tackle the N ridge head-on from Llanuwchllyn, a pearl of a walk with Benllyn's rocky crown in your sights all the way. Having achieved that, why not press on to Fawddwy across the bouldery neck (too wide to be a ridge, too narrow to be a plateau) which is dotted with vestigial tarns and mildly reminiscent of the Glyders?

The S cwm, Cywarch, is grander altogether, exuding a rugged appeal. You can do one of two things. Either climb directly out of the head of the cwm (easier than it looks), close to the tumultuous crags and with only the music of the stream for company. Or you can walk up the side of the subsidiary cwm of Hengwm, where the dark drama of crags is replaced by grassy slopes that plummet unhindered into one of the most poignantly lonely scenes in Wales.

By comparison with these the E approaches are terra incognito. (Only from the W do the Arans fail to tempt.) Start from Llanymawddwy and it matters little whether you trek Llaethnant, Cwm Dyniewyd, or Darren Ddu; the likelihood is that the only sound you will hear will be the bleating of sheep! Yet Llaethnant and Dyniewyd can hold their own in any company and are well worth exploring. Give them a chance and they will reveal aspects of the Arans that few suspect.

For instance, you can divert N out of the Llaethnant Valley into Bwlch Sirddyn. From there you can walk over to Cwm Croes, or have an easy pull up to Esgeiriau Gwynion. Esgeiriau and its environs looks a dully spongy quagmire from the road at Bwlch y Groes, not at all the sort of place to waste time on. However first impressions are not always right, and if you keep to the W rim your reward will be views of the Hirnants (not to speak of the Arans themselves) that will live in your memory. And dry feet too!

S of Glasgwm the landscape is different again, with velvety rounded ridges linking the lonely, rolling uplands that resemble the Dovey hills across the pass more than they do the giants that bear down so harshly on Creiglyn Dyfi and Cywarch less than two miles away.

As you can see, the Arans are hills of many parts.

Note: For many years the Arans suffered from difficulties over access. The problems have recently been resolved by the landowners agreeing a number of so-called 'permitted paths'. These are clearly marked on OS maps, in addition to which they are prominently displayed on notice-boards at strategic points around the Arans (eg at the start of the N ridge route at Llanuwchllyn, at Cwm Cywarch, at 875205 where the permitted path up Drysgol begins and at Esgair-gawr Farm). As the arrangements are subject to regular review I have not detailed them in this book. You should therefore always check the current situation before setting out. Please also note that many of my routes go beyond the permitted paths as defined at the time of writing. Special permission should therefore be sought from landowners before you use them. Acting in this way you will help ensure the continuance of harmonious arrangements for the future.

ARAN BENLLYN

Aran Benllyn fully justifies the high hopes it raises from Bala. The N ridge (the usual ascent) is a beauty with views that reach a thrilling climax as you finally mount the airy boulder-strewn top. The slumbering giant N is Arenig Fawr, chaperoned by Moel Llyfnant and its lesser half, Arenig Fach (guardian of the marshy Migneint). Behind them lies the long tapering line of Foel Goch and Carnedd y Filiast, and the hazy outline of Snowdonia. W are the rambling moors that rise to Rhobell Fawr and Dduallt before culminating in the Rhinogs.

In contrast to this, the outlook E is a case of 'all passion spent'. No pinnacles, no crags, just the rounded slopes of the Hirnant hills with the Berwyns arcing the sky beyond, dreary when the sky is overcast but strangely enticing when speckled by shafts of sunlight or powdered with snow.

To the S a spacious stony ridge leads on to Aran Fawddwy giving glimpses of Cader Idris, the Tarren and Dovey hills, and Plynlimon. The ridge is a grand walk, nowhere difficult and de

Aran Benllyn from Erw y Ddafad-ddu

rigueur if you have got this far. Never dropping below 2700ft and graced with tiny tarns, it conveys an infectious 'top-of-the-world' feeling similar to the Glyders, despite the difference in scale.

A word of warning. The E face of Aran Benllyn is not to be trifled with. You should stick to the ridge when mist is about. There are some spectacular lunch spots tucked away in the rocks above the cliffs, but searching them out in thick weather would be asking for trouble.

N ridge (AN1)

Pont y Pandy, 880298, is the jumping-off point. A footpath sign indicates the way down a farm lane. After half a mile a bridleway sign directs you up rich green slopes to the ridge. Should you miss this, wait until you pass a cottage, Garth Uchaf, when you can clamber up to the ridge beside a dilapidated wall just beyond. Once atop the ridge a well-trodden path follows a fence in a series of giant steps. Stiles and arrows on rocks are there in abundance to discourage any straying. The views, meanwhile, mature with every step.

Benllyn's rocky pyramid looms impressively ahead, while if you divert L you will have a rare chance to observe Llyn Lliwbran slumbering in its cold, silent hollow far below.

A short sharp rise brings you to the shores of Llyn Pen Aran and its tiny acolyte, idyllic on a calm sunny day when the only sound is the gentle lapping of waves, but unfortunately often whipped up by scurrying winds. Soon after this the path abandons the faithful fence, veering L to climb the final bouldery pile on its own.

Llyn Lliwbran route (AN2)

The N ridge can be combined with Llyn Lliwbran, one of the most inhospitable lakes in Wales. Walk down the road that penetrates Cwm Croes from 895270. Shortly before Nant-y-Llyn Farm, cut across the fells for half a mile of trackless, tussocky bog to reach the lake. When you have had your fill of the austere beauty of this desolate sun-starved hollow, head N until the slopes ease. Steep screes and cliffs rule out a direct pull up to the ridge from the lake.

Creiglyn Dyfi route (AN3)

The Cwm Croes road continues to the head of Cwm Llwydd (though it is not marked on the map) whereupon a grassy trail continues to the shores of Creiglyn Dyfi. The backdrop to the cradle of the famous Dovey could scarcely be more thrilling as the shattered face of Aran Fawddwy soars aloft in an angry intrigue of buttresses, gullies and terraces. Yet the lake itself seems strangely lack-lustre from this viewpoint - too open, too square - and it is only from the nearby Drysgol ridge that it begins to take on the romantic aura its name leads you to expect.

The key to the ascent is the grassy nose that slopes down from Erw y Ddafad-ddu. This provides a quick way home for tired legs in the evening, raises quite a sweat in summer (there is nearly 900ft of it) and needs care in winter. Snow gives it a wicked innocence - witness the crags that buttress it N and E. Once up, you are virtually midway between Benllyn and Fawddwy.

Instead of plodding up Cwm Llwydd you could leave the road to climb via the shoulder of Foel Hafod-fynydd, with splendid views all the way (AN3,1).

Llaethnant route (AN4)

The Llaethnant Valley walk, starting from the gate at the bend in the road at 905212, used to be a real charmer. However, on returning to it recently after a break of some years I was disappointed to find that the green path of old had given way to an ugly, grey, bulldozed road. It is still a beautiful walk, though sadly something irreplaceable has been lost. It begins in great style, hugging the slopes beneath the poetically named crags of Nyth-yr-eryr (nest of the eagle), and soon leaving the vivacious stream tumbling from chasm to chasm in its tiny gorge far below. Across the valley the hillside is fringed with crags and dappled with trees and gives a dazzling blaze of greys, greens and coppery reds when the bracken is at its height.

A steepish rise brings you alongside the stream with bleaker, more open terrain ahead. Unfortunately the grassy mound of Foel Hafod-fynydd shuts out all but the most tantalising glimpses of the high Arans beyond. The track starts to veer N now, and if you stayed with it would take you across Bwlch Sirddyn to Cwm Croes via the abandoned farmstead of Cwm-fynnon, 883243. (On grit all the way apart from a sketchy patch over the Bwlch - see AN19.) However, for today's walk you should leave the track now for one of the oozy little trails that wend across the S flanks of Hafod to Creiglyn Dyfi, before pulling up to Erw y Ddafad-ddu to finish as in AN3.

ARAN FAWDDWY

It is a moot point whether Benllyn or Fawddwy is the finer viewpoint. Rather like Mahler and Bruckner, it all depends on your mood. Fawddwy frames Creiglyn Dyfi, the birthplace of the Dovey, in its giant turrets; but otherwise there is precious little in it. Benllyn, with its focus on the rugged wilder N, plays King to Fawddwy's Queen and the softer hills of the S. Happily both peaks have the gift, shared by so many of the mid-Wales hills, of transporting you into a world where the works of man are subsumed in a blue-green fantasy of hills, woodlands and dales extending as far as the eye can see.

Cwm Cywarch route (AN5)

Driving up the twisty road to Cwm Cywarch the urge to get out of the car and onto the fells is almost irresistible. The sight of that familiar cirque with its massive buttressed crags piercing the sky is an inspiration, even to the most indolent. Park in the field where the unfenced road ends at 854185. March on, ignoring the footpath sign to Hengwm, past the farmstead of Blaencywarch, over a ford and up a springy band of green that cuts through bracken and boulders. (Many signs and arrows on rocks render detailed directions superfluous.) Before long you are hemmed in by lowering crags, serenaded by the music of the brook and marvelling at having climbed so quickly out of the lush pastures below.

Unless you want some awkward scrambling be sure to spot (near the top) where the path crosses to the stream's true L bank. Once across, the path fades and the best plan is to head slightly E of N until you meet a fence with a well-trodden path alongside. This is a squelchy, oozy mess at first (so much so that long white planks have recently been laid over the worst sections) but it firms up later as it winds up the mountain's bouldery slopes to a large cairn marking the S top at 860220. The trig point is then a short walk NE across a stony plateau.

On the way, shortly before you meet another fence coming off the hillside R, you pass a junction of fences at 851208. This gives a much needed clue to the whereabouts of Waen Camddwr some 150 yards to the S.

Cwm Hengwm route (AN6)

Hengwm is the most popular route up Aran Fawddwy. However my advice for the perfect day would be: out via Cwm Cywarch; home down Hengwm when the long slopes that can seem endless on a muggy morning are perfect for a relaxed afternoon.

A footpath sign at 853187 directs you across a bridge, through a rickety kissing-gate and up a rough muddy track beneath a canopy of trees. Turn L when you meet a gravelly farm road and in a few minutes you will join the long, carefully graded path that slants across the N flanks of Pen yr Allt-uchaf. The trough of Hengwm deepens with every step. Colossal green slopes, smooth and bare, gaze silently down on an empty cwm that curls round as if to feed on its own monumental loneliness.

Above Hengwm the path toils up to the Drysgol spur and a teardrop tarn where, on a still day, you may glimpse the Aran tops reflected round its tussocky shores. The spur caries on to the slender neck of Drws Bach (Little Door) where it narrows to a whisker and a cairn at 863214 commemorates an RAF member who was killed by lightning in 1960. The views are tremendous: a 1000ft drop into Hengwm on one side; the Arans' E face on the other, as majestic and thrilling as anything in Wales. Beneath the cliffs lies the sparkling Creiglyn Dyfi, flat and bland looking as you stand by its shores, but the very quintessence of a mountain lake from this lofty eyrie (never more so than in winter when it mirrors the blacks and whites of the snow-capped peaks all round).

Stay with the fence that straddles the spur beyond Drws Bach until you are invited to cross it at a ladder-stile. (The tarns at 860215 scarcely merit a diversion, short though it would be.) The terrain changes abruptly from grass to rock hereabouts and the well-worn path that scales the mountain's final defences, leading first to the knuckly S top and then to the breezy trig point, is amply cairned.

Cwm Dyniewyd route (AN7)

For a day with a difference try starting from Llanymawddwy. You can choose from two routes, both of which are all but forgotten. Darren Ddu is perhaps best saved as a steady downhill trek for tired legs in the evening, but Cwm Dyniewyd gives good sport either way. Both join the Hengwm route at Drysgol.

The lane by the chapel at 902190 is easily missed as you drive through the village, but it is there all right, climbing steeply beneath an awning of pines, then cutting through bracken before entering Cwm Dyniewyd above a glen (mauve with rhododendron flowers in spring). The cwm is still as nature intended; the black slippery rocks at its head festooned with the silver thread of Pistyll Gwyn. At some point you must gain the ridge. Probably the easiest course is to make for the tiny col just W of Pen Foel-y-ffridd, one of the hills that stand guard over Llanymawddwy. A stiff slog but worth every pant.

Follow the forest boundary as it curves above the falls and then let your compass guide you across the barren moors to Drysgol. Be sure to inspect the gaunt unknown cliffs of Gallt Ceiniogau and Llam Llai as you glance back across the Dovey.

Darren Ddu route (AN8)

Leave Drysgol on a bearing of 120 and set out across the peaty fells of Gwaun Lydan. Before long you will see a track wending through the grass near the S rim of Darren Ddu. This will see you safely down to the road at Bryn Hall (907194) via Brynuchaf Farm. In contrast with the friendly tranquillity of Cwm Dyniewyd the harsh gash of Darren Ddu is lifeless and sombre, but impressive nonetheless.

Llaethnant route (AN9)

Follow AN4 to Erw y Ddafad-ddu and then advance L across the stony waste to cross a stile over the fence around Aran Fawddwy's N approaches. A cairned path then weaves up the final rocky pyramid to the summit.

Drysgol N approach (AN10)

You would not care to tackle this trackless route every day, but it is worth noting that you can use it to make a direct descent from Drysgol to the Llaethnant Valley. To do this proceed E from Drysgol for a few minutes until, at about 878212, an easing in the slopes permits a roughish descent over mosses and stone-encrusted grass. You can then either cross the stream to link up with AN4, the Llaethnant route (thus regaining the road at 905212) or follow farm tracks to Pont y Pennant at 904203.

W approach (AN11)

The Arans present a dull face to the W. They are prettily wooded, it is true, but the ridge looks rounded and whale-backed with no hint of excitement. This more or less sums up the long tramp which is given here for completeness (and because it is one of the permitted paths) rather than on merit. The final nail in the coffin is that it is impossible, unless you have a friendly chauffeur, to combine it with any other route that would form a worthwhile round.

The route starts from Esgair-gawr Farm, 816224, where a car park has recently been constructed and where a mounted Mosquito engine commemorates two airmen who crashed in the Arans in 1944. Pass through the farm and then bear R on a Land-Rover track which leads across fields and a forest plantation (where the path is wet and scrappy) before finally emerging on the open fells. The

Aran Fawddwy from Erw y Ddafad-ddu

Arans are by now clearly impressed on the skyline ahead, but the best views are of Dduallt and Rhobell Fawr behind you. As on all the permitted paths there is a proliferation of arrows on rocks and markers on fences to prevent straying - so it is only a matter of time before you meet the fence and path mentioned in AN5 at 856216.

ERW Y DDAFAD DDU

The name (Acre of the Black Sheep) says it all. The stony top with its sprawling cairn may not literally occupy an acre, but it certainly has that sort of feel about it as you come across it - an unexpectedly flat interlude on the high-level tramp between Aran Benllyn and Aran Fawddwy. It is a superb viewpoint, on a par with the two Arans themselves but with the added advantage that they are also included. As for routes, anything leading to the two senior Arans will do.

WAEN CAMDDWR

Seeing it on the ground it is scarcely credible that Waen Camddwr should be rated a 2000 footer in its own right. It is a pleasant enough little hillock in the midst of the damp undulating moors separating Aran Fawddwy from Glasgwm, and it sports a tiny cairn. However, that is all there is to say, indeed without some prior homework the chances are that you would walk right by without even noticing it!. Waen Camddwr is easily reached from Gwaun y Llwyni by descending NW along a new fence, but it is most naturally tackled en-route to Aran Fawddwy on AN5.

PEN YR ALLT-UCHAF

Pen yr Allt-uchaf is the slender grassy finger that gazes down on Cwm Cywarch from the NE. It is a featureless top. The highest ground is at the NE tip of the ridge but there is no cairn, no rock, nothing except fresh untrampled grass. Yet the views compensate: Cwm Terwyn S, Cwm Hengwm N, with pride of place going to the gigantic splintered slopes of Gwaun y Llwyni and the distant line of the Rhinogs delicately framed in the jagged head of Cywarch.

Cwm Hengwm route (AN12)

Start on AN6 but double back where the gradient eases near a fence and a signboard indicating the Arans' permitted paths. Advance across the spongy top of Waun Goch to claim the ridge from there.

Cwm Terwyn route (AN13)

A path crosses the fields from the road at 860175 to give access to a beautifully engineered path that slants across the cwm's S slopes. As the ground levels off near a corner of some woods, bear L to join the ridge close to its topmost point. Another track (AN13,1) tackles the cwm on its N side.

GWAUN Y LLWYNI

Gwaun y Llwyni is not one of the Arans' big names, it is not even marked on the 1:50,000 map although it is certainly one of the most recognisable from a distance. Many is the time, gazing E, trying to fathom out what was what, that I have suddenly spotted the tilted, grassy wedge (rather like Rhinog Fach, but longer and not so dramatic) that characterises Gwaun y Llwyni. Then everything fell into place.

Nearer to hand Gwaun y Llwyni sports a dashing front, lording it over Hengwm with massive slopes of grass, scree and shattered crags that curl round the head of the cwm while plunging a dizzy 1400ft to the green solitudes below. Perched on the brink of the abyss is a small cairn beside a line of lonely poles that are the sole remains of an ancient fence.

Cwm Hengwm route (AN14)

Except for AN9 virtually all the routes for Aran Fawddwy serve Gwaun y Llwyni equally well, but the most natural is AN6. Follow it to Drws Bach and then bear L on to a playful little track that hugs the NW rim of Hengwm before bounding up a heathery bank to the cairn.

SE face (AN15)

As you tramp the edge of Gwaun y Llwyni round from Drws Bach you will notice a slim, shaly path ribboning across the screes towards the head of Cwm Cywarch. This provides a toe-burning escape to a farm track that leads close to the mountain hut of Bryn Hafod.

FOEL HAFOD-FYNYDD

Foel Hafod-Fynydd is a triangular-shaped afterthought to the grassy nose that Erw y Ddafad-ddu sends down to Creiglyn Dyfi. Apart from the sharp craggy fangs it shows to Bwlch Sirddyn, it is grassy. As an island of high ground it is also a splendid viewpoint, especially of the Arans' E face.

Cwm Croes route (AN16)
See AN3.

Bwlch Sirddyn route (AN17)
See AN19.

LLECHWEDD DU/ESGEIRIAU GWYNION

Llechwedd Du (the Black Hillside) is a thrilling sight when you see it towering over the tiny hamlet of Llanymawddwy. It only needs a light dusting of snow or frost on the shattered cliffs guarding its S and E flanks to create a scene of true Alpine splendour. However, just as early morning sun does not necessarily herald a fine day, so the early promise here is not fulfilled. The top is a huge tableland of soggy moors, ridden with peat hags, wet and cheerless, especially when mist clamps down. A narrow neck at 894232 leads to a second top, Esgeiriau Gwynion (cairnless like the first), and by following a fence it is a simple matter to progress from one to the other. Hence this combined entry.

If you have been put off, please read on because, as I shall now relate, there is at least one walk of outstanding merit.

N ridge (AN18)

I had been walking the Arans for many years before I first sampled Esgeiriau Gwynion's N ridge. Many were the times I had seen it across Cwm Croes and rejected it as too featureless and dull. Then, one sunny afternoon in spring, having lunched by the shores of Creiglyn Dyfi and seeking a change from the long trek down Cwm Croes back to Llanuwchllyn, I climbed Esgeiriau Gwynion from Bwlch Sirddyn (AN19) and set off down the N ridge.

Apart from a short break in the middle, a fence accompanies you all the way and provided you stick with it the going is pleasant and dry and the only decision (which matters little) is where to drop down to the farm road in the valley. So far a walk like many others. The difference lies in the views. Nowhere reveals the Arans in more heroic vein as they stand rugged and wild, tall and proud, across Cwm Croes. Not even the Glyders strike a more regal pose. In sun the dark drama of the crags is leavened by the glitter of Llyn Lliwbran - one of the few occasions when it is enticed out of its rocky lair. To the W Hirnants and Berwyns ripple away in a mosaic of pastel hues, and then there is Foel Figenau, the conical hill directly ahead which, despite its modest stature, delights the eye just as surely as any Sugar Loaf or Tryfan.

Bwlch Sirddyn route (AN19)

The Llaethnant Valley approach from 905212, walking beneath the splintered crags of Tap Nyth-yr-eryr (the Eagle's Nest), has already been described in AN4 when the objective was Aran Benllyn. However, by staying with the track as it curves round the W flanks of Llechwedd Du, following it over Bwlch Sirddyn rather than continuing up the Llaethnant Valley, the way is open to capture three of the Arans' outliers. As its name implies, Bwlch Sirddyn is a mountain pass and a walk from Llanymawddwy to Llanuwchllyn (or at least part of it) is a good choice when the elements dictate a low-level day. Apart from a sketchy patch near the top of the pass where it is little more than a shadow in the grass, the track is wide and gritty throughout.

The first landmark, 890225, is a fence rambling up the slope L across the stream. This leads directly to Foel Hafod-fynydd (AN17). It is too steep hereabouts to scale Llechwedd Du with comfort, so carry on until you meet the Nant y Fuddai, the first of three streams that come tumbling down R. You could pull up here (AN19,1) to the narrow neck linking Llechwedd Du to Esgeiriau Gwynion to claim either top. However the easiest course is to press on a few more minutes until a fence crosses your path at 885230. You then follow this to claim either Foel Hafod-fynydd L (AN17,1) or Esgeiriau Gwynion R.

The track, meanwhile, leads via the deserted homestead of Cwm-fynnon (883243) and the E bank of the Afon Croes to the road at 895270. Alternatively you can follow a path that proceeds due N from Cwm-fynnon to the farm of Nant-y-barcut at 884263, there to join the road referred to in AN3 (unmarked on the map) that leads up the W side of Cwm Croes.

Bwlch y Groes route (AN20)

Any walk that takes off from nearly 1800ft as this does should be popular; but not in this case. It starts from a stile by a cattle-grid at 913233, the highest point on the mountain road from Llanymawddwy to Llanuwchllyn, and provides the simplest way by far to Llechwedd Du. Unfortunately it lacks interest and, after a short spell along a Land-Rover track, degenerates into a trackless tussocky slog through peaty bog.

GLASGWM

Glasgwm is a tilted plateau of rough billowy moorland and small rocky knuckles, extensively wooded to the S and guarded to the E by the mighty battlements of Craig Cywarch. Its tall, elegantly rounded cairn is situated just off the N rim and has a distinctive beehive appearance (like the cairns on Glyder Fawr) when viewed from afar. A few steps N of the cairn is the shallow, rocky hollow that cradles the diminutive Llyn Bach. An equal distance S is the larger, more exposed Llyn y Fign, a lake that really needs blue skies to bring it alive.

Most Arans walkers stick pretty solidly to the main highways and Glasgwm is left in relative peace. All the more reason then, if you are contemplating a visit, to go the whole hog and tackle it from Dolobran in the S. This gives you the opportunity to link it with Pen y Bryn-fforchog and have a relaxing away-day in attractive country that is seldom visited save by the occasional shepherd (see AN H4).

Dolobran route (AN21)

I offer a couple of less strenuous variants later, but let me begin with what, for my money, is the best approach of all from this side, despite some early collar work. Start from the junction at 841165 and proceed E down a lane to a couple of adjoining gates. Go through the R gate into a field where a farm trail brings you by an idyllic cottage at 846163 to the foot of a prominent green path. Climb up the hillside on this until you reach a gate at the second switchback, 850160. Go through the gate and then follow the fence up to Foel Benddin's breezy top. A stiff slog, quite as demanding as Pen yr Ole Wen ever was, or so it seemed the last time I took it on!

The rewards are immediate with tremendous views of Maesglasau, Cribin and Bwlch Oerddrws. Ahead lies a seductive undulating grassy ridge that leads first of all down to a narrow neck, Bwlch yr Anges, then up to Y Gribin at 1975ft and finally down to a second neck at 842179 (where the forest trail of AN21,1 joins you L and the Gesail farm path, AN23, clears the edge of Cwm Cywarch R). The centre of attention has by now switched to the N, to the harsh serrated buttresses of Craig Cywarch and to Aran Fawddwy itself, riding astride Drysgol and the round of Hengwm. Stay with the fence that straddles the ridge, climbs a small rise and then heads

The last habitation on AN21: Y Gribin on the skyline

across moorland flats until it makes a sharp L turn at 837188. Here strike out almost due N for the top, aided by a flinty track and the occasional stunted stake.

Now for the less strenuous variants I promised. For the first (AN21,1) start from the junction as before but work your way across a field to pick up a path that enters a coppice at 842167. After twisting round the head of a stream this meets a new forestry road which zig-zags easily (but at some length!) up the hillside to join AN21 at the neck NW of Y Gribin. The other option (AN21,2) is to join the forest track at its source, picking it up from the lane that leads to Pentrewern Farm at 825164.

Cwm Cywarch route (AN22)

Stay with AN5 until you meet the fence crossing the fells above Creigiau Camddwr. Follow this L up a slope of rocky debris direct to the cairn.

Gesail Farm route (AN23)

The coarse bulldozed track that zig-zags its way so brazenly between the crags backing Gesail Farm, 852184, is no substitute for the wisp of a trail that once followed much the same course. At least not in aesthetic terms, however helpful it may be in simplifying route-finding. To be fair it still retains a sense of occasion. How could it be otherwise in the august surroundings of Craig Cywarch? Who knows, perhaps one day the grass will grow again! On top you join AN21 at 842179.

PEN Y BRYN-FFORCHOG

It may seem a bit 'cart-before-horse' to give only one route for a hill and then suggest it is best used for descent, but no one is likely to climb Pen y Bryn-fforchog (Top of the Forked Hill) for its own sake with so much else around. After all it is merely the top of a grassy shelf that bounds, yet barely surmounts, the SW periphery of the Glasgwm plateau. However if you tackle Pen y Bryn-fforchog from Glasgwm, having spent the morning tramping AN21, and then use the Bwlch Oerddrws route to get down again, you are assured of an enjoyable day in peace and solitude, seeing old friends from new angles and discovering untrodden ground.

Bwlch Oerddrws route (AN24)

A fence makes a right-angled bend where it straddles the top at 818179. Follow it SW down a fresh grassy slope that is a joy on a sunny afternoon with Cribin staring you full in the face from across the valley. As you approach a hillock at 810174 you must decide whether to bear L or R. Pleasant ridges continue either way; it all depends on where you want to join the road.

HIGH-LEVEL WALKS
Cwm Croes horseshoe (AN H1)

If I had to recommend just one walk in the Arans it would have to be this, despite the omission of Cwm Cywarch. Start from Llanuwchllyn and climb Aran Benllyn's N ridge (AN1). Carry on over the central spine to Aran Fawddwy. Backtrack to Erw y

Ddafad-ddu, scamper down the grassy nose to Creiglyn Dyfi and then tackle the gentle rise up to Foel Hafod-fynydd. Descend S of E along the fence until you meet another fence dropping away more steeply N. Use this (AN17,1) as your guide to cross Bwlch Sirddyn and for the pull up to Esgeiriau Gwynion (AN19). Next follow the N ridge (AN18) back to the road at 895270, leaving a 2.5-mile slog along the road to regain your car. You could shorten the day by returning down Cwm Croes (AN3) but the views from Esgeiriau Gwynion are so dramatic that it would be a shame to miss them.

Cwm Cywarch/Hengwm circular (AN H2)
This runs the Cwm Croes horseshoe a close second. The kernel of the walk is scaling Aran Fawddwy via Cwm Cywarch on AN5 and then returning down Hengwm on AN6. However this is easier than it looks and three additions should be considered. The first is to branch out to Pen yr Allt-uchaf, maybe using Cwm Terwyn rather than Hengwm for the way home. The second is to include Gwaun y Llwyni en-route to Aran Fawddwy in the morning. Gwaun does not look exciting but as a vantage point over Hengwm it is second to none. Thirdly you could start on AN23, climbing Glasgwm first before following the fence down its NE slopes to join AN5 on the moors above Cwm Cywarch. The trouble with this is that you miss the best part of the cwm.

Llanymawddwy horseshoe (AN H3)
Put simply this combines two routes on Aran Fawddwy, AN7 and AN9, and it is a toss-up which is the better way round. What you can be sure of are charming valleys at either end of the day, the grandeur of the high Arans in the middle, solitude and the excitement of treading self-effacing little tracks that normally only see sheep and the odd shepherd. A walk for the connoisseur!

Dolobran circular (AN H4)
Climb Glasgwm from Dolobran (AN21), follow the edge of the woods round to Pen y Bryn-fforchog and then descend on AN24. These are the bare bones of a walk that offers more than you might think from the map. It is more like a day in the Dovey hills or the Tarrens than the Arans, with wide grassy ridges predominating

and only sheep for company. Having said that you pass close by the massive crags of Craig Cywarch and the views, both of the distant Arans and of the Dovey hills across Bwlch Oerddrws, are magnificent. Another walk for Aran devotees seeking new pastures.

N/S traverse (AN H5)

This is an obvious walk and a grand one, taking in the core of the Aran massif in its entirety; provided your logistics can cope. Simply combine AN1 and AN5.

LOWER-LEVEL WALKS/EASIER DAYS

Bwlch Sirddyn (AN L1)

See AN19. A good walk for clearing the cobwebs away on a wet or blustery day when you hanker after a sniff of the fells but the tops look just too uninviting!

Cwm Croes (AN L2)

This is essentially a valley walk with a road (or near road) most of the way. It should not raise too much of a sweat to get as far as Creiglyn Dyfi. See AN3.

THE ARENIGS
OS maps
1:25,000 - Sheet 18/23 1:50,000 - Sheets 124/125

Peaks	Height (ft)	Map Ref	Page
Arenig Fawr	2802	827369	50
Moel Llyfnant	2464	808352	52
Rhobell Fawr	2408	787257	66
Arenig Fach	2260	821416	55
Carnedd y Filiast	2195	871446	58
Dduallt	2172	811274	62
Carnedd Llechwedd Llyfn	2110	857446	60
Foel Boeth	2031	778345	55
Foel Goch	2005	953423	60
Mountain Lakes			
Arenig Fach	1500	828417	
Arenig Fawr	1326	846380	
Dywarchen	1400	763420	
Hesgyn	1400	885443	
Nameless (Craig y Bychau)	2200	825355	
Serw	1475	780428	

THE ARENIGS

Untrodden heather-clad tops, wild moors, scattered hills, uncluttered views, the marshy Migneint, generous variety and vast solitudes: these are the lures of the Arenigs, some of the least known hills in Wales. When I last visited them only one of the nine cairns, Arenig Fawr's, carried the tell-tale signs of human desecration. That surely says it all!

Are there really nine tops? Surely the map shows only two

Arenigs? That is so, but like others before me I am taking the liberty of using 'Arenigs' to describe a diffuse group of hills that owes no allegiance to a recognised range and which, without a name, would remain unsung and unknown. Arbitrary this may be, presumptuous perhaps, but tidy and defensible certainly, as all eight of the other tops rise in the shadow of Arenig Fawr.

The Arenigs domain is a vast quadrilateral of some 200 square miles bounded by the Afon Eden and the A470 W, the Bala gap and the A494 E, and by the B4407 and the A5 N. Open windswept fells predominate in the N, bleak in winter but a dazzling aromatic array of pinks and purples in summer. Farther S the terrain becomes more broken with scattered outcrops and extensive afforestation. Rarely, however, does the walker tread rock and nowhere is the use of hands even remotely in question. Tracks, faint but reliable, ease the way most of the time. Stay with these and the Arenigs can be kind; stray and you may find bog and jolty tussocks lying in wait although even then, to be fair, their impact is muted and nowhere does the errant walker suffer as he may in the Rhinogs!

The Arenigs wear their hearts on their sleeves: simple hills, hiding little. It could scarcely be otherwise with nine peaks scattered so widely, yet there are a few secrets left to uncover. Who, from the road, would suspect the sparkling lakes that snuggle beneath the E ramparts of Arenig Fawr and Arenig Fach? Who would anticipate Arenig Fach's craggy E face? Then there is the sprinkle of little tarns adorning Craig y Bychau, the austere but wistfully beautiful Hesgyn Valley and the pristine joys of Dduallt and Rhobell Fawr.

Arenig Fawr is the unquestioned doyen of the range, a large elephantine peak of 2800ft with a regal bearing. Unsightly quarries offend its N face but these are of small moment. Its rambling fells offer excellent sport, especially if you walk the full length of the ridge from Craig y Bychau to Pen Tyrau. Across the road Arenig Fach is a much underrated hill; looking deceptively dull, its soft heathery top is ideal for munching bilberries on a sunny afternoon and for views of the Migneint it is second to none.

Moel Llyfnant is in many respects the more logical 'Fach', being linked to Arenig Fawr by a grassy col. Like the official Arenig Fach it is a languid grassy mound from most viewpoints, but still worth the occasional away-day. Some two miles W again lies the last top

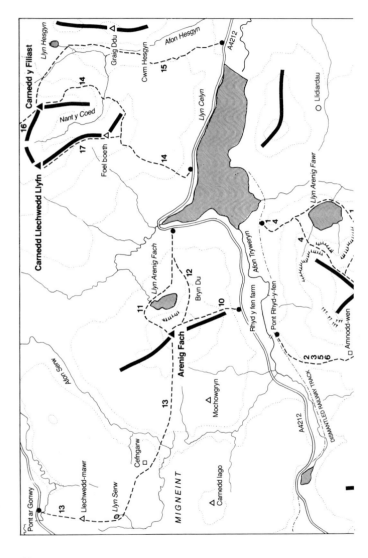

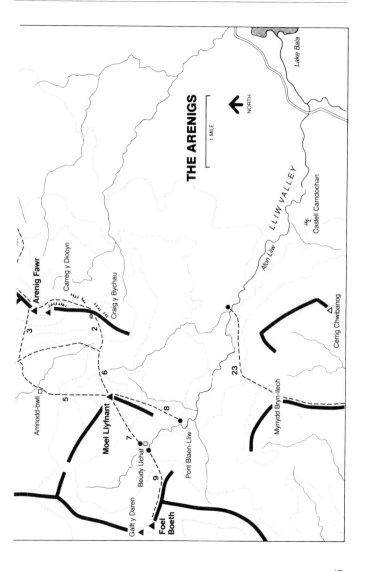

*Arenig Fawr and Moel Llyfnant across the Migneint
with Llyn Serw in the foreground*

in this cluster, Foel Boeth. King of a dull shallow ridge it is all but forgotten, and understandably so.

Three more hills rise to the NE. Carnedd y Filiast and its satellite Llechwedd Llyfn are gently curved hillocks of rampant heather. Foel Goch is a loner, surrounded by roads, barely lifting its head above the prestigious 2000ft barrier. Study the map, though, and you will find it is a big mountain, fully endowed with ridges and cwms and well worth the occasional day.

The two remaining tops, Dduallt and Rhobell Fawr, lie well S. Set apart from their peers and the world, both revel in a happy harmony of fells, woodlands, rock and marsh. Like good wine these are peaks to relish on a special day.

The Arenigs glory in vast open views. Rising apart, unclustered, there is little to deflect the eye. Take the view from Arenig Fawr (and rather than reciting the panorama each time let this speak for the other peaks too). Arenig Fach and the Migneint lie to the N. The NE skyline is filled by the rounded swell of those two lonely outliers,

Carnedd y Filiast and Foel Goch. Rising beyond Lake Bala are the Hirnant hills and the distant Berwyns. The urgent thrust of Aran Benllyn kindles the spark SE while SW the sharpness of Dduallt complements the soft curve of Rhobell Fawr with the Dovey hills and Cader Idris arcing the horizon. The scene is stolen W by the Rhinogs, with Moel Llyfnant providing a massive foreground. The circle is completed NW by the ranges of Snowdonia, with Snowdon itself, Tryfan, the Glyders, Moel Siabod, the Moelwyns, Cnicht, and the Ffestiniog hills all competing for pride of place. Set this in your mind's eye within a mosaic of moors, forests and glittering lakes (for you should count yourself unlucky if you cannot see at least Llynnau Conwy, Tryweryn and Y Garn) and you have a picture to treasure.

The Migneint

This is a book on hills, but no essay on the Arenigs would be complete without an introduction to that remote wilderness, known as the Migneint, over which they preside.

The Migneint is an expanse of windswept moorland, cupped in a shallow depression with higher ground all around. No ridges or hills gladden the eye. Instead you have the austere beauty and solitudes of virgin moors and their secret places: a haven of tranquillity for quiet contemplation with a unique ethereal charm that, once experienced, long casts its spell. The sense of other-worldliness is enhanced by the absence of landmarks in the long miles of marsh and heather. There are no tracks and scarcely a cairn; even one solitary stone astride another, marking a spot height, is an event!

The Migneint has acquired a harsh reputation as a confusing and squelchy bogland, full of knobbly tussocks and deep trackless heather. While this has some truth, it can often be exaggerated. Treat the Migneint with respect, you must. There will be few, if any, fellow walkers to help in case of trouble. Plenty of map and compass work is needed, and when mist swirls it is an eerie place, best avoided. Yet there are ways through which are easier than you might suppose. During the wet summer of 1985, for instance, I crossed the Migneint in both directions, a walk of some 14 miles, in an unhurried seven hours. I had ample time for pictures and a leisurely lunch on Arenig Fach, and ended the day with dry feet! I was alone that day, incidentally, and that is the best way to appreciate the Migneint's delicate charms. Despite the rigours, it is no place for groups.

Arenig Fach is the unquestioned king of the Migneint, looking a veritable giant and reassuringly familiar as it towers over its wild and marshy serfdom. Combine it with a crossing of the Migneint and you have a pearl of a day in country that is both wild and serene, remote yet evocative.

ARENIG FAWR

Arenig Fawr is not a mountain you can ignore. Set apart from its fellows and totally dominating the surrounding moors, its twin-topped summit makes it an impressive and familiar sight for miles around.

Most visitors form their first impression from the W when its smooth, uncluttered slopes suggest a simple straightforward peak. However when you see it from the E, from Llidiardau at 874382 (say), you may well have second thoughts. For though the profile is little changed, with the conical top as pre-eminent as ever, a craggier face is now evident, especially S. Even then, neither of these lowland viewpoints reveals either Llyn Arenig Fawr or the cluster of little tarns near Craig y Bychau. To observe these you must take to the fells - which you may do with confidence. The senior Arenig is a friendly giant offering easy going. Even in mist it is safe, provided you stay on the main tracks and only leave the top alongside the remains of the old wire fence that crosses it.

Sad to relate the trig point on this lofty summit faces a memorial to eight American airmen who died on the mountain in 1943 when their Flying Fortress crashed on the final stage of its flight from the USA.

Llyn Arenig Fawr route (AG1)

The classic route up Arenig Fawr starts over a stile at 846396. A slow rise up a stony road is dreary and quite uneventful until, after half a mile, the desolate Llyn Arenig Fawr comes into view below the frowning bastion of its guardian peak. A sombre, melancholy scene. The road ends by an old sluice house and weir but a track carries on, rambling up the heather-clad slopes of the ridge that rises enticingly before you.

The scars of civilisation now yield to the wild of the fells with views of the crags that threaten the lake improving with every step. Higher up the ridge the path crosses a fence, then a second one. The summit is in view by now and you can see that it is well set back with still some way to go.

The path now sweeps round to the R to maintain height before gradually curling back L towards the summit where it runs below, but parallel to, the main ridge. The path never reaches the ridge so you must therefore abandon it and work diagonally up the grassy slopes to a ridge path that follows a wire fence to the top. Better still, aim direct for the ridge immediately after the second fence. That way you gain height sooner with an overview of the lonely Pen Tyrau uplands and their scattering of teardrop tarns.

Craig y Bychau route (AG2)

At 823393, just E on Pont Rhyd-y-fen, a gritty spur road breaks away from the country road from Bala, heading W. Follow this for a short half-mile to a sheepfold adjoining a disused quarry. (You are spoilt for choice because a dismantled rail track parallels you R while a green path contours across the hillside up-slope L.) At the quarry change to a stony path that moves away S to curl round Arenig Fawr's W flank with Moel Llyfnant building up imposingly ahead.

Keeping L after passing the ruined homestead of Amnodd-wen where a farm road curves round before you. The R fork leads to Moel Llyfnant (AG6). Carry on for about a mile until the road peters out by an old stone wall high up on the exposed col between Arenig Fawr and Moel Llyfnant. Turn L and follow the wall (no track) to the skyline. Topping the rise brings quite a surprise; a secluded enclave of outcrops, grassland and lakelets, snuggling serenely beneath Arenig Fawr's protective bulk.

A steep trudge up the S ridge follows with grass gradually yielding to scree and impressive views of the crags of Carreg y Diocyn. It is hard work and you will be glad of the excuse of a last view of the lakes to take a brief rest when you reach Arenig Fawr's subsidiary top at 828366. Only a quick down-and-up then remains to put you on main top.

Arenig Fawr from the W

W face direct (AG3)

Just beyond Amnodd-wen you can struggle directly up the hillside to gain the summit ridge slightly N of the cairn, using a shallow groove that slants across the face of the mountain and which you can discern from almost anywhere to the W of it. A brute!

N approach (AG4)

Follow the fence from the trig point until, after a mile, you come to a plateau of clumpy heather, rocky terraces and scattered tarns not unlike one of the more benign parts of the Rhinogs. Keep E for views of the crags towering over Llyn Arenig Fawr, then march on to the NE corner of the plateau at 839382 where a break in the crags permits a rough but practical line of descent to AG1. Care is needed as the slopes are covered in deep tussocky heather with half-hidden boulders and the occasional pothole; not unlike one of the more tiresome parts of the Rhinogs!

MOEL LLYFNANT

It is never easy to live in the shadow of a famous relation and that is Moel Llyfnant's problem precisely. Seen from the Lliw Valley, Arenig Fawr and Moel Llyfnant stand very much on equal terms. From the more usual N viewpoints, however, Moel Llyfnant is totally outclassed - small, grassy, smooth and round where Arenig Fawr is vast, rugged and photogenic. However it is still a worthy addition to a day spent exploring its better half. Although it is a predominantly grassy hill, Moel Llyfnant is capped with a small rocky crown and sprouts minor crags on its S and W flanks that demand respect in mist.

N ridge (AG5)
Walk to Amnodd-wen as in AG2 and then branch R through the forest. After a second deserted farm, Amnodd-bwll, stay with the path as it curls round Llyfnant's N ridge and peters out. Now take to the hillside for a short slog up to the summit cairn. This simple walk can also be commenced from the A4212 at 806385 where a forest road signposted to Nantddu leads to Amnodd-bwll (AG5,1).

E face (AG6)
Follow AG2 to the col between Arenig Fawr and Moel Llyfnant, then prepare for a hard grind up the hillside. The col is marshy in places and dry feet are best ensured by staying close to the remnants of a tumbledown wall. Tiring though it can be in hot weather, this is the best way up Moel Llyfnant as there is something about this lonely col that makes the ascent a strangely rewarding experience. Arenig Fawr is tremendous across the valley.

SW face (AG7)   (See maps pages 47 & 54)
A SW descent is useful if you wish to move on to Foel Boeth. It is simply a matter of rambling down the rough broken slope until you meet the bulldozed road that penetrates the upper reaches of the Lliw Valley near the farmstead of Beudy Uchaf at 797344. In mist proceed N from the summit for about 200 paces before dropping down in order to avoid some minor crags.

S approach (AG8)   (See maps pages 47 & 54)
Follow the summit fence S until you are clear of crags R. It is then a straightforward but soggy trek down to the road near Pont Blaen-lliw.

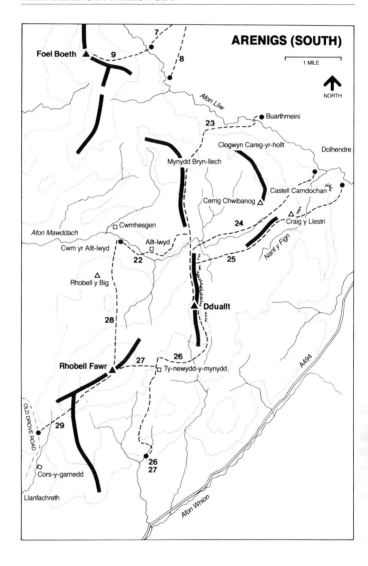

FOEL BOETH

Seekers after excitement should look elsewhere. Foel Boeth is the undistinguished top of a dull featureless ridge that rambles on for nearly two miles without any significant variation in height or, indeed, much at all to set it apart from the drabness of the surrounding moors. The most likely reason for tackling it is simple 'peak bagging'. Strictly speaking it is, like Arenig Fawr, a twin-topped peak with Gallt y Daren at 778345 marginally higher than Foel Boeth itself (but this is merely hair-splitting when there is so little of character on either 'top').

S and E approaches (AG9)   (See maps pages 47 & 54)
Foel Boeth can be plodded up almost anywhere from the mountain road to the S or from the stony road that penetrates the upper Lliw Valley from Pont Blaen-lliw at 802336. With damp tussocky grass the staple fare, there is much to be said for keeping the tramp as short as possible!

ARENIG FACH

Arenig Fach looks singularly uninspiring from Arenig Fawr or the road; not worth climbing. What a contrast when it is viewed from the Migneint or Carnedd y Filiast! Then it assumes a dominating air and looks every inch a mountain, even though there is still no sign of the craggy E face that watches over the almost unknown Llyn Arenig Fach. This is a shy hill and one whose treasures must be coaxed.

The vast summit plateau is ideal for sunbathing: cushions of heather to lie on, bilberries to feast on, dips for shelter from the wind plus views to uplift the spirit. All the Arenigs are splendid viewpoints but Arenig Fach is twice blessed, towering as it does over the Migneint's wilderness of moorland and bog. Even a dull day cannot entirely dispel the magic, while in sunlight the mosaic of purples and greens, yellows and browns, hillocks and dips, pastures and streams, casts an ethereal spell that will live in your memory.

Caution is de rigeur in mist; on three sides slopes are steep and quickly lead to rough trackless terrain. When in doubt steer a SE course, later trending E, to let the gentle Bryn Du ridge (AG12) bring you safely down.

S approach (AG10)

Leave the A4212 through a gate at 826400 (opposite the entrance to Rhyd-y Fen Farm) and climb steeply N over ancient pastures, crossing several tumbledown walls on the way, until you meet a more substantial wall beyond which grass succumbs to unbroken heather. Continue slightly W of N, keeping to the crest of a shallow ridge. There is no track but despite the heather the going is a joy, with only the occasional hidden boulder to watch out for.

Avoid the urge to forge ahead when the trig point peeps over the skyline. Instead bear R above the lowering crags that cradle Llyn Arenig Fach in the stony depths below. Follow the N rim of the plateau round to the trig point with ever-widening views of the Migneint.

Llyn Arenig Fach route (AG11)

Leave the A4212 through a gate at 845418 and thread your way up gently wooded slopes until the crags guarding Llyn Arenig Fach rear ahead and you stand on its shoreline. Lack of a path is barely noticed. Continue to the N tip of the lake where a playful track snakes up the bilberry/heather-clad slopes with consummate ease, breasting the summit plateau close by the cairn.

Bryn Du ridge route (AG12)

This is the best way off in thick weather. Leave the trig point in a SE direction but bear E after half a mile for the ridge. The only problem is gaining access to the road. You could do worse than aim for 845418 and AG11.

Migneint route (AG13)

Here is a walk through the Migneint that follows the grain of the land (in so far as there is one), takes in most of the sights and throws in an ascent of Arenig Fach for good measure. The round trip involves a good 12 miles of trackless walking and should not be underestimated. On the other hand there are obvious shortcuts, so have a go but choose a fine day!

Start from Pont ar Gonwy, 778446, keeping W of the stream. The first objective is the minor top of Llechwedd-mawr, 779436, and its small cairn. Then on to the first of Migneint's two lakes, Llyn Serw,

The unsuspected crags of Arenig Fach overlooking Llyn Arenig Fach

where a five minute diversion W reveals one of the few rocky outcrops in this vast morass - an unsuspected little cliff watching over the infant Afon Serw.

Spot height 479m at 786425 is the next target, bringing the second cairn of the day. You are now on the crest of a shallow rise. Follow this SE until it falls away to a broad marshy depression. Nearby is an isolated farmstead, Cefngarw, still used for sheep shearing. Keep well S of it to ensure an easy crossing of the Serw.

So far, though trackless, the going has not been at all bad. However reaching the next checkpoint, the cairn at Carnedd y Gorsgam (813417), involves a mile of deep heather. Pretty to look at, but an ankle-twisting tormentor with only the odd sheep track for respite. Panting up the steep slopes beyond (past a primitive shepherd's hut) seems welcome relief and you will enjoy lunching on Arenig Fach's breezy top, reclining on springy cushions of heather and bilberries while marvelling at the mottled splendour of the Migneint below.

For a fresh way home head for Mochowgryn (tussocky heather

again) and then Carnedd Iago (easier going restored). Iago is the highest point of the day apart from Arenig Fach and a splendid vantage point for admiring the arc of encircling hills. When you resume, follow a faint track along the perimeter of the woods W, trending N of W. As you do this, look out for a line of boundary stones. Follow these for three-quarters of a mile after the woods desert you L, then strike out W for Llyn Dywarchen. Lying in a shallow, windswept hollow it is as cheerless a sheet of water as any in Wales.

For tired walkers the easiest way home is N to regain the road near Rhyd Cerig-gwynion. However purists may prefer to take a compass bearing and keep to the moors via Llechwedd-mawr.

CARNEDD Y FILIAST

The simple heathery mound called Carnedd y Filiast seldom merits a second glance, yet first impressions can deceive. It may have no mountain ruggedness, but for crisp moorland walking with long vistas, peace and solitude it ranks among the best.

The view from the twin-cairned summit (one cairn encircling the trig point, the other sporting a boundary stone) is dominated by the Migneint and the two Arenigs, while E Foel Goch displays a shapely pyramid above the glittering blue of Llyn Hesgyn. The W foreground is filled by Carnedd Llechwedd Llyfn and it is an easy task to combine the two peaks. Simply follow the fence from Carnedd y Filiast W until, after a mile, you come to a rounded cairn marking the start of the spur ridge to Carnedd Llechwedd Llyfn.

Llyn Celyn route (AG14)

Park by the lakeside at 857410 and walk E along the road for quarter of a mile, looking for an overgrown path that slants up the embankment and disappears into the forest through a rickety old gate. You are soon enveloped by trees and ferns while moss-encrusted boulders abound in the dank, dark air. An evocative start, especially when shafts of light pierce the shadows after a shower and the scents of the earth vie with the glistening raindrops.

The path leaves the forest at a gap in a wall, 857413. Proceed half-R now, under power lines, to pick up a white Land-Rover track that cleaves a sea of heather so vast that in summer the air is heavy with its scent. After a mile the path bears E beneath the minor top of Foel Boeth before descending to cross the Nant y Coed. Bear L where it divides (the R fork leads into Cwm Hesgyn). You can save time at the end, where the path arcs round in a long curve, by heading direct for the cairn as soon as it comes into sight.

Alternatively (AG14,1) leave the path around 865427 to walk over wiry stone-studded heather to Foel Boeth. Next make a bee-line for Carnedd y Filiast, first crossing the Nant y Coed over a footbridge at 867434 and then scrabbling up Brottos over more trackless heather.

Cwm Hesgyn route (AG15)

Go through the gate off the A4212 at 884403 and follow a farm road through pastures. On topping a small rise at 882414 the long secluded Hesgyn Valley comes into view. It has more than a hint of the Pennines or the back of Skiddaw about it with gently rounded heather-clad hills enclosing it on three sides; a gorgeous sight on a bright autumn day.

Another half a mile brings you to a lonely dwelling R, the last habitation you will see - only sheep and wind from here on! Keep R where a track breaks away L to skirt the slopes of Foel Boeth, and cross the Hesgyn by a bridge at 884428. The scene is wilder now and soon your cup is filled as Llyn Hesgyn springs into view. Set in a hollow, dotted with trees, it is a pretty sight and as blue as the best on a sunny day.

You must now cross the valley. It looks simple but there is no track and the intervening ground is an energy-sapping morass of bog and squirmy tussocks. Allow half-an-hour to an hour for this sample of purgatory. If you are in any doubt, rather than risk spoiling a pleasant day, why not settle for exploring Cwm Hesgyn instead?

N approaches (AG16)

Carnedd y Filiast can also be approached from either Ysbyty Ifan, 842488, or Blaen-y-cwm, 882472. However these routes start a long way from the usual walking centres and involve mainly trackless moorland walking.

CARNEDD LLECHWEDD LLYFN

Carnedd Llechwedd Llyfn tops the minor ridge W of Carnedd y Filiast. It is unlikely to feature in anyone's plans apart from Carnedd y Filiast, so try combining the following descent with AG14.

Llyn Celyn route (AG17)

Leave Carnedd Llechwedd Llyfn on 150, aiming for Foel Boeth on grass and stubby heather. Glimpses of the Hesgyn Valley and Craig Ddu enliven the scene L with Llyn Celyn to the fore. However it is the two Arenigs that steal the show, looking veritable giants with Arenig Fach, for once, yielding nothing to its senior colleague. If the sun is out you may see Llyn Arenig Fach sparkling high up (or so it seems) on its slopes, one of the rare occasions when it is coaxed out of seclusion. From Foel Boeth stay on 150 and AG14,1 back to Llyn Celyn.

FOEL GOCH

Foel Goch is a loner, surrounded by roads and looking its best towering over Bala from the N. Although its S and E slopes are prettily wooded it is a bare windswept hill of empty grassland. Peak-bagging apart, it is best kept for a quick blow on a rain-shortened day. However it is a fine viewpoint with Snowdonia, the Berwyns, Hirnants, Arans, Dduallt, Rhobell Fawr, the Rhinogs and Arenigs all splendidly arrayed.

The top is thrice crowned, sporting a trig point, a cairn and a boundary marker. Yet despite this proliferation there are few landmarks. No wall or fence crosses the summit, and if stranded the wisest course is to drop down to the col just E of the top where a fence quickly leads to lower ground, N or S.

S approaches (AG18)

Walk up the narrow road to Pentre-tai-yn-y-cwm Farm at 957403 and follow the tree-lined lane that accompanies the chattering Nant Cwm Da until you come to a bridge after about half a mile. You then have three choices. Firstly to stay with the stream, eventually reaching the col at 959425 after some mild bog-bashing following the disappearance of the path. Secondly (AG18,1) to strike out L for

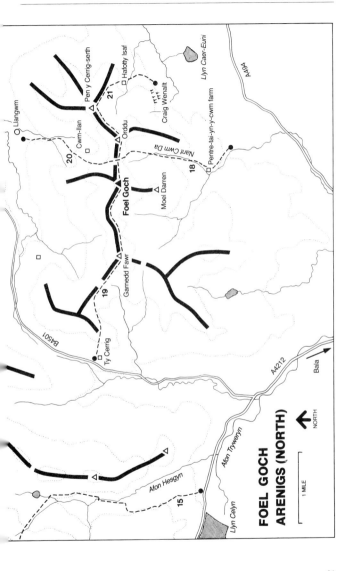

FOEL GOCH
ARENIGS (NORTH)

Moel Darren, 952414, and the S ridge. Thirdly (AG18,2) to bear R for Bryn Bras whence the top is reached via Orddu and the col as before. Bryn Bras offers fine views, not least of the picturesque Llyn Caer Euni.

NW approaches (AG19)

Leave the B4501 at 914429 and walk down the lane towards Ty Cerrig. Turn L just before the farm and follow a grassy track up the hillside. When this peters out pull up to the NW ridge where a wire fence accompanies you to Garnedd Fawr. The main top, hidden so far, now comes into view about a mile away E over undulating grassland with a scattering of boundary stones pointing the way.

Alternatively (AG19,1) start by following a footpath sign at 912426 and then bearing NE to join the ridge as before. The ridge can also be reached from Aeddren at 938442 by following a new bulldozed track that curves round its N tip (AG19,2).

N approaches (AG20)

From near Llangwm a track runs S towards Cwm-llan, 961430, from where the col at 959425 can be reached after a short rise.

SE approaches (AG21)

A track climbs steeply alongside the woods just to the E of Craig Wenallt at 976415. By proceeding N from there via the old homestead of Hafotty Isaf the E ridge can be gained around Pen y Cerrig-serth, 971429.

DDUALLT

Dduallt is a favourite of mine. Lest I eulogise too much, perhaps you should discount just a little of what I say, but not too much for here is one of the jewels of the Welsh hills.

My first awareness of Dduallt came while walking the Arans. I was struck, one brisk sunlit morning, by a huge triangle of naked rock across the valley which I later discovered to be the E face of Dduallt. My excitement was all the greater as this was terra incognita; who ever tramped the wilderness S of Arenig Fawr? Later I also came to recognise Dduallt's distinctive thrust from the Arenigs; a

Dduallt rising over Lake Bala

perfect foil to Rhobell Fawr's curvaceous top. When I eventually climbed Dduallt I was not disappointed. The precipitous E face (not unlike Pavey Ark in Lakeland) which truly earns Dduallt its title of Black Height when in shadow, is balanced by gentler W slopes just as the N ridge balances the equally attractive S ridge.

The summit is an airy perch of heather and bilberries, miniature rocky outcrops and playful pools (one close by the cairn, a cluster a short way down-slope SE). To gild the lily, just below the beautifully sculptured cairn, a cleft in the rocks provides the perfect shelter from the wind.

It is easy to list the peaks on display - Snowdonia, the Arenigs, Hirnants, Berwyns, Arans, Cader Idris, Rhinogs - but that is only the hors d'oeuvre. The majesty of the scene owes at least as much to the virgin wilderness, where works of man are subservient to Nature's creation; to the blend of rustic vales with rounded hills and the multi-coloured patchwork of marsh and heather, forest and rock.

Allt-lwyd route (AG22)

Cwm yr Allt-lwyd has a strangely forbidding air. Maybe it is the bleak treeless slopes; treeless, that is, apart from the man-made forest higher up the vale. Perhaps it is the absence of human settlement; for there are more ruins than inhabited dwellings.

Whatever the reason it deserves to be better known for it offers both the easiest line of approach to Dduallt and a base for a superb round taking in Rhobell Fawr as well.

Park by the bridge at 788293 and follow the stony track along the S bank of the river before crossing to the derelict homestead of Allt-lwyd. Next follow a gritty track that climbs steeply out of the valley, weaving over bleak moors to a ford at 810293 whence the foot of N ridge is but a short step away.

Despite the difference in scale, the walk assumes a character reminiscent of Tryfan. Grass yields to sprightly thickets of heather and bilberry that cloak emergent terraces of rock. Rhobell Fawr beckons temptingly W, with Rhobell y Big in the foreground hoisting a perfect cone. To the N Arenig Fach rises slowly in the arc spanning Arenig Fawr and Moel Llyfnant. When the slope eases cross the fence and walk along the cliffs, above a dizzy drop L, to gain the summit of one of the finest tops in Wales.

Buarthmeini route (AG23)

Park W of the farm at 827325, where the road bridges a tiny stream. Cross a field to the footbridge over the Lliw at 827325. The falls upstream are a grand sight when in full spate. Over the bridge a faint path, little more than a sheep track, wends W or slightly S of W, with the Afon Lliw keeping you company R and the shattered crags of Clogwyn Careg-yr-hollt L. Across the valley Arenig Fawr is completely overshadowed, for once, by the brooding dome of Moel Llyfnant.

After about a mile a deepish gully looms ahead with a break in the crags L, 813322. This is your signal to desert the valley and to scramble up to the flat marshy 'badlands' that guard Dduallt's N and E approaches. Once aloft, bear R for drier ground along the shallow ridge of Mynydd Bryn-llech that bounds the depression W.

The scenery is the very archetype of wild Wales; Arenigs N, Rhinogs W, Arans E, Cader Idris S. No hint of civilisation intrudes as the gaze leaps to the far blue haze. Nothing disturbs the fantasy of hills and heath, bog and woodland that overwhelms as much by its spaciousness as its calm beauty. For lovers of the wild this is a treasure-place. Keep S along the ridge. You should meet the banks of the Mawddach, near the ford at 810293, to finish on AG22.

Cerrig Chwibanog route (AG24)

A magnificent day awaits anyone coupling this with the previous walk. Navigation needs watching and there are a few wet patches, but nothing to deter an ardent fellwalker with a keen eye. The key is to plan your descent while resting by the cairn on Dduallt. Take a bearing of 15 or 20 and try to spot the whitish rock-strewn slopes of Cerrig Chwibanog from among the shallow line of hills hiding the Lliw Valley. Just in front you will notice a slight depression. This is the next objective and on a clear day you may even glimpse the woods to which it leads. In between lies a mile spattered by emerald marsh and you need to plan your route using odd gates, fences and islands of dry ground as landmarks.

Near Cerrig Chwibanog the bog relents and a track appears in the depression. This passes through a gate and descends steeply through the forest, joining a farm road at 843313 by another gate and a giant boulder. Walkers based on Buarthmeini, having started on AG23, should bear L for the farm at Craig y-tan. A path, exiguous in places, continues up this sylvan vale to a bridge at 831323 and then Buarthmeini (AG23,1), a beautiful ending to a memorable day! For Dolhendre turn R to regain the bridge at 853308 in an easy ten minutes with Castell Carndochan casting an aura of mystery and romance to the very end.

Craig y Llestri route (AG25)

This rough 'sporting' walk starts along the SW fork of the crossroads at 853308, S of the bridge at Dolhendre. Where the road swings L (almost at once), carry straight on through a gate and progress along a grassy lane to a spoil heap at 848306. The lane continues through a rusty old gate but you must leave it here and bear R on a green track through a gap in the wall that parallels the slopes of Castell Carndochan. Stay with the wall as the crags of Craig y Llestri rear ahead, then cross the Afon Fwy (you may have to head upstream to a bridge when it is in full spate) to climb one of several bracken-clad breaches in the crags. As you top the crest the great wedge of Dduallt appears in all its dark, brooding splendour.

A shallow ridge falls away from Craig y Llestri before rising again to spot height 493 at 820281. This is the next objective. At the time of writing the intervening ground is newly afforested but there are plenty of fire breaks and, whatever their demerits, at least they are relatively dry and certainly preferable to the quagmire around Nant y Fign. As you approach Dduallt trend N to a grassy rake for an easy pull up to N ridge and AG22.

S ridge (AG26)

The entrée to this route is the mountain road that leaves the A494 at 798217. It winds through foothills to what used to be the old stone cottage of Ty-newydd-y-mynydd (recently demolished). However you should park well down the valley as there is scant space higher up.

Just short of the cottage site is a fire break where old forestry plantations give way to new. Continue along the road for another quarter of a mile until, at the top of a small rise, by a stone gate-post and a fire station, there is a further fire break where the new plantation ends and the old is resumed. Turn R here and walk through the fire break until you meet a fence bounding the forest at its far end, 804259. Turn L along the fence and walk down and up two depressions until, at a little knoll following the second, the forest boundary leaves you L and the S ridge comes into view half-L, 806259. Stay with the fence to another gate but then strike out direct for the ridge.

It is trackless, marshy and tussocky at first but the going soon improves as height is gained in a series of rocky steps. Higher up a fence comes in R, with a faint track which leads to the cairn. Avoid the temptation to stay with this too long in descent as it would eventually land you in difficult boggy country well to the SE. On the other hand (AG26,1) you might well decide to cross the forest using the more S of the two fire breaks mentioned earlier. You would then be ideally placed, at 799257, for an ascent of Rhobell Fawr on AG27

RHOBELL FAWR

Where Dduallt is sharp, precipitous and severe in its ridges and the plunge of its E face, Rhobell Fawr exudes a quiet dignity, presenting a gently rounded profile to the world. Nevertheless there is power too, albeit power with serenity, for Rhobell Fawr is as rugged as the best. Only close by the summit cairn do boulder-strewn slopes succumb to grass. The view rivals that from Dduallt in scale, but is more easily achieved. It would be hard to take an hour over the climb from Ty-newydd-y-mynydd, a small price to pay for such a pearl.

Ty-newydd-y-mynydd route (AG27)

The shortest way to Rhobell Fawr starts from 799258 where the old cottage of Ty-newydd-y-mynydd used to stand (see AG26). The cottage has gone but the site is still identifiable since it is on the boundary between new and mature forestry plantations. Across the road is a gate. Go through this and walk up the gentle rise W. This brings you to a small depression with a wall climbing the bouldery slopes beyond. Follow this until the gradient moderates and another wall crosses your path. Now bear slightly S of W, across increasingly grassy terrain, until the trig point springs up on the skyline behind yet another wall.

Allt-lwyd route (AG28)

By steering N from the cairn a descent can be made to Cwm yr Allt-lwyd. There is no track and knobbly tussocks and a succession of drainage leats make for tedious walking.

Cors-y-garnedd route (AG29)

The old drovers' road that skirts Rhobell Fawr's W flanks, crossing Bwlch Goriwared on its way to Cors-y-garnedd and Llanfachreth, offers connoisseurs a novel route in wild country. Leave the trig point SW, threading through boulders until you meet a wall descending in much the same direction. This carries on to the drovers' road with a sketchy track alongside and beautiful views over the Mawddach Estuary.

HIGH-LEVEL WALKS
Arenig Fawr/Moel Llyfnant circular (AG H1)

If you only have time for one walk in the N Arenigs this should be it. Start by scaling Arenig Fawr on AG1, viewing Llyn Arenig Fawr en-route. Continue S for lunch at the tarns near Craig y Bychau, AG2. Cross the col to Moel Llyfnant, AG6. Descend Llyfnant's N ridge, AG5, and carry on via Amnodd-bwll and Amnodd-wen to the road at 823393, leaving a one and a half mile trudge back to base.

Arenig Fawr/Foel Boeth circular (AG H2)

For peak-baggers after Foel Boeth's scalp, or anyone seeking a moorland hike with guaranteed solitude, this fits the bill. Follow AG H1 to Moel Llyfnant but then cross the Lliw Valley to Foel Boeth (AG7/11). Follow the ridge N, passing over Bwlch y Bi and Moel y Slates (785364) before freelancing R across rampant heather to join the dismantled rail track near Nant Ddu with a three mile march to regain your transport.

Carnedd y Filiast/Llechwedd Llyfn circular (AG H3)

This combines the Llyn Celyn route to Carnedd y Filiast with a return over Carnedd Llechwedd Llyfn (AG14/17). Another option would be to approach Carnedd y Filiast from the Hesgyn Valley (AG15), provided you are prepared for the rough scramble around Llyn Hesgyn and a longer road walk in the evening. Second to none for rolling moors and scented rampant heather!

Afon Gelyn horseshoe (AG H4)

Climb Carnedd y Filiast from Llyn Celyn (AG14) and then stay with the fence that straddles the skyline as it weaves somewhat unadventurously across the moors. A faint track eases the way and Arenig Fach grows majestically with every stride. Around 825432 you must leave the fence and cut across boulder-strewn heather to pick up the playful little path that climbs Arenig Fach's N face (AG11). A descent over Bryn Du (AG12) returns you to the road at 844418 within a mile of your start.

Dduallt/Rhobell Fawr circular (AG H5)

This magnificent walk deserves a special day, so choose a fine one. You warm up on Dduallt's N ridge, starting from Cwm yr Allt-lwyd (AG22). Next you coast down the S ridge to Ty-newydd-y-mynydd (AG26,1) where you are perfectly positioned to claim Rhobell Fawr on AG27. The long wettish tramp down the N slopes of Rhobell Fawr (AG28) is an anti-climax but a small price to pay for a day with two of Wales' most charismatic peaks.

*The headwaters of Afon Lliw with the long rambling ridge of
Foel Boeth on the skyline*

LOWER-LEVEL WALKS/EASIER DAYS

Craig y Bychau lakes (AG L1)

Many pleasant hours could be spent pottering among the lakes near
Craig y Bychau, AG2. Arenig Fawr towers above, Moel Llyfnant
plays the giant W and there are lovely all-round views. Outcrops,
hollows and a sprinkling of rocky terraces guarantee plenty of rest
spots.

The Migneint (AG L2)

AG13 describes one of the best walks in the Migneint but there are
plenty more, starting from either the B4407 or the B4391. You will
find it less marshy than is often claimed and there are clumps of
springy heather to lunch on. However do not stray too far afield
unless you are expert with a compass: landmarks are a rarity! You
could do worse than start from Pont ar Gonwy as in AG13. Even if
you only went as far as Llechwedd-mawr or Llyn Serw you would
still get a good taste of this unique wilderness.

Foel Boeth heather slopes (AG L3)

This is the Foel Boeth beneath Carnedd y Filiast, not the dreary hump W of Moel Llyfnant. The object is unashamed laziness: a day luxuriating in a sea of scented heather with Llyn Celyn shimmering in the valley and the Arenigs ranging larger than life on the skyline. Follow AG14 as far as energy allows.

Lliw Valley (AG L4)

The Lliw Valley is ideal for filling the odd two hours, maybe on a day when the sun only peeps through late in the afternoon. Start from the bridge at Dolhendre, 853308, and continue beneath Castell Carndochan along the footpath to Buarthmeini, 828325. The path is little used nowadays and capricious; but it is there, given patience! A restful blend of woodlands and pastures, crag and brook all the way, plus the falls at 823325 if you get that far (see AG23/24).

Hesgyn Valley (AG L5)

Another walk for filling the odd hour. Start on AG15 and go as far as the spirit is willing. There are picnic spots aplenty, though it would be a pity to stop short of the secluded valley head and Llyn Hesgyn.

Afon Mawddach Falls (AG L6)

For a day out of the wind try a walk from the wooded picnic site on the banks of the Mawddach at 730234. Follow the forest trail N, keeping a weather eye open for white-water enthusiasts, until you reach the dark plunging falls of Rhaeadr Mawddach at 736275. Cross Pont Gilrhyd and then, almost at once, a second bridge beneath the foaming cataracts of Pistyll Cain. Return down the true R bank of the Mawddach, regaining your original line over the bridge at 734251.

THE BERWYNS

OS map 1:50,000 - Sheet 125

Peaks	Height (ft)	Map Ref	Page
Cadair Berwyn (S top)	2723	072324	78
Moel Sych	2713	066319	76
Cadair Berwyn (N top)	2713	072327	78
Cadair Bronwen	2572	077347	79
Tomle	2431	085336	81
Foel Wen	2263	100334	81
Mynydd Tawr	2234	113324	81
Godor	2224	095307	81
Post Gwyn	2165	049294	82
Moel Fferna	2066	116398	86
Nameless	2037	089369	84
Glan-hafon	1991	082273	90

Mountain Lakes

Lluncaws	1900	071317	

Note: All previous literature on the Berwyns seems to refer to Moel Sych and Cadair Berwyn (N top) as being jointly the highest points in the range at 2713ft, although larger scale maps give Moel Sych the benefit of the doubt by one foot. No reference is made to what I have called the S top of Cadair Berwyn although it is quite clearly higher than either Moel Sych or the N top when seen on the ground.

In autumn 1988 the Ordnance Survey announced that the S top is indeed the highest point of the Berwyns at about 2723ft, the exact elevation not being known. As a result it is being suggested that S top be given its own identity and Craig Uchaf has been mentioned as a possible name. In the midst of this uncertainty I am listing N top and S top separately above, but treating them as two crests of the

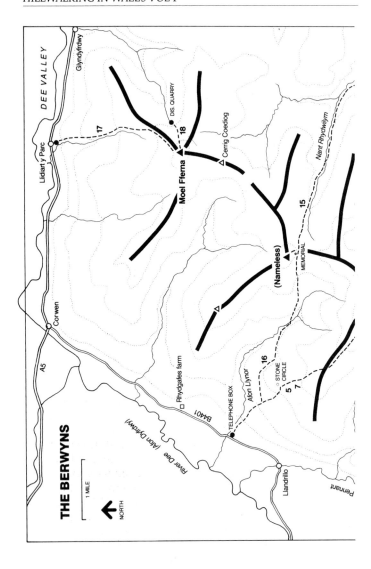

THE BERWYNS

NORTH

1 MILE

DEE VALLEY

Glyndyfrdwy

Llidiart y Parc

Corwen

A5

River Dee (Afon Dyfrdwy)

Rhydgates farm

B4401

TELEPHONE BOX

Llandrillo

Pennant

DIS. QUARRY

17

18

Moel Fferna

Cerrig Coediog

15

16

5

7

(Nameless)

MEMORIAL

STONE CIRCLE

Afon Llynor

Nant Rhydwlym

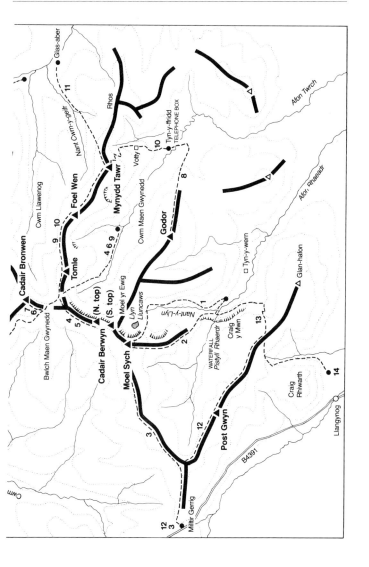

same peak in the route descriptions that follow. The two tops are in any case too close together, in my view, to merit separate recognition.

THE BERWYNS

Mention 'Berwyns' and I immediately think of landscapes, but not in any dramatic sense for the Berwyns are reticent to a fault. Only along their scarped E edge does a truly mountainly aura shine through. Here we have a more elusive charm; to do with spaciousness, peace, solitude and timelessness. The Berwyns are friendly restful hills, made for lingering and mediation, a haven for hill-lovers. Rock-hounds and peak-baggers should look elsewhere.

There is no better way to imbibe the character of the Berwyns than to tramp the ridge from Mynydd Tawr to Cadair Berwyn on a sun-dappled day in high summer with drifting white clouds above. Across Cwm Maen Gwynedd the Godor ridge, rounded and broad, is a tapestry of tussocky mossy turf, speckled with peat hags, crowned in purple and fringed with ferns, while to the E the land declines in a mosaic of hillocks and meadows to the Shropshire plains and a fleeting glimpse of the Long Mynd.

The best comes as you turn N: ripples of gently swelling ridges and green sheltered glens, dappled with copses and woods, form a memorable palette of colour. Mottled greens and browns vie with seas of purple heather until all is lost in the haze of the Denbigh moors and the lonely Clwydian hills beyond Llangollen. Mounting the main Berwyn ridge and gazing W the scene is similar, but now the long view is enhanced by the shapely profiles of the Arans, Arenigs, Rhinogs, and, when the air is especially clear, by the Snowdonia giants themselves.

The Berwyns occupy a vast area, from the foothills of the Dee N and W to the Vale of Tanat in the S. Thus they lie astride the backbone of Wales since the Dee flows into the Irish Sea while the Tanat feeds the Severn. However the area of most interest to the walker is confined to a long undulating ridge of stubby heather, stretching from Moel Fferna in the N to Milltir Gerrig (the high point of the B4391 as it crosses the moors from Welshpool to Bala) in the S.

There are five 2000 footers straddling the ridge. Moel Fferna and a nameless top some three miles farther S are little known. The

Berwyn ridge from the crags NW of Mynydd Tarw

others - Cadair Bronwen, Cadair Berwyn, Moel Sych - form the heart of the range. A compelling triumvirate, provided they are approached from the E, that is. From the W they sell themselves short, revelling in featureless monotonous slopes. How different from the E when the dark broken precipice of crags and heather-clad steeps, four miles long and breached in only three places by walkers' tracks, kindles a tingle of anticipation.

The anticipation is amply rewarded! The breezy walk along this lofty edge is a gem, the crowning glory of the Berwyns. From Moel Sych's bald dome to Cadair Bronwen's mighty cairn the land never falls beneath 2300ft while the views maintain an Olympian breadth and majesty. Some 700ft below the ridge, nestling in a lonely hollow in the shadow of Moel Sych is the Berwyns' only lake, the placid Llyn Lluncaws.

There are two subsidiary ridges abutting on the main massif from the E. Mynydd Tawr, Foel Wen and Tomle form an elegant trio on one while Godor squats in solitary isolation at the tip of the other. Either gives an attractive entrée to the heartland, facing the escarpment all the way. Link them in a horseshoe of Cwm Maen Gwynedd and you have a round to remember. Yet, strangely, you can almost guarantee having it all to yourself. The reason is simple: Pistyll Rhaeadr.

The famous falls of Pistyll Rhaeadr are one of the seven wonders of Wales. Set in a shady glade they enjoy a romantic setting: two torrents of sparkling white tumble headlong to a splash of spraying cascades, before plunging again to a narrow (natural) arch where they unite in a single foaming plume to feed the bubbling cataracts nearly 300ft below. Such is their fame that few walkers consider starting their day from anywhere else. So while the crowds toil up Moel Sych's S ridge or congregate beside the Nant y Llyn, the rest is left in peace.

The Berwyns' remaining top, Post Gwyn, lies above the falls to the W. It is this solitary outlier, on a remote spur, that I fancy has given rise to the fiction that the Berwyns are harsh opponents, consumed by waist-high trackless heather. W of Post Gwyn, on the slopes down to Milltir Gerrig, and to a lesser extent N of Moel Fferna, this is certainly so. The beautiful rash of pinks and mauves, so appealing to the eye, is a snare for the unwary and purgatory for tired limbs. However, elsewhere you can relax and stride to your heart's content, enjoying to the full these incomparable landscapes. In the words of Gilbert and Sullivan the man-eating heather of the Berwyns is a myth that has been 'prodigiously exaggerated.'

MOEL SYCH

Moel Sych (the Dry Hill) is a bare exposed top where I once stood in the sun counting seven separate showers in full spate all around. Lest you think I have the luck of the devil I hasten to add that I am usually on the receiving end! All you will find here is a large cairn sitting at a junction of fences where three ridges meet: SW to Milltir Gerrig (BN3); S to Pistyll Rhaeadr (BN2); NE to Cadair Berwyn and all points N along the main Berwyn spine.

Much more interesting is Cadair Berwyn's rocky S top, a short step away up a broad grassy arm, to which most walkers proceed without more than the briefest of pauses on Moel Sych. Half-way along, in a transient dip, try and spot a shy wisp of a path, part grass part shale, that sidles away beneath the crags to a fence. This would lead you over Moel yr Ewig and on to Godor. But that is for another day.

Nant y Llyn route (BN1)

Pistyll Rhaeadr is a popular haunt for weekend motorists. It is also the starting point for two of the most popular walks in the Berwyns and by combining these - preferably out on BN1, home on BN2 - an enjoyable day is there for the taking. You can either park by the café at the foot of the falls or on grass verges by the stream. Either way you will have to backtrack a little to pick up the firm green path that leaves the road by a gate at 079291.

The path curls round the slopes above the true L bank of the Nant y Llyn. The valley is wide and empty but the spiky ramparts of Cadair Berwyn keep the adrenalin flowing, looking from this distance more impressive than they really are. The green path gives up the ghost once you cross the stream at 076310 but a damp peaty track takes its place, winding above the S shores of Llyn Lluncaws before climbing steeply up a heathery edge to the cairn.

S ridge (BN2)

Leave the cairn S down a heathery slope beside a fence. Where the angle eases cross to the E side of the fence, keeping above the crags that frown down on Nant y Llyn. A budding path darkens the grass, bringing you to within sight of Pistyll Rhaeadr and a Land-Rover track that descends towards the café at the foot of the falls. (This track starts as a green path beside the Afon Disgynfa and links up with BN1 at 076299.) However, before descending you should first enter the woods to view the falls at the top of their dizzy plunge.

If you choose this route for ascent, follow the path behind the café to the old iron bridge that crosses the stream below the falls. Do not cross the bridge: that leads into BN13 and Post Gwyn. Instead follow the footpath sign R.

SW ridge (BN3)

Moel Sych's tapering SW ridge looks a natural. It aims straight for the top, climbing gently from a high 1500ft start. On a sunny day in late summer with the heather in bloom few scenes are more

N top of Cadair Berwyn from S top

appealing, its purple slopes, blending with the valley greens of Dee and Pennant. The only problem is that it is wet, very wet. It shows all the signs of degenerating into a gluey black quagmire that can only get squelchier and wider with each succeeding year. The best time to tackle it is during a drought - if they have droughts in Wales!

You can park at 017305, just above the Powys boundary sign, where the road levels off after the long climb out of Llangynog. You should then backtrack down the hill until you see a cart track at 018302. Follow this for 250yds until it splits, whereupon it is straight ahead for Llandrillo, R for the ridge, with bootmarks in the oozy peat making further directions quite superfluous.

CADAIR BERWYN

The shapely peak that gives its name to the range is unquestionably the king of the Berwyns. Its S top is enticingly capped with a tumble of boulders and a generous windshelter, and it boasts a rugged, broken E face that rivets the eye as you approach it from S or E. The

N top, beyond a vestigial tarn, carries the trig point.

Sandwiched between Moel Sych and Cadair Bronwen, Cadair Berwyn is usually tackled as part of a traverse of the big three. However, as well as this and the two direct routes indicated below, there is another option - to ascend via Godor on BN8, a beautiful walk with the S top glittering like a coronet in the morning sun. The fence along the Godor ridge turns sharp R, almost directly below the S top, at about 074322. From there you can either struggle up beside the fence or follow a playful slip of a track that shelves adventurously, but quite safely, across the face of the mountain to join the ridge in a slight depression midway between S top and Moel Sych.

Bwlch Maen Gwynedd route E (BN4)
See BN6.

Bwlch Maen Gwynedd route W (BN5)
See BN7.

CADAIR BRONWEN
Cadair Bronwen is the most N of the Berwyns' big three. Since its capture involves little short of a three-mile round trip from Cadair Berwyn, and most walkers start from Pistyll Rhaeadr in the S, it is less frequently visited. However the extra effort is well repaid for here you can experience your first impression of the encompassing silence and wildness of the Berwyns' N moors and the vast carpet of purple that sweeps on, remorselessly, to the very gates of Llangollen. The summit is capped with a massive cairn, a six-foot-high dome implanted with a wooden cross which, from many viewpoints, resembles nothing so much as a shark's fin.

Bwlch Maen Gwynedd route E (BN6)
Walk up Cwm Maen Gwynedd, past some woods much frequented by pheasant, until at 084327 you spot a green path wending up the hillside R. This brings you to an iron gate in a fence at 081338. A short digression R then gives you Tomle (BN9). Tigers may pull steeply up L to gain the ridge direct, midway between Cadair Bronwen and Cadair Berwyn (BN6,1). More circumspect folk will go through the

Looking across to Arenig Fawr from Cadair Bronwen's massive cairn

gate and follow the well-used path that curls round the headwall of Cwm Llawenog to Bwlch Maen Gwynedd where there is another gate, nowadays sadly languishing in an ugly splodge of black mud.

Cadair Bronwen is a simple ten-minute walk along the fence R: Cadair Berwyn (BN4) a slightly longer stroll L with a peaty little tarn en-route. The path follows the fence. It is wet and becoming badly churned up by motor-cyclists. Far better to cross the fence and stroll along the edge. The views are superb: Arans and Arenigs to the W, backed by the Rhinogs and a distant glimpse of Snowdonia; long green valleys rolling away E to the lowlands of England.

Bwlch Maen Gwynedd route W (BN7)

The best that can be said for this lonely route is that, together with BN16 it makes it possible to plan a round based on the Dee Valley. On its own it lacks interest; but for a quick, easy-on-the-legs way home after a day exploring the N fells it is perfect. You could hardly miss the start, a black muddy morass by the iron gate at the bwlch midway between Cadair Berwyn and Cadair Bronwen. Shortly after the start the trail divides. The L fork drops down to Cwm Clochnant, passing a lone square copse before eventually joining forest trails that bring you down through Cwm Pennant to Llandrillo (BN7,1).

The R fork contours round above the cwm and is never in doubt as it alternates between N and NW. It is level for long periods (disconcertingly so in mist), doubles up as a Land-Rover track lower down, and eventually joins the start of BN16 on the B4401 at 043385. Do not miss the stone circle at 056372.

GODOR

Godor is an unassuming grassy hump at the tip of a peaty/tussocky ridge that leaves the main massif above Llyn Lluncaws. A small clutch of rocky slabs is all that confirms its mountainly status, but the views are vintage Berwyn. Nevertheless its only possible interest is as part of a horseshoe of Cwm Maen Gwynedd with Mynydd Tawr as the other terminus.

Tyn-y-ffridd route (BN8)

From the road junction at 118309 take the S fork and plod steeply uphill to the first farm gate you come to, marked as point 362 on the map. Follow a white stony track round the edge of some fields until it fizzles out at the corner of a field at 113305. Then proceed half-L across a couple more fields to the fence that straddles the W ridge where a faint track leads uneventfully to the top.

TOMLE/FOEL WEN/MYNYDD TAWR

These three simple grassy tops are the highlights of an easy ridge that runs E from the col separating Cadair Bronwen from Cadair Berwyn. As a glance at the map makes clear, it would be pedantic to distinguish them in route-finding terms. Tomle is marked by a small cluster of flat white stones at a point where the fence that straddles the ridge makes a sharp right-angled turn. Foel Wen is the more W of two unmarked humps. Mynydd Tawr (the Hill of the

Bull) boasts a large rambling windshelter and is becoming increasingly wooded on its E flank.

A faint path hugs the crest - the sort that tries to suck your boots off when wet! That apart it is a jolly hike with glorious views of adjoining ridges and Cadair Berwyn's spiky crown forever urging you on. In such benign surroundings the rocky outcrop W of Mynydd Tawr comes as quite a surprise.

Bwlch Maen Gwynedd route E (BN9)
See BN6.

Tyn-y-ffridd route (BN10)
Start from the phone box at 118309 where a farm road climbs up towards a forestry plantation and the homestead of Votty. The road becomes a typical forest trail after a while, twisting this way and that but open enough to enable you to enjoy the views and so well graded that it makes the 1000ft rise seem much less. It is a warm route too, sheltered by the bulk of Rhos on one side and tucked into a fold in the hillside on the other. Thus it is protected from the prevailing wind and acts as a trap for the morning sun. A final break in the trees, delicately fringed with banks of heather, brings you to a boundary fence with the cairn 100yds L.

Nant Cwm-y-geifr route (BN11)
This provides a useful way off Mynydd Tawr if you are attempting a horseshoe of Cwm Llawenog, say in conjunction with BN15. From the windshelter follow the forest edge until you can make a bee-line down easy slopes (easy for descent that is) to the confluence of two streams at 127334. Now select one of the higher tracks that cleave the bracken above the true R bank of the Nant Cwm-y-geifr. You need to keep fairly high because later on the stream tumbles through a deep, darkly wooded, impenetrable gorge: one of the highlights of the day. You eventually join a more prominent track that merges into a quarry road to bring you down by Glas-aber at 140339.

POST GWYN
The B4391 from Llanfyllin to Bala makes a welcome change from the

A5 when travelling to Wales from London and few stretches are more inspiring than the moors N of Milltir Gerrig. Seas of heather rising to gently rounded hills are hard to resist, and what better foray could there be than Post Gwyn? Less than an hour from the road, up an easy ridge (or so it seems from the map), with lovely views of the Berwyn and Hirnant hills thrown in for good measure. There is just one snag, the ridge in question, the W ridge, is virtually trackless. The heather may look appealing, especially in its autumn finery, but one and a half miles of deep squirmy tussocks with every step a step into the unknown, is a long way! Such walking dampens enthusiasm in the morning and is certainly not for tired legs in the evening! Not that I want to put you off Post Gwyn. On the contrary it is a jolly objective for an easy half-day, but only if you tackle it from the E where the sting is drawn.

W ridge (BN12)

If you nevertheless feel game for the W ridge, start along BN3. After about 20 minutes, when you come to a second little rocky outcrop, break away E. Despite what I have said there is a wee whisper of a track here and there but, even if you are lucky enough to find it, I would not fancy your chances of keeping it for long.

Pistyll Rhaeadr route (BN13)

Cross the bridge beneath the falls and follow the yellow waymark signs. A rustic path that is almost engulfed by bracken in summer skirts the woods beneath the ramparts of Craig y Mwn before turning SW to breast the grassy saddle between Post Gwyn and Glan-hafon near 072280. On the way you weave across an old quarry track which you could also pick up from Tyn-y-wern at 085288 (BN13,1). From the saddle it pays to pull up to the crest where it is easy grass with the cairn beckoning you on from afar and Cadair Berwyn displaying a perfect cone N.

Llangynog route (BN14)

It is hard to credit that Llangynog was once the hub of a thriving industry based on slate quarrying and lead mines. Today, despite being surrounded by beautiful unspoilt countryside, it is all but forgotten, even by the hillwalking fraternity. Yet one of the best

*Craig Rhiwarth and the pass between Post Gwyn and Glan-hafon
from near Llangynog*

short rambles in the Berwyns starts on its very doorstep, at 059265 just off the narrow lane that shadows the B4391 N of the Tanat. There you will find a waymarking sign inviting you across the toes of the battlements of Craig Rhiwarth. It clips the corner of a fairy glen before descending through rampant ferns to a farm track that comes in from the R by a gate at 064268. Continue up-valley, via a stony zig-zag, to the shallow col dividing Post Gwyn and Glan-hafon. Either top can then be claimed by a crest walk on springy grass enlivened by extensive views: Nant y Llyn and the Berwyns massif N; the Hirnants, at their most rugged, S.

NAMELESS

The nameless top at 089369, marked by a semi-collapsed cairn on a rocky shelf, is a scrappy mess of burnt heather, tired grass and soggy peat. Were it not a staging post on the traverse of the Berwyns from Moel Fferna to Milltir Gerrig, and for the reference on the map to the memorial plaque beneath its S flank to an unnamed 'Wayfarer, A

Lover of Wales', it is probable that it would be totally forgotten. That would be a pity for it is a good vantage point for the prairie-like landscape and mottled colours of the N Berwyn moors and its ascent from either E or W via a shallow pass is one of the easiest of any of the Welsh peaks. The continuation to Cadair Bronwen is only slightly more taxing, and then only because of the glutinous bog to which the path is gradually succumbing.

Nant Rhydwilym route (BN15)

Although it is a pleasant stroll up the valley from Llanarmon Dyffryn Ceiriog, it is still a longish way and pretty meadows do nothing to make roads any softer! So it pays to try and park by the farm buildings at 136348. Even then you still have a mile of road work before a stony track takes over to climb the wooded slopes above the stream and its tumble of little falls. By the time you pass a shooting hut the views are really opening out with the slopes of Cadair Bronwen and the nameless peak enclosing the shallow notch of the pass in waves of rolling barren moors. At the pass the plaque is set in the rocks on the R, just beyond a bright metallic storage shed. The nameless peak is five minutes due N.

Dee Valley approach (BN16)

If you have done the popular routes up the Berwyns from the E, try this for a change and take the opportunity to explore the Dee Valley. Drive up the B4401 from Llandrillo and park near the phone box at 043385. Walk down the lane beside the vibrant Afon Llynor and then trudge up a sharp incline, beneath a leafy canopy of trees, to a gate at 051376. The gritty track straight ahead leads to Bwlch Maen Gwynedd and BN7. However for today's walk bear L towards a coppice, noting the Arans and Arenigs W. You are soon trending E, skirting two more woods in friendly bracken-clad countryside dotted with heather that is more akin to the E Beacons than N Wales. After the second wood the path dips to cross a stream where playful cascades and clusters of gorse provide the last vestiges of calm before the desolate windswept fells ahead.

The only other landmark - striking a slightly incongruous note for such a remote spot - is a tall metal signpost at 083367 where another track comes in from the L. This offers an alternative routing (BN16,1) starting from the B4401 by Rhydgafes Farm at 050398.

MOEL FFERNA

Like Post Gwyn in the S, this most N of the Berwyns is a heather hill, with the difference that this time there is a track through the heather - all the way if you possess an eagle eye, most of the way if not! Only the heather fields between Llyn Celyn and Carnedd y Filiast in the Arenigs, or around Pen-twyn-mawr in the Black Mountains, can compare with these as they sweeten the air deliciously with their scent. For a quiet reflective walk alone with nature this is worth half a day of anyone's time.

The trig point shown on the map no longer exists; just a large rambling shelter atop a grassy mound, a curious oasis in such a vast sea of heather. If you are aiming for the nameless peak all points S start on 160. You soon come to a junction of fences where a Land-Rover trail heads E and a stile gives access to a pencil-thin track S to the minor top of Cerrig Coediog. This is glutinous and slippery when wet, suitable only for single-file walking, and relatively slow going.

Llidiart y Parc route (BN17)

There are two lanes which head S from the A5, opposite the B5437 junction at 119432. Take the most W. The bustle of the road is soon replaced by the calming burble of a stream down in a glen R. When you come to an ancient moss-coated bridge where the track splits - one half plunging into the woods, the other switching back on itself - follow the latter to a turning circle and then switch back again to your original direction. Follow this for 115 paces and then break away L along a green path that burrows into the woods beneath a tunnel of trees. This brings you to another forest road. Follow this for 25 paces until it also splits, then make off L again up another forest trail. This soon becomes a stony lane skirting the edge of the woods with the smooth silken mound of Moel Fferna proudly hogging the skyline before you.

A gate at 122417 brings you to open country and a lush band of bowling-green quality turf that swathes through bouncy cushions of heather and bilberries with the Clwydian hills resplendent to your rear. Shortly after you become level with a shooting hut down-valley R, the main track turns sharp L. Ignore this and carry straight on along a faint Land-Rover trail that soon veers to 240 (near a wooden pole) to ascend the hill in a shallow groove. This develops into a slim stony path higher up and is never in doubt if used in descent. However it is easily missed on the way up, for which the penalty is a spell of knee-high heather stomping - very tiring!

Glyndyfrdwy route (BN18)

A shorter, but less interesting approach can be made from the disused quarry at 124400. This involves struggling up through the heather to a fence crossing the skyline E to W, beside which is the summit Land-Rover trail referred to earlier.

HIGH-LEVEL WALKS
Pistyll Rhaeadr circular (BN H1)

Anyone hiking the Berwyns for the first time should have this at the top of their list. My recommendation would be to start with the Nant y Llyn route to Moel Sych (BN1); carry on along the ridge over the twin tops of Cadair Berwyn to Cadair Bronwen; backtrack to Moel Sych and then wend your way home down the S ridge (BN2). If you try it the other way round I think you will find the S ridge a bit of a grind, whereas coming down it provides the perfect finale.

Cwm Maen Gwynedd horseshoe (BN H2)

This is one of my favourites. It omits Pistyll Rhaeadr but otherwise captures the essence of the Berwyns to a T, with varied views all day. Except for the middle section you will probably be on your own with shy little trails that are enough to make the walking pleasant but no more. No peaty quagmires. Let's try and keep it that way!

Start from Tyn-y-ffridd and climb Mynydd Tawr on BN10. Follow the ridge via Tomle to Bwlch Maen Gwynedd, then head S to the dip between Cadair Berwyn's S top and Moel Sych. At this point you should look out for the path that slants back across the mountain face to the Godor ridge at 074322 (see Cadair Berwyn). Next make for Godor. The path follows a fence most of the way but cavorts off to the N towards the end. Finish on BN8.

Cwm Llawenog horseshoe (BN H3)

Try this for a change when you have done BN H1 and BN H2. It is a combination of BN15 and BN11 linked by a tramp along the main ridge from the nameless peak at 089369 to Bwlch Maen Gwynedd.

Dee Valley circular (BN H4)
This is virtually the mirror image of BN H3 formed by coupling BN16 and BN7, preferably in that order.

Milltir Gerrig circular (BN H5)
Provided you can face up the the rigours of the trackless heather coming off Post Gwyn, and a virtual re-ascent from Pistyll Rhaeadr, this has a lot going for it. Up Moel Sych on BN3; down the S ridge to the falls on BN2; up BN13 to Post Gwyn (hard to take if you succumb to tea in the café); then the final challenge of BN12 back to Milltir Gerrig. To be fair the going on this last stretch may be rough, but late summer colours and the sense it conveys of sailing alone on an ocean (so all-embracing is the isolation) can make the toil worthwhile!

Berwyn ridge traverse (BN H6)
It is always exciting to cross a belt of wild open country, remote from roads and the other trappings of civilisation, and when you can combine it with a tramp across the backbone of one of Wales' loftiest mountain ranges, then it becomes even more exciting. All you need is freedom from wheels and the ability to face up to a roughish tramp of some 15 long miles because, once you are committed that is it! BN17 up Moel Fferna gets you going, and though BN3 down to Milltir Gerrig could be a bit more sympathetic to aching limbs at least it is all downhill by then!

LOWER-LEVEL WALKS/EASIER DAYS
So easy is the walking in the Berwyns (with the notable exception of the W slopes of Post Gwyn) that it calls for fine judgement to decide what tips the balance between an easy day and something more exacting. None of the approaches from the Dee should trouble the average pedestrian provided he is well clad and shod. BN15 up the Rhydwilym Valley is equally mild and so is BN1 as far as Llyn Lluncaws. Any of these are pleasant walks with a touch of the wild

Pistyll Rhaeadr

you normally only get in higher realms. However, with that said, here are a couple of suggestions. One is fairly vigorous since it tackles Glan-hafon, a hill which only misses the 2000ft barrier by a mere 9ft. The other, inevitably, is Pistyll Rhaeadr which, at best (or worst, depending on your point of view) demands little more than a quick saunter from the car.

Glan-hafon (BN L1)

Glan-hafon is an excellent viewpoint and the walk up from Llangynog is a little gem with a succession of rocky battlements adding interest as you tramp the long summit ridge to the trig point (BN14).

Pistyll Rhaeadr (BN L2)

There are several options once you have admired the falls. One is to climb the top of the falls as in BN2 and then wander up the Disgynfa Valley. Another is to follow the green track above the Nant y Llyn as in BN1. Less well known, but a pearl of a walk all the same with enchanting views, is to start along the waymarked path beneath Craig y Mwn (as in BN13), aiming for the col between Glan-hafon and Post Gwyn.

The Black Mountains

THE BLACK MOUNTAINS
OS maps 1:25,000 - Sheet 13 1:50,000 - Sheet 161

Peaks	Height (ft)	Map Ref	Page
Waun Fach	2660	215300	102
Pen y Gadair Fawr	2624	229287	105
Pen Allt-mawr	2360	207243	100
Pen Rhos Dirion	2338	212334	111
Black Mountain	2306	255350	115
Twyn Tal-y-cefn	2303	222324	110
Pen Cerrig-calch	2300	217223	97
Twmpa	2263	225350	112
Chwarel y Fan	2228	258294	108
Pen y Beacon	2219	244366	118
Mynydd Llysiau	2173	207279	102
Pen-twyn-mawr	2153	242267	108
Pentwynglas	2115	213257	101
Black Hill	2102	275348	117
Red Daren	2003	281308	114
Mynydd Troed	1998	166293	124
Mynydd Pen-y-fal*	1955	273187	123
Mynydd Llangorse	1666	158263	124
Crug Hywel**	1480	225207	125

*	Sugar Loaf	
**	Table Mountain	

Mountain Lake

Grwyne Fawr	1634	230308

THE BLACK MOUNTAINS

Hills cast their spell in many ways. Sometimes the mere thought of the naked rock of Crib Goch or Tryfan is enough to set the pulse racing. At other times inspiration comes from lonely valleys, or the strange solitude of the Migneint. There are days when the spark is lit by the rugged Rhinogs, where vigilance of foot is repaid with glimpses of their secret places. Then there is the exhilaration of striding long open ridges, free as the wind, subduing the skyline time and again, master of all you survey. For days such as these the Black Mountains have treasures in abundance.

The Black Mountains form a rough quadrilateral running NW to SE. On three sides they are bounded by an escarpment while to the S they gradually taper away to foothills where the Sugar Loaf stands supreme. No less than four lofty, whalebacked ridges cross the range. Each offers miles of superb walking because, once you are launched, there is little variation in height to break your rhythm.

The ridges are deployed like the fingers of a hand with the N arm of the escarpment acting as the 'knuckles' that bind them together. The W boundary is the Rhiangoll Valley from which a variety of approaches lead to the first of the ridges where Pen Allt-mawr is the unquestioned king. Cupped between this and the Pen y Gadair Fawr ridge that comes next is the Grwyne Fechan Valley. Untroubled by roads, this is perhaps the most beautiful of the vales; a haven of peace where pastures and woodlands mingle with heath and fells in a medley of colour that transcends the seasons.

The Grwyne Fawr Valley is less fortunate. Here the works of man intrude - the road, the man-made forests, the picnic areas, the reservoir. Yet, while denying the valley the pristine freshness it once enjoyed, these intrusions are relatively muted and have not destroyed the rustic charm. The Chwarel y Fan ridge that bounds it E is little known. No shapely peak graces its long flat expanse; nor does it enjoy the magic of a name like Offa's Dyke as does the fourth and last ridge beyond the Vale of Ewyas. Despite the road that runs its entire length and crosses Gospel Pass at its head, Ewyas is a beautiful vale, where the ruins of Llanthony Abbey and the lush pastures beside the Afon Honddu are the perfect foil to the bleak ridges that rise either side. Finally, to the E of Offa's Dyke lies the Olchon Valley, unspoilt and forgotten despite an appealing old-

Pen Cerrig-calch and Pen Allt-mawr from Sugar Loaf

world charm.

Superimposed on the main pattern are four subsidiary ridges, all of which are of interest to the walker. The Darren Lwyd runs SE from Twmpa to Capel-y-ffin where the Vale of Ewyas divides. The short Tal Trwynau ridge slopes SE from Pentwynglas. Then there are two of the finest ridges in the whole of S Wales; the Black Hill ridge in the NE and Y Grib, which joins the massif N of Waun Fach.

The 15 2000 footers are spread fairly evenly over the ridges. One of them, Black Hill, is wholly in England while another, Black Mountain, is right on the border. (Both are regarded as Welsh for the purpose of this book.) Few of them are particularly 'peaky' in appearance although Pen Allt-mawr commands attention with its steeply plunging N face, Pen y Gadair Fawr sports a distinctive wedge-shaped top, Pen Cerrig-calch stands aloof at the end of a ridge, while Chwarel y Fan occasionally takes on the pinnacled mantle of a true mountain. Otherwise there is little in the rest to set the adrenalin flowing. Some are no more than shallow mounds rising lethargically from the surrounding moors.

Take Waun Fach. Highest point in the Black Mountains it may be,

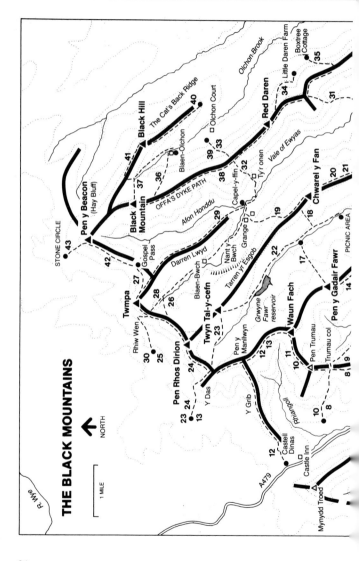

THE BLACK MOUNTAINS

NORTH

1 MILE

R. Wye

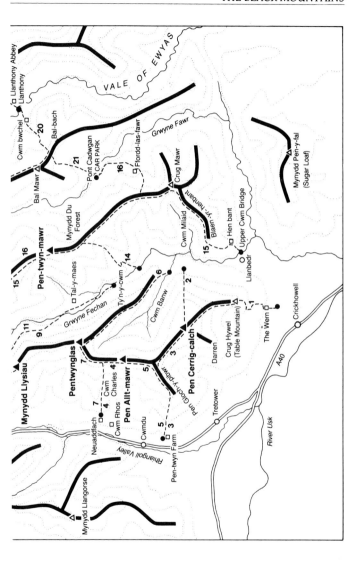

but on the ground it is just a wet, featureless, spongy plateau. Indeed it would be difficult to spot it, were it not for the more distinguished Pen y Gadair Fawr just to the S giving the clue to its whereabouts. Oddly enough several of the shapelier tops are to be found among the lesser brethren below 2000ft: hills like Mynydd Pen-y-fal (the Sugar Loaf), Mynydd Troed, Mynydd Llangorse and Crug Hywel (Table Mountain), all of which give excellent walking too.

Perhaps 'peak' is too evocative a word to use in the Black Mountains, conjuring up as it does images of serrated edges and spiky tops that are far removed from these soft flowing lines. Ridges, not peaks, are the key to the Black Mountains. In Snowdonia you will usually set out to climb (say) Tryfan or Cnicht, while in the Black Mountains it is more likely to be the choice of ridge that determines the day's outing with peaks following almost as incidentals.

Tracks abound. They may be a squelchy mess of black peat or pink mud when wet, but they are never difficult. Moreover after the initial pull up there is usually little ascent and descent so progress is rapid, the miles melting away almost before you know it. Above all the Black Mountains engender a feeling of well-being and spaciousness. With peaks and ridges varying but little in height the gaze is cast far and wide, to distant horizons and the blue beyond. Accompanying the spaciousness is solitude. You will not find crowds in the Black Mountains, even in summer there are days when the sheep will be your sole companions.

The ideal day in the Black Mountains is cool and breezy, the sort of day when sun and cloud send shadows scampering across the fells and a dappled skyline. Late summer gilds the lily with rampant heather that creates a sea of purple and sweetens the air with its heady aroma. The valleys are especially lovely when the browns and golds of autumn irradiate the scene.

As an island of high ground surrounded by valleys (the Wye, Olchon, Usk, and Rhiangoll) you expect wide-ranging views from the Black Mountains. They do not disappoint you. N the gaze extends to the Radnor Forest and is halted short of the Cwmdeuddwr plateau only by the Mynydd Eppynt uplands. E the view sweeps over the Herefordshire foothills to the Wye. The S skyline is filled by

Mynydd Llangatwg and Mynydd Llangynidr, the last bastions of high ground before the valleys that slope down to the Bristol Channel. W are the flowing lines of the Brecon Beacons, Fforest Fawr and the Black Mountain, treasures for another day.

Inwards the best views are found to the S and W of the range. The N 'knuckle' is a vast prairie of shaggy grassland with little variety while the line of sight from Offa's Dyke jumps over Ewyas without so much as a peep. On the other hand the view from Pen Allt-mawr, spanning the Rhiangoll and Grwyne Fechan valleys, is one of ineffable loveliness. But wherever you go the bleakness of the N gradually moderates as you move S and gentle pastures and woodlands increasingly mellow the scene.

As always, care is needed. These giant whalebacked ridges, friendly enough in fair weather, must never be treated with less than full respect. Their very openness exposes them to the worst that Nature can muster. In winter, with a gusting wind, they can be bitter and bleak while in high summer there is little shelter from the scorching sun. Mist brings its own problems because of the paucity of landmarks and the lack of variation in height along the ridges. Then is the time to keep to the S half of the range or along the N escarpment. Unless you are an expert the environs of Waun Fach and Twyn Tal-y-cefn can be particularly confusing.

PEN CERRIG-CALCH

Pen Cerrig-calch is the most S of the Black Mountains and is often the first port of call for walkers setting out from Crickhowell. It has the stoniest top of any of the Black Mountains, a feature that gives it an odd 'frosty' look when viewed from afar. It is also a splendid viewpoint.

Of all the riches on display, nothing surpasses the curvaceous Sugar Loaf - a rounded green hill, pure in line, stately and aloof, arcing the sky in flawless beauty. Round to the S, more prosaically, the eye jumps Crickhowell and the Usk to the barren moors of Mynydd Llangattock and Mynydd Llangynidr. The E skyline is dominated by the Brecon Beacons with the Black Mountain peeping over their shoulder. The NW belongs to Mynydd Troed and the distant Wye Valley. The circle is completed N and E by the Grwyne

Pen Cerrig-calch from near Crug Mawr

Fechan Valley adding a touch of pastoral charm to the wedge of Pen y Gadair Fawr which, as so often, overshadows its higher neighbour, Waun Fach.

Table Mountain route (BS1)

The shortest way to Table Mountain, the first port of call on this route, is via Perth-y-pia Farm and is waymarked from the road at 234207. However the following route to Table Mountain is also worth noting as combining the two gives a pleasing after-dinner stroll, returning along the country road.

Start from 223193 and walk up the lane to 'The Wern'. Turn R through a gate with a yellow waymark, cross the field to a second gate similarly marked, then turn L along a grassy lane between two hedges. When you reach yet another gate, follow a line of trees across two more fields. Climb over a stile to join a short section of tarmac which quickly bears R to take you into another field. This leads uphill to a copse at 224203 where there is a further stile and an old sign, 'FP To Mountain'.

Turn R through the copse but leave it when you reach a gate with Table Mountain rearing up L with surprising vigour. The route is now obvious, a green path climbing steeply through thick bracken. Table Mountain belies its name, its spacious top noticeably tilting from S to N. However it yields little to Pen Cerrig-calch as a viewpoint except where the latter's own vast bulk restricts the outlook N.

From Table Mountain a pleasant track, distinct without being obtrusive, wends steadily N on to Pen Cerrig-calch with the crags of Darren off L. It is superb in late summer when the mauve of the heather, the yellow of the gorse and the red tips of the bilberry leaves combine in a glorious palette of colour. Regretfully, bleakness is just around the corner, for the ground is still black and lifeless from a fire some years ago. However the desolation is short-lived, for when you reach the trig point the whole Grwyne Fechan Valley bursts into view in all its verdant splendour.

Cwm Banw route (BS2)

'Route' is perhaps too strong a word to describe what is essentially just a jolty rough scramble down the mountain's steep E slopes. Leave the cairn on a bearing of 80, aiming for the foot of the Pentwynglas ridge opposite. About half-way down try to spot a track that slants across the hillside. If you are lucky it will give welcome relief to your knees and legs and take you to within a field's width of the road at about 236223.

I have climbed up from Cwm Banw several times but the slanting track is not easy to find from below, and even if you are able to locate it there is still a hard unremitting grind after it peters out; not recommended.

Pen Gloch-y-pibwr route (BS3)

This enchanting route reveals the Black Mountains at their most serene but is virtually unknown, no doubt because starts from the Rhiangoll Valley seem curiously out of fashion. Yet for the connoisseur they offer new insights into old friends amidst some of S Wales' most attractive scenery where softly wooded pastures and deep cwms blend with bracken-clad slopes and crisp, heather tops.

To avoid parking problems you will probably find it best to start from Cwmdu, in which case you must walk up the narrow lane towards Pen-twyn Farm, 182229. However, just before entering the farm turn L through a gate to pick up a muddy farm track straight ahead. Follow this through two further gates, each with waymarked stiles at the side, before passing a ruined barn L followed by a third gate, also with a stile. Next walk alongside a small wood L until, after yet another gate, a small rise L at last brings you to open country.

This is a good spot to pause and admire the view. The splintered, rather aggressive looking rocks straight ahead are Pen Gloch-y-pibwr, for once totally upstaging the usually charismatic Pen Allt-mawr. The N horizon is consumed by a huge arc of Mynydd Llangorse, Mynydd Troed, Castell Dinas and Y Grib. Further afield, W and S, there are the Brecon Beacons and the moors of Mynydd Llangattock.

When you resume, a wide grassy track wends through the bracken to a shallow ridge that ascends to Pen Gloch-y-pibwr. From there follow a path SE along the edge of the elongated plateau linking Pen Cerrig-calch to Pen Allt-mawr, with glorious views down to the Usk. This is also a fine route for descent. Indeed if you are ever lucky enough to be homeward bound as the sun is setting, the golden glow of the Beacons and the shafts of sunlight reflecting off the roof-tops of Cwmdu and Tretower will surely live in your memory.

PEN ALLT-MAWR

Pen Allt-Mawr is the most shapely of the Black Mountains, its N face plunging dramatically down to reveal a profile not unlike Pen y Ghent in the Yorkshire Dales. Whether seen from the A40, the Rhiangoll Valley or Waun Fach, it has an aura of 'mountainliness' that many of its fellows lack. As a vantage point it rivals Pen Cerrig-calch, particularly round the head of the Grwyne Fechan Valley. However it is less formidable than it looks. The pull up the N face is a ten-minute affair at worst, while the approach from the S is level going.

Pen Allt-mawr is usually climbed via Pen Cerrig-calch as part of a longer ridge walk. As a result the two routes below are seldom used. Both are gems.

Cwm Charles route (BS4)

Some of the most rewarding approaches to the Black Mountains start from the Rhiangoll Valley and this is one of them. For the easiest start cross the field behind the farmhouse of Neuaddfach at 188251. There you will find a green track slanting enticingly up through the bracken E. Follow this, first through an iron gate and then as it runs in a groove, towards the crest of the ridge that encloses Cwm Charles from the N.

Down to the R is a tumbledown stone wall (quite a rarity hereabouts). This shadows a line of trees down to Cwm Charles, a lovely vale where woodland blends with bracken in a near parkland setting. Foxgloves in profusion and moss-encrusted stones create a pastoral atmosphere where time stands still; valley and fells in perfect harmony.

Higher up the ridge coarse grass and heath take over, but the going is easy and the views superb. It is not long before you meet the well-trodden path linking Pen Allt-mawr to Pentwynglas with both peaks but a few minutes away.

Pen Gloch-y-pibwr route (BS5)

Climb Pen Gloch-y-pibwr as in BS3 and then follow the edge of the plateau N, an exhilarating tramp with a wide stony path underfoot and glorious views W with Mynydd Troed and Mynydd Llangorse looking especially tempting.

PENTWYNGLAS

Like its near neighbour, Mynydd Llysiau, Pentwynglas is essentially a 'technical' peak, qualifying only by possessing the requisite configuration of contour rings. On the ground both are minor humps, mere transit stops for hikers striding the long ridges (and for that reason alone neither lacks visitors). A tiny rocky outcrop and an ancient boundary stone mark the top.

Tal Trwynau ridge route (BS6)

Park by the bridge at 234229 and cross a stile at a white waymark sign. Follow this uphill across a field (the bearing is 30/40) until you come to a gate at 235230 where four tracks meet. Carry on straight ahead along a lane, hedged on both sides, that doubles as a watercourse in wet weather. Shortly after passing some new woods R another gate gives access to the open hillside with a clear trail on to Pentwynglas.

Some old quarry workings introduce a tinge of nostalgia higher up, but this is soon dispelled by fine views of Grwyne Fechan and Cwm Banw, both pleasantly wooded. Further afield Pen y Gadair Fawr is, as usual, prominent on the E skyline while N Mynydd Llysiau displays an aggressively craggy E flank that is rarely seen to such effect. Combined with a circuit of Pen Allt-mawr and Pen Cerrig-calch this lonely little ridge guarantees a pleasant day.

Cwm Charles route (BS7)
Follow BS4, the Cwm Charles route for Pen Allt-mawr, until you meet the ridge path that links that peak to Pentwynglas. Turn L and in ten minutes the top is yours.

MYNYDD LLYSIAU
Like Pentwynglas, Mynydd Llysiau is of little interest except as a transit point on the long ridge that stretches from Pen Allt-mawr to the Trumau col. Indeed so gentle is the rise to its rambling, heathery crown that the highest ground would be in considerable doubt were it not for a colourful little cairn that has recently appeared.

Rhiw Trumau route (BS8)
Follow BS10 to the Trumau col at 204287. Turn S up a small rise to gain the ridge. The top is then a simple five-minute stroll further along.

Grwyne Fechan route (BS9)
Follow BS11 to the Trumau col at 204287; finish as in BS8.

WAUN FACH
Waun Fach may be the highest peak in the Black Mountains but it is scarcely the most attractive. Its huge flat top is a morass of coarse grass, dank, featureless and too wide to permit more than odd

glimpses into adjacent valleys. Even the cairn is set in a sea of peaty mud. To add insult to injury, not only does Pen y Gadair Fawr look the higher peak from afar, it even upstages Waun Fach from its very own top, quite belying the fact that it is actually 36ft lower. Yet Waun Fach will continue to be a popular objective. It stands at a nexus of routes and is effectively the hub of the range. To be fair, if you stroll E from the cairn for a couple of minutes you will be rewarded with fine views of the Chwarel y Fan and Offa's Dyke ridges to complement the distant view of the Brecon Beacons in the W.

The absence of features can cause problems in mist. The safest options are then either on a bearing of 330 towards Pen y Manllwyn or on 240 for Pen Trumau. Either way ensures a clear path that soon brings you to lower ground. Continuing on to Pen y Gadair Fawr is not recommended as the path starts faint and boggy and is bereft of landmarks.

Rhiw Trumau route (BS10)

This is one of the most attractive ways into the fastnesses of the Black Mountains. It starts with a lane that leaves the road at 186289. With care you can park nearby, but probably the best plan is to leave the car by the Castle Inn at 174296. In any case, if you are planning a round trip including the exhilarating Y Grib ridge (BS12) it won't make a lot of difference.

The lane sports a canopy of trees and is thickly hedged either side with hollies. Now four gates come and go in quick succession before you join a pleasantly graded green path that climbs the side of a softly wooded vale. Pen Allt-mawr rears up impressively R - a tasty hors d'oeuvre.

As you reach more level heathland a cairn appears directly ahead, trapped in the V formed by the minor top of Pen Trumau L and Mynydd Llysiau R. This marks the col at 204287 which is a popular crossroads, not least for pony-trekkers. From the col proceed N then NE over the breast of Pen Trumau, following any of a number of well-trodden tracks. As you pass a cairn with boulders daubed orange and blue marking Pen Trumau (does anyone know the significance of these coloured cairns in the Black Mountains?) spare a moment to admire the Sugar Loaf, beautifully framed between Pen y Gadair Fawr L and Pen Allt-mawr R. Perfect balance and symmetry. After this the dull plod up the marshy slope to the marshy top of Waun Fach is an anticlimax.

Another rather more circuitous way to reach the col (BS10,1) is to follow a sign 'To the Hill' which directs you off the minor road at 191270, just short of Ysgubor Ganor Farm. After an initial climb this makes a bold sweep across the W face of Mynydd Llysiau.

Grwyne Fechan route (BS11)

A bridleway runs the length of the Grwyne Fechan Valley. Starting from the road-head at Ty'n-y-cwm at 231247 it provides as leisurely an entrée to the hills as you could wish for - firm, dry and gently graded. Lowland meadows and woodlands slowly give way to the harsher calling of the fells, though on hot days you may find the temptation to linger and bathe in the pools near the Tal-y-maes bridge well nigh irresistible. When you reach the col between Mynydd Llysiau and Pen Trumau carry on as in BS10.

Y Grib route (BS12)

Y Grib gives the best mile of ridge walking in the area. Walk down the lane that heads NE from the A479 at 173301 and stay with it until a gate at 180304 gives access to a pinkish and often muddy path which cleaves its way up a bracken slope to the ridge. What follows is vintage stuff. The ridge, narrow without ever being exposed, rises in an exciting cascade of twists and undulations. The occasional rocky outcrop adds a touch of authenticity while, as with all the best ridges, there is more than a hint of evil in the air when mist swirls around.

In fair weather, however, it is a very different story, particularly if you keep to the crest. The sharpness of the ridge permits glorious views: the verdant lowlands of the Wye L; the gently wooded Rhiangoll Valley R, with the W slopes of the Black Mountains beyond.

All too soon the ridge peters out and succumbs to a dull trudge through coarse grass to the undistinguished top of Pen y Manllwyn, identified by a small cairn with red and white painted stones. From here a wide peaty scar of a path - virtually a quagmire in wet weather - leads unerringly to Waun Fach. Even Rhiangoll looks

Looking W down Y Grib across the Wye Valley

sombre as you progress round its head and the main interest lies in the distinctive reddish hue of the local grass.

Y Das route (BS13)

Proceed as in BS24 to the plateau near Y Das. Next follow a track that heads in a S direction towards Pen y Manllwyn, a small rise on the skyline about one mile away. Finish as in BS12.

PEN Y GADAIR FAWR

Only Waun Fach of the Black Mountains' peaks exceeds Pen y Gadair Fawr in height, and then by a mere 36ft. However, from most viewpoints Gadair Fawr actually looks higher, its distinctive windswept top gaining it pride of place on the skyline for many miles around.

Sadly there is only one direct route (BS17) and even that lacks distinction (its main use being for crossing to/from the Chwarel y Fan ridge). However all that stands in the way of more direct routes is the minor top of Pen-twyn-mawr, so if we ignore that nicety then

Pen y Gadair Fawr is well served! A word of warning; it can be confusing in mist and the safest escape then is SE to join the broad stony track that enters the NW tip of the Mynydd Du Forest. The trail N to Waun Fach should certainly not be trusted in mist. It starts off clearly enough but fades as it nears a boggy wasteland midway between the two peaks.

Grwyne Fechan route (BS14)

Park on the grass verge at 236237, cross the bridge at the bottom of the hill and follow the trail into the forest. As with most forest trails there are a number of U turns, but at least you gain height without too much effort. Before long you see open country ahead, where the trail makes a sharp R turn to hug the edge of the forest (243249). This is your signal to leave the trail, and the forest, by crossing an old wire fence and toiling up a heathery slope on a bearing of about 30.

It is hot work with only fragments of sheep track to ease the way and you will be relieved, when the slope at last moderates, to see a wide, white stony path running parallel to the W boundary of the Mynydd Du Forest along the crest of the ridge. Follow this W of N and after about a mile look out L for the slight rise that is all that indicates the heather-clad top of Pen-twyn-mawr. After another mile you enter the forest itself for a brief spell of what may be very welcome shade. On leaving the woods Pen y Gadair's smooth scalp is 300yds NW.

Blaen-yr-henbant route (BS15)

From the church at Llanbedr take the lane that descends to Upper Cwm Bridge at 242204. Cross the river, climb over a stile L and then ascend the peaty path that zig-zags up through the woods. Before long you reach a large, flat, upright stone where the path leads into a field. Cross this, keeping close to a wire fence L, and then cross a road by two further large, flat stones. Enter the field on the far side and bear R along a faint track until you reach yet another flat stone, this time in a corner of the field. The farm of Hen-bant is now in view half-L. Head for this, still on a shadowy track, but keep it to your R and look out for a sign, 'To the Mountain', by an iron gate behind the farm (fierce dogs). This gives access to a rough and overgrown trail through some more woods.

If this seems complicated Hen-bant can also be reached, a little more circuitously though quite possibly in a more relaxed frame of mind, by one of the minor roads shown on the map.

The trail through the woods soon improves and after half a mile follows a wall R as it gradually veers from N to E to climb the upper slopes of the charming Cwm Milaid, keeping just below the crest of Blaen-yr-henbant and skirting to the L of the trig point on Crug Mawr. At this point the vast expanse of the Mynydd Du Forest comes into sight N, with the delectable Grwyne Fechan Valley far below L and the intervening ground a spectacular rash of colour when the heather is out. You can also pick out the stony track referred to in BS14 as it follows the forest edge towards Pen-y-Gadair Fawr.

Mynydd Du Forest route (BS16)

Park at 266252, cross the road and take the trail that climbs through the forest on a bearing of about 130. Stay with this as it alternates between forest and pasture until you reach the ruined cottage of Ffordd-las-fawr at 266237. Turn L behind the cottage and then, almost at once, bear R along the edge of more woods. You now have a steepish pull up through the forest to reach the boundary fence and emerge into open country at 260236. There you join the stony path mentioned in BS14 to finish as before.

If descending by this route use the 'kink' in the forest's boundary fence at 260237 as a landmark, else you may well find the start of the path down through the woods hard to find.

Forest trails are not to everyone's taste and sometimes they are an eyesore. However this route is pleasant enough, and the spell round the old cottage conveys a curious sense of well-being as if from a bygone world. Be prepared for some improvisation since tree felling can sometimes hide or deflect forest paths.

Grwyne Fawr route (BS17)

Start from the bridge at 243296. This is reached by walking up the Grwyne Fawr Valley unless, of course, you are crossing to/from the Chwarel y Fan ridge. The bridge is a bit of a diversion and it is often possible to cross the stream further down. Often but not always!. Once across you are faced with a hard slog up the steep grassy slope, marginally easier if you keep to the breast of the rise rather than hugging the forest. Either way you will be glad of a flop round the rambling cairn.

PEN-TWYN-MAWR

Pen-twyn-mawr is never likely to be a prime objective as it is merely the highest point of an almost imperceptible swell in the surrounding moors, and quite featureless. Featureless, that is, except in high summer when the air is sweet with the scent of the heather that proliferates for miles around. It is best visited en-route to Pen y Gadair Fawr on BS14, 15 or 16. Having spotted it from the track (for it really is a very slight rise) strike out across the heather. A little diligent searching, and a bit of luck, should then reveal the two or three flattish stones that serve as the cairn.

CHWAREL Y FAN

Chwarel y Fan is a strange mountain. On the map it scarcely rates a second glance. On the ground, too, it often looks no more than a benign little hump - but not always! Seen from the N on the ridge extending to Twyn Tal-y-cefn, Chwarel rears up to a sharp point that becomes a dazzling pinnacle of white when snow falls in winter.

Reality, alas, is more prosaic. The top is indeed a minor hump, capped by a small rocky platform. Alas? Perhaps not. Tops are not everything. The ridge over which Chwarel y Fan presides is made for walking, with long striding miles and wide rambling views. It is at its best towards Bal Mawr (see B20) where the crest narrows and the rough grass of the N yields to soft cushions of heather.

Grwyne Fawr route (BS18)

This route is handy for switching ridges (eg from Pen y Gadair Fawr) but that is about all. It starts at the N edge of the forest at 292249 from where it is simply a matter of toiling up the open hillside, helped by a couple of scrappy tracks, one of which keeps to the side of the forest.

Capel-y-ffin route (BS19)

Start off down the minor road that leads from Capel-y-ffin into Cwm Nant y Bwch but leave it L at 252316 and follow the signs to Grange (shown as Plas Genevieve on the map). Bear L again at the house to join a stony farm track that rises to a gate and then climbs steeply alongside some woods. This is a quagmire of pink mud in wet weather. Fortunately the rise is a brief one and you soon reach easier ground with grass and bracken.

The next objective is a prominent cairn perched on top of the escarpment ahead. This looks quite a challenge but some easy rocky steps (quite a rarity in the Black Mountains) make light work of it and you are soon marching on across a lush heathery plateau. After half a mile you meet the well-trodden path that straddles the ridge all the way from Pen Rhos Dirion to Bal-bach. A large cairn adorned with blue and gold painted stones marks this spot, which it is essential to identify if you are descending by this route. Chwarel y Fan is now an easy three-quarters of a mile to the S, with views into the wooded Grwyne Fawr Valley to lighten every step.

Cwm Bwchel route (BS20)

Leave Llanthony near the telephone kiosk and follow the footpath sign to Bal-bach. Cross over the footbridge (blocked at the far side the last time I was there, but still passable) and then be guided by some rather erratic yellow waymark signs to the farmstead of Cwm Bwchel. This part of the walk is unpleasantly muddy and slippery when wet, but the discomfort is short-lived and perseverance well rewarded. Once past the farm a gritty path climbs the steep-sided Cwm Bwchel in a setting that is wild yet serene; the music of the brook busily tumbling away in the depths of the desolate ravine, the timeless abbey framed in the V of the valley.

A large straggly cairn marks a crossroads of tracks at Bal-bach. Take the track that twists NW up the slope to the trig point at Bal Mawr, passing two black and white iron posts on the way. The magic returns as the track cleaves its way through seas of close-cropped heather along a ridge now sharp enough to give superb all-round views, with Offa's Dyke, the Pen y Gadair Fawr ridge, the reservoir and the Sugar Loaf all vying for attention. Perfect loitering country, and on a hot day Chwarel y Fan may be just a shade too far!

Pont Cadwgan route (BS21)

This route is useful to have in the locker for planning longer rounds. The tedium of the forest is then just about acceptable. Otherwise it would be a waste of time with so much else to do.

From Chwarel y Fan follow BS20 to Bal-bach. Turn R and stay with a boggy track until you reach a dilapidated stone wall running along the edge of some new woods at 270263. Bear L until a gap in the woods enables you to drop down to join a forest road that you will doubtless have spotted from higher up. This eventually brings you down to the car park at 266251 near Pont Cadwgan.

TWYN TAL-Y-CEFN

Twyn Tal-y-cefn is another of those Black Mountain 'peaks' whose sole claim to fame rests on their possessing the necessary contour rings to qualify as a top, despite lacking any presence of their own. There is absolutely nothing there; nothing, to be precise, save a small cairn with stones daubed red, white and blue that rests languidly in a vast expanse of open moor. Not a good place to be in mist!

Grwyne Fawr route (BS22)

Park by the picnic area at 252286, where many peaceful hours could be whiled away on a sunny day by the cascading stream. Shortly before this a sign by the roadside indicates the start of a green track to the reservoir. This is gently graded and runs just below the line of the wood, with Pen y Gadair Fawr for company on the W skyline. Stay with it until you are about half a mile beyond the reservoir and then branch out N over the open fells until you meet the wide peaty path that links Pen Rhos Dirion to Chwarel y Fan. If your navigation is sound Twyn Tal-y-cefn's cairn should soon be in sight to guide you the rest of the way. This is not a walk for a misty day.

Alternatively continue up the road from the picnic area until it terminates beneath the reservoir. A short pull up R then gives you the green track as before.

Y Das route (BS23)

Climb Y Das as for BS24 and then proceed on a bearing of 100 along a trail leading to the Grwyne Fawr reservoir. Leave this after about a mile and strike out on a bearing of 80 over the open fells until Twyn Tal-y-cefn's rounded mound comes into view.

PEN RHOS DIRION

Pen Rhos Dirion is an airy staging post for walkers hiking the N rim of the Black Mountains. A trig point near the plunging edge is the sole adornment on its sprawling bare top, but the views are quite superb. A fresh green mosaic of bridleways, meadows and woodland stretches away to the Wye. This is also one of the best vantage points for imbibing the sheer scale and desolation of the dour and sombre N moors; a tangled expanse from which Twyn Tal-y-cefn and Pen y Manllwyn emerge with surprising stature given their total lack of character nearer to hand.

Y Das route (BS24)

The landscape near the bend in the road at 188333, where this route begins, is a picturesque blend of heath and woodland more like the New Forest than Wales. This illusion is maintained (apart from the hills soaring up ahead!) as you advance down a double avenue of trees passing the Wern-Frank Wood and thickets of gorse L.

Memories of softer climes quickly fade. Off R Mynydd Troed, pointed and aloof, raises a mighty crown. The path bears L to mount a broad grassy shoulder before joining a well graded stony track cut into the slopes above Cwm Cwnstab. Easy, steady going and a tasty aperitif for the choice of routes that awaits once you gain the plateau by a cairn with a protruding pole. Slightly R, on 180, is a path leading to Pen y Manllwyn and Waun Fach (BS13). A second track crosses the moors on 100 to the Grwyne Fawr reservoir (BS23, BS L1). Finally, turning sharp L to follow the escarpment edge leads into a wide peaty track to Pen Rhos Dirion, an easy 20-minute walk with impressive views of Chwarel y Fan and the Grwyne Fawr reservoir on the way.

Rhiw Wen route (BS25)
See BS30.

Nant y Bwch route (BS26)

Follow BS28 to the head of Nant y Bwch where the track from Capel-y-ffin fades. Cross the stream L to pick up another track heading off W. This brings you to the escarpment at 216340 whence Pen Rhos Dirion is a few minutes' walk away L after a small rise.

TWMPA

Twmpa gazes down on Gospel Pass from the W just as Pen y Beacon does from the E. In fact there is more than a passing similarity between these hills. Both are spectacular belvederes perched on the edge of a dizzy escarpment; both also give a quick start to a day in the hills (or an easy way down for tired legs in the evening). Like so many tops in the Black Mountains Twmpa sports a cairn adorned with coloured stones, on this occasion pink and yellow.

Gospel Pass route (BS27)

With a start from nearly 1600ft this shares with the similarly named route to Pen y Beacon the distinction of being the shortest and easiest climb in the Black Mountains. There is only a mile to walk and under 700ft of height to gain. Unfortunately it has become so popular that the track is now a black peaty scar, defacing the once lush grassy slopes. To offset this the timeless peace of the meadows nestling in the valley, and the sense of solitude as the bustle of the road is left behind, quickly kindle a feeling of well-being which deepens as you breast the breezy, heathery top to gaze down on the world below. Twmpa is often the first port of call of a long expedition and it is nice to have a top under your belt so early!

Nant y Bwch route (BS28)

Leave your car near the bridge at Capel-y-ffin, 255315, and advance down the leafy lane that skirts the monastery L before wending its way up one of S Wales' most delectable vales. Cross a ford and look out for a bank of wild caltha R, just before the lane climbs to more open country with bracken slopes close by R and the rugged escarpment of Tarren yr Esgob frowning down L.

Once past the farm at Blaen Bwch the vale narrows and a bridleway follows the chattering stream amid clumps of bracken and heather. A scene with more than a hint of Devon about it, especially where the Nant Ganol, the second of three streams that come tumbling down the hillside L, joins the main stream by shady green banks to give an idyllic picnic spot. Rest there at your peril; you may find it hard to leave!

At the vale head, beyond Nant Uchaf, the trail disappears for a while in a morass of bog. However you have only to press on in the same direction (ignoring the path that rambles away L across the stream towards Pen Rhos Dirion) for it to reappear and lead you to the escarpment at Rhiw Wen where a view of electrifying intensity awaits. Far below a colourful mosaic of green and yellow pastures stretches away as if to infinity. W the Beacons, Fforest Fawr and, on a clear day, the Black Mountain itself all rise tall and proud. S is a veritable desert of rambling bleak moors. Once you have feasted on this magnificent vista it is but a short walk along the edge to Twmpa.

Darren Lwyd route (BS29)

Slow starters beware; the initial scramble onto Darren Lwyd is excruciatingly steep, but at least it completes the hard work in one fell swoop so that you can then relax and enjoy the delicate charms of this sadly forgotten ridge. The shortest approach is up the lane from 254317 to Pen-y-maes where a gate leads to the open hillside. Alternatively a bridleway leaves the Nant y Bwch road at 242323 and you can follow this as it curves beneath the tip of the ridge until you find a suitable place to scramble up the slopes. Either way it is a severe test of lungs and legs to pant up to the two ancient cairns that gaze over Ewyas.

Once rested you have two and a half miles of the best, with a playful track to guide you through the springy heather and inspiration from the glorious views. To the R Offa's Dyke and Pen y Beacon display a massive bulk. L the Chwarel y Fan ridge seems to stretch on forever, with the dour crags of Tarren yr Esgob standing guard to the fore and Pen y Gadair Fawr and Waun Fach silhouetted on the skyline beyond. Spare a glance to the rear, too, to bid fond farewell to old friends before they gently slip from view; the sylvan Vale of Ewyas and the far-off Sugar Loaf.

Partway along the ridge look out for a large cairn adorned with green, yellow, blue and gold painted stones; lavish (some might say

113

gaudy) even by Black Mountains' standards!

Rhiw Wen route (BS30)

This is ideal for a day spent pottering along the N escarpment, followed by a descent from one of the other N heights and a return to base along the network of trails below the N rim. The bend in the road at 209345 is a good place to start. A bridleway sets out on a bearing of 75 before gradually curling back on itself to scale the plateau at 220347. Despite the 800ft gain in altitude the gradient is moderate throughout, with a good stony grip underfoot, and you will be pleasantly surprised at reaching the top so easily. Pen Rhos Dirion is one mile away R, Twmpa about half a mile L.

RED DAREN

Red Daren may be only a minor 'blip' on the vast expanse of Offa's Dyke, but it commands as fine a view as any in the area with the lowlands of England rolling away E and Pen y Gadair Fawr and Waun Fach dominating the W skyline.

Llanthony Abbey route (BS31)

No other hillwalk in Wales starts from an abbey (apart from the easy day stroll from Strata Florida in the Cwmdeuddwr hills, CR E2) and this alone accounts for its deserved popularity. On entering the Abbey forecourt look out for a stile L that gives access to a Land-Rover track across a field. Half-way across the field bear L, as directed by a sign for Offa's Dyke. This takes you in a N direction across two further fields, keeping above and parallel to Cwm Siarpal. Next you must veer L again to the N tip of a copse, 288286 (not shown on the 1:25,000 map). The slope steepens, spawning a network of tracks any of which will land you on the ridge where the Offa's Dyke trail is unmistakable as a gross peaty scar in the otherwise prolific heather. If it is clear you will have no difficulty spotting Red Darren's trig point, an easy one and a half miles away NW.

Ty'r Onen route (BS32)

Just short of a mile along the ridge NW of Red Daren stands an old signpost. The post remains but the signs have long since disappeared. A little further along at 270319 is a cairn that used to anchor a pole (now lying on its side) with faint tracks leading away either side. The track to the R (NE) is the start of the Olchon Court route (BS33); that to the L is the Ty'r Onen route.

In spite of some ancient cairns this path is all but forgotten nowadays and badly overgrown. Care is needed. It is important to drop down to one of the trails in the vale head L, then aim for the gap in the woods near Ty'r Onen at 264311 (from where a dirt track leads to a footbridge at 258311 and hence the road). Otherwise it is all too easy to be seduced by a green track that maintains height and contours round NW, above the woods, only to leave you high and dry above Blaenau near a notice warning you to beware of snakes! Even if you were to survive these you would still have some trackless cross-country work to reach the farm trail near the river to get back to Capel-y-ffin.

Olchon Court route (BS33)
The key to this lonely route is the footpath sign at 276327. This directs you through two iron gates to a track that snakes its way up the bracken-clad hillside to join the Offa's Dyke path opposite the start of the Ty'r Onen route (see BS32). Red Daren is then about a mile along the ridge L.

Little Daren Farm route (BS34)
An attractive picnic area just S of Little Daren Farm at 296299 marks the start of this neglected route. The trail is clear enough in its early stages and joins the Offa's Dyke trail about half a mile SE of Red Daren's trig point.

Boxtree Cottage route (BS35)
This trail is signposted at 302296 as a crossing to Llanthony. It intersects the Offa's Dyke track at 299285, so if you use it for climbing Red Daren you will have a two-mile tramp along the ridge before gaining your objective.

BLACK MOUNTAIN
Black Mountain is situated at 255350. This needs to be said because

The Head of the Olchon Valley from the Olchon Court trail; route BS41 can be seen climbing the flank of Black Hill on the far side

the OS maps do not use the name, showing it as point 703 on the 1:50,000 metric map and as point 2306 on the 1:25,000 version. This really says it all, for despite its grandiose name Black Mountain is far from being a true mountain. It is distinguishable on the ground only by a cairn of large flat stones placed at the top of a tiny rise on the Offa's Dyke path.

Blaen Olchon route (BS36)

Follow the lane at 273338 to the deserted farmstead of Blaen Olchon. Bear L into a field on a bearing of 290 and then strike out, via some woods, for a track that is clearly visible rambling up the bracken, rock-encrusted slopes ahead. It is advisable to check your bearing when the slope eases as the track becomes a bit capricious in the shaggy heather. When you meet the Offa's Dyke path Black Mountain is but a short stroll away N.

Olchon Valley route (BS37)

Climb to the head of the Olchon Valley on BS41. Then, instead of bearing R for Black Hill, stride out L through trackless but friendly heather on a bearing of 270 until you meet the Offa's Dyke ridge. You should then be very close to the cairn marking Black Mountain, provided your navigation is sound.

Ty'r Onen route (BS38)

Use BS32 to gain the ridge at 270319. A rousing two-mile tramp along its crest then gives you Black Mountain.

Olchon Court route (BS39)

This route also joins the Offa's Dyke path at 270319, but this time the start is from the Olchon Valley as in BS33.

BLACK HILL

Black Hill hides on an isolated spur remote from the main Black Mountain highways and so is rarely visited. This is a pity for the panorama of the Wye Valley that it reveals is second to none, while the ascent of its narrow, rocky SE ridge is a real delight. A good idea is to combine the two routes given below and then to extend what would otherwise be a short day by exploring the little-known and unspoilt Olchon Valley.

The Cat's Back Ridge (BS40)

Do try to find time for this exhilarating walk. It begins from the imaginatively sited picnic area at 288329, an ideal starting point with glorious all-round views of hill and dale to whet the appetite. Cross the stile and thread your way up the grassy slope, with thickets of gorse here and there, until you reach a succession of rocky slabs. These carry you aloft for the next half mile while the ridge narrows to create a more mountainly atmosphere than anywhere in the range except Y Grib (BS12). Seen in snow it has a real micro-alpine character and care is required. Sadly the magic is all too brief. A large cairn heralds more conventional fare where the ridge widens and the trig point can be seen half a mile away with an easy track swathing through the heather.

Olchon Valley route (BS41)

Leave the road at 274337 and follow the public bridleway sign down a grassy lane. After passing an old iron gate this continues by a line of trees with a wire fence L before beginning a gentle climb to the vale head. The change from the quiet pastures of only a few moments before could hardly be more marked. Steep banks of bouncy heather, scattered outcrops and the desolate boulder-strewn ravine forged by the tumbling Olchon combine to evoke memories of Snowdonia itself. Once the ridge (or plateau) is reached bear R across the open moor to pick up one of several tracks that lead to Black Hill.

PEN Y BEACON

Pen y Beacon, or Hay Bluff as it is sometimes called, rises at the NE tip of the Black Mountains. It is a magnificent viewpoint with the Wye Valley and the Herefordshire plains spread like a map below. Despite this its ascent is a simple afternoon stroll, ideal for a family outing or a day when mist clears too late for a full expedition.

Gospel Pass route (BS42)

This is a doddle with only 450ft of ascent in just over a mile along a well-used peaty path. There is a short, steepish section to begin with, but thereafter the gradient is almost as gentle as a seaside promenade as the path hugs the escarpment edge. Moreover the patchwork of fields surrounding the Wye can be enjoyed while reclining on soft cushions of heather; a nice way to blow the cobwebs away because there is usually a breeze blowing.

North ridge (BS43)

Little need be said. From the car park by the stone circle at 240374 the way is all too obvious; an unremitting 650ft grind up the steep grassy slope directly ahead. The agony can be relieved a little by picking up a track, half-way up, that slants across the hillside to the R. This climbs more gradually and joins the Gospel Pass route a short distance below the top.

HIGH-LEVEL WALKS
Grwyne Fechan horseshoe (BS H1)
This is arguably the most rewarding ridge walk in the Black Mountains. It is also one of the longest, but the going is good throughout and strong walkers should have a field day. Start from 227196 and take BS1 to Pen Cerrig-calch. You then have a choice of ways over the elongated plateau to Pen Allt-mawr; either to hug the E edge, looking down over Cwm Banw and the Grwyne Fechan Valley, or to veer W to take in Pen Gloch-y-pibwr with glorious views of the Rhiangoll Valley and the foothills around Mynydd Troed. Or, best of all, take to the stubby heather and cross the narrow neck at 205234 to enjoy the highlights of both worlds.

The country N of Pen Allt-mawr is perfect for striding out, the way clear and the views superb. The minor peaks of Pentwynglas and Mynydd Llysiau come and go (see if you can spot the mound of turf shown on the 1:25,000 map at 212267!), then it's down to the Trumau col and up the oozy slope to Waun Fach for the highest ground of the day.

The path on to Pen y Gadair Fawr is not clear at first in the squelchy bog, but you have only to follow a bearing of 150 and dry firm walking is soon restored. Just SE of Pen y Gadair Fawr pick up the white stony track that goes initially through, and then later along the top of Mynydd Du Forest. This skirts just E of Pen-twyn-mawr from where BS15 takes you back to Llanbedr to leave you with a long mile of road bashing to regain your base.

Grwyne Fechan bridleway circular (BS H2)
For lesser mortals the full Grwyne Fechan circular, BS H1, can be aborted at the Trumau col and an easy low-level return made along the bridleway described in BS11. The only trouble is that you then have a long tramp of about four miles along the road. It is a quiet pretty road, but four miles is four miles!

Cwm Banw horseshoe (BS H3)
For anyone not relishing the rigours of the full Grwyne Fechan horseshoe, here is an attractive hors d'oeuvre. Follow BS H1 to Pentwynglas, but then make for home down the Tal Trwynau ridge as in BS6. Mile for mile this gives as good a return as you will find

in the Black Mountains. A little gem of a walk.

Rhiangoll horseshoe (BS H4)

This combines BS12 and BS10, climbing Waun Fach via Y Grib and descending Rhiw Trumau. It should only take a good walker half a day; but what other half-day expedition starts with the finest ridge in the area, scales the highest peak, returns down a delightfully secluded green track, and encircles the head of one of the Black Mountain's loveliest valleys, the Rhiangoll? As the map shows there are plenty of lanes for regaining your starting point and you should still have enough time (and energy) left to explore the ancient fortress of Castell Dinas at the foot of Y Grib.

Grwyne Fawr horseshoe (BS H5)

Apart from the environs of Waun Fach, the Black Mountains' two inner ridges lie outside the average walker's repertoire. This round combines them. Once you are launched the route is remarkably flat and much easier than it looks from the map. Nevertheless, despite the exhilaration of being on the tops all day there are long stretches of desolate moors and the walk can easily degenerate into a route march in dull weather. So do choose a fine day.

Park at 266252 and climb through the woods to Pen-twyn-mawr as in BS16. Stay with the white stony path along the edge of the forest until it peters out near Pen y Gadair Fawr. A lesser path continues to Waun Fach, clearly at first but fading as you approach the bog around the summit plateau. Beyond Waun Fach a badly eroded, peaty path takes over. This follows the escarpment edge over Pen y Manllwyn and round Y Das to Pen Rhos Dirion. The views are tremendous by now and this is a good place for lunch. Just before this, incidentally, there is an abort point in the form of a well-trodden track (BS L1) that crosses the range from Y Das, 203327, to the road-head beyond the Grwyne Fach reservoir.

For the homeward half pick up the faint track that sets out SE from Pen Rhos Dirion's trig point. This becomes more distinct once you have passed the undistinguished mount of Twyn Tal-y-cefn, by which time Chwarel y Fan is beginning to take shape to urge you on across the bleak fells. The final stretch beyond Chwarel (see BS21) is one of the highlights of the day, the ridge narrowing to give beautiful all-round views in the golden glow of evening.

Mynydd Du Forest circular (BS H6)

This is a shortened version of BS H5 that manages to retain most of the highlights at the cost of some loss of height half-way through when, having claimed Pen y Gadair Fawr, you cross over to Chwarel y Fan using BS17 and 18. The return follows BS21 as before.

Ewyas horseshoe (BS H7)

The third of the Black Mountains' horseshoe classics begins on a high note at Llanthony Abbey. It starts with a pull up to Offa's Dyke that is stiffer than it looks (BS31). Then comes a six-mile hike to Pen y Beacon, perfect fellwalking all the way with scarcely any variation in height, and with the flowing lines of the Black Mountains W balancing the rolling plains of England E until Black Hill constrains the view.

After such level going the 400ft descent to Gospel Pass and back up again to Twmpa seems harsh medicine, but this is but a brief interlude as once you are past Twmpa and Pen Rhos Dirion you have another six miles of the best along the Chwarel y Fan ridge (see BS H5). The day ends on as high a note as it began, the beautiful walk from Chwarel back to Llanthony (BS20) providing a fitting finale as the shadows lengthen.

Capel-y-ffin horseshoe (BS H8)

The Ewyas horseshoe can be shortened by basing it on Capel-y-ffin rather than Llanthony. It is then best done clockwise, so begin by following BS19 as if set for Chwarel y Fan. However turn away from Chwarel y Fan as you approach the ridge and strike out for Twyn Tal-y-cefn. Then it's across to Offa's Dyke (BS H7 in reverse) before returning to Capel-y-ffin on BS32. Be careful not to miss where BS32 leaves the ridge.

Darren Lwyd circular (BS H9)

Here is a pearl of a walk, revealing a lush side of the Black Mountain that few walkers even suspect. It is ideal for one of those days when, after mist or rain has prevented an early start, fresher and brighter conditions eventually light up the hills.

Walk up the enchanting Nant y Bwch to Twmpa (BS28) admiring countless falls as you wend through the bracken. Next drop down to Gospel Pass, scramble back up to Pen y Beacon and continue along Offa's Dyke; varied scenery and far horizons all the way. You end by zig-zagging down to the woodlands around Ty'r Onen (BS32) with the evening sun casting its golden glow over the beautiful Vale of Ewyas if you're lucky.

Nant y Bwch/Darren Lwyd ridge walk (BS H10)

For a short day, but a grand one, try climbing Twmpa via Nant y Bwch before returning to Capel-y-ffin along the Darren Lwyd ridge. This is simply a combination of BS28 and BS29 and the walk could equally well be done anti-clockwise. It all depends whether you prefer the hard work first and want to avoid a knee-jerking descent at the end of the day. Few rounds can match this for variety and beauty. By nightfall you will have tumbling falls, Twmpa's lofty top, the pastoral loveliness of the Wye Valley and the purple moors of Darren Lwyd all firmly enshrined in your memory.

Olchon Valley horseshoe (BS H11)

The Olchon Valley is far removed from the main highways of the Black Mountains and sadly neglected as a result. Yet it offers fine walking, especially if you like to get off the beaten track. Start by claiming Black Hill on BS40. Next follow the well-used track that skirts the edge of Crib y Garth on its way to Pen y Beacon, another superb vantage point. Turn SE along a wide peaty path that quickly links up with the main Offa's Dyke track. Follow this over Black Mountain and continue on towards Red Daren but, about a mile before the trig point, look out for the cairn marking the top of the Olchon Court route (BS33/39). (This lies a few hundred yards short of an old wooden signpost.) Follow the route down into the valley where the map reveals a variety of ways to regain your base.

The day can be shortened by bee-lining across the fells from Black Hill to Black Mountain (cutting out Pen y Beacon), or by regaining the valley from Black Hill on BS36. Equally it can be extended by continuing beyond Red Daren to descend via the Little Daren Farm route (BS34). You then have a longer walk back to base but a most pleasant one, the softly wooded landscape of the Olchon

Looking across the Olchon Valley to Black Hill

Valley creating a near parkland setting.

LOWER-LEVEL WALKS
Grwyne Fawr reservoir and beyond (BS L1)
For a simple walk that gets you 'away from it all' and into the fastnesses of the hills on a good firm track (and with a pleasant picnic area to start from too) try BS22. You can extend the walk as far as you like since the path crosses the range before descending near Y Das as in BS24. A day for quiet contemplation where you can imbibe the vast solitudes of the fells, rather than for thrills.

The Sugar Loaf (Pen y Fal) (BS L2)
Sugar Loaf is probably the most frequently climbed hill in S Wales. To newcomers approaching Abergavenny from the E its elegantly rounded crown, perfect in its symmetry, is often their first glimpse of the Black Mountains. What better aperitif could there be?

Numerous paths criss-cross Sugar Loaf's lush bracken-clad slopes.

One of the best begins high up near the car park overlooking the Usk at 269167. A green path wends its way lazily along the broad ridge of Mynydd Llanwenarth before beginning a climb so temperate that nothing prepares you for the vast panorama that strikes the eye the moment you mount the rocky terrace at the top.

The entire Black Mountains, from Pen Allt-mawr in the W to Offa's Dyke in the E, are arrayed in all their splendour. A scene of breathtaking grandeur and intensity where gently swelling heights, cool green valleys and scattered woodlands come together in close alliance. Yet of all the riches on display nothing surpasses the inviting arc of heights girdling the Grwyne Fechan Valley, beckoning seductively with the promise of joys to come.

Mynydd Troed/Llangorse (BS L3)

Mynydd Troed presents a stern face to the Rhiangoll Valley. Shapely and imposing, yes; but steep, bare and isolated too. Not the stuff from which good days in the hills are made. However, try taking one of the pretty lanes to the head of Cwm Sorgwm at 161284. When you do, you will find a path cleaving its way through a carpet of bracken. It rises gently at first but steepens later, though the worst can be avoided by switching to a bridleway that traverses the slope a little way below the crest. Soon you are on top of the world, with bouncy pillows of heather to rest on and gentle dips offering shelter from the breeze. An hour would be ample even for a dawdler.

The view is fit for a king. The Black Mountains stretch from Y Das to Pen Gloch-y-pibwr with the Y Grib and Rhiw Trumau trails both prominent and Pen y Gadair Fawr, as so often, hogging the skyline. An extraordinary patchwork of fields stretches unhindered to the Wye and carries the eye to the distant Beacons. Nearer to hand Mynydd Llangorse looks tempting with its lake glimmering in the sun. How can such temptation be resisted! Troed is too short even for a half-day, so what better complement could there be than its neighbour? Just head back down to the road and then up the track on the far side for another pearl of a top.

EASIER DAYS
Table Mountain (BS E1)

Table Mountain is perfect for an easy half-day; simply follow BS1. Few excursions repay such a modicum of effort with such a satisfying climax because the 'Table', modest height though it may be, always rewards you with the bracing air and views of a true mountain. You can extend the walk in several ways: up the slopes towards Pen Cerrig-calch which is a pageant of colour in late summer; across to the rocky outcrop of Darren or back via Cwm Cumbeth.

Rhiangoll Valley (BS E2)

Follow BS12 to the foot of Y Grib. After passing through the gate bear R on a path that wends its way up the gently wooded valley. All too soon the flanks of the hills close in to create a feeling of wildness and abandon far removed from the parkland charm of only moments before.

An inspection of the ancient ramparts of Castell Dinas could be included at the start; better still (or as well) walk up the ridge itself for a while to savour its magic and the views. When you have had enough, the maze of lanes and footpaths shown on the map offers innumerable options for returning to your car.

Grwyne Fechan bridleway (BS E3)

For a sound, easily graded trail penetrating directly to the heart of the hills, you cannot do better than BS11. Lowland pastures gradually yield to the severity of the high fells and you should easily get to the Trumau col which is within ten minutes of Mynydd Llysiau.

Nant y Bwch Valley (BS E4)

The Black Mountains have no lovelier vale than this, yet in all probability the pony trekkers will be your sole company. Start as for BS28. Reaching the N escarpment is easy enough, but the lower valley is so bewitching with playful tracks through the bracken and gently tumbling falls, it is highly likely you will eat your lunch there and progress no more!

Beneath the N escarpment (BS E5)

Many days could be happily spent exploring the network of paths and bridleways nestling beneath the N escarpment. Gorse, heather, bracken, little glades, waterfalls and secret nooks to escape the breeze - all are there, set against the backdrop of the hills. In summer it is ideal picnic country, but do not discount it in winter. With a powdering of frost or snow to boost the heights, and the golden glow of autumn lingering in the bracken, there are still treasures here in abundance.

It matters not where you start or how you wander. Let the map, or your intuition, be your guide. Among the best access points are the meadows at 188333, the bend in the road at 209345 and the stone circle at 240374.

THE BRECON BEACONS

OS maps 1:25,000 - Sheet 11 1:50,000 - Sheets 160

Peaks	Height (ft)	Map Ref	Page
Pen y Fan	290	012215	137
Corn Du	2863	007213	134
Craig Gwaun-taf	2704	005206	136
Cribin	2608	023213	139
Waun-rydd	2522	061208	143
Gwaen Cerrig-llwydion	2450	055203	147
Craig Cwareli	2393	042197	146
Fan y Big	2358	036207	142
Allt-lwyd	2143	079189	147
Cefn yr Ystrad	2025	087137	149
Y Gyrn	2010	989216	133

Mountain Lake

Cwm Llwch	1910	002220

THE BRECON BEACONS

Beacons! The very name carries a challenge, a hint of adventure. No wonder they are the most popular hills in S Wales. You can tramp all day on the nearby Black Mountains (not to mention Fforest Fawr or Mynydd Du) with only the sheep for company, even on a sunny weekend in August. Not so in the Beacons where the wide peaty tracks on Corn Du and Pen y Fan bear witness with their scars to the crowds who flock up from the Storey Arms all year round. These are probably the easiest ascents of major peaks anywhere in Wales.

To the occasional walker, out for the odd day on the fells, the instantly recognisable decapitated tops of Corn Du and Pen y Fan are the Beacons. Not for him the shapely cone of Cribin or the softly

Pen y Fan and Cwm Sere from the N

wooded cwms of Sere, Cynwyn and Menasgin; much less the lonely hills and rolling moors over to the E where purity and solitude reign supreme. These are the treasured retreat of the connoisseur, quiet and unspoilt. Long may they remain so. (Strictly speaking the term 'Beacon' only applies to the Big Three: Corn Du, Pen y Fan and Cribin. However it is widely used to refer to the whole area and I shall do the same.)

There are 11 tops which exceed 2000ft in this heart-shaped region and apart from Cefn yr Ystrad (a lonely outlier well to the S) they form a magnificent ridge five and a half miles long which stretches from Y Gyrn in the W to Allt-lwyd in the E. To tramp the whole ridge end to end is one of the S Wales classics, a hard day's work but a grand one. In only two places, and even then but momentarily, does the land fall below 2000ft. Pen y Fan at 2906ft is the senior peak, and you would need to travel as far as Cader Idris or the Arans to find higher ground.

Like Fforest Fawr and Mynydd Du the Beacons are bare,

windswept hills with an austerity which borders on harshness. Neither tree nor hillock nor hollow breaks the smooth uniformity of their higher slopes. This is at once a weakness and a strength. A weakness because with their clear simple lines it is easy to underrate them - easy but dangerous. Navigation, so simple when skies are clear, acquires a whole new dimension in mist. As in the Carneddau there are few landmarks to steer by. Lazing on the tops on a balmy spring day it is hard to imagine what fiends roam these hills in winter. Yet nowhere does the wind gust with greater ferocity (adding a laying of clothing is a major task!) and shelter is non-existent. In blizzards only fools set forth.

On the other hand, few lovers of the wild can fail to be stirred by the classic simplicity of the Beacons' uncluttered skylines; the stark awesome grandeur of the long N escarpment; the vast empty rim round Cwm Oergwm or the 'lost world' desolation of Waun-rydd.

Five subsidiary ridges converge on the Beacons from the Usk Valley in the N. Each leads directly to one of the main peaks. All are linked by a network of leafy lanes whose tall hedgerows, alight with colour in early summer, provide an idyllic prelude to a day in the hills. The simplest leads over Pen Milan to claim Y Gyrn, the Beacons' most W bastion. The two most popular ridges attack Pen y Fan and Cribin. Cribin is a rounded conical peak requiring a stiff pull-up whichever way you tackle it. However, nothing can compare with the scarped N-facing cliffs of Corn Du and Pen y Fan. Heavily corniced in winter, they plunge to the valley unhindered by crag or ledge. Ribs of rock cleave the dank green of grass and moss. Deep furrows rend the face in gullies hundreds of feet long.

The fourth ridge, sharp and airy, ends on Fan y Big, a lively little peak with a defiant knuckle of rock on top. Between Cribin and Fan y Big the land falls away to Bwlch ar y Fan, commonly known as The Gap, where an old Roman road, now a bridleway, exploits a weakness in the cliffs to offer another way into the hills (or, if you prefer it, a complete N/S traverse from Brecon to Merthyr Tydfil). It is here, too, that a subtle change in character begins to manifest itself. So far the peaks have exuded a true mountainly aura with finely sculptured tops that are aloof from the surrounding fells. Now, as you venture E, the slopes are gentler with hill and fell more united, the tops merely the crests of the gently rounded moors

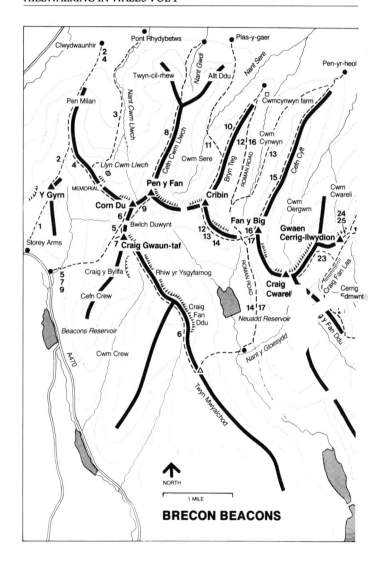

BRECON BEACONS

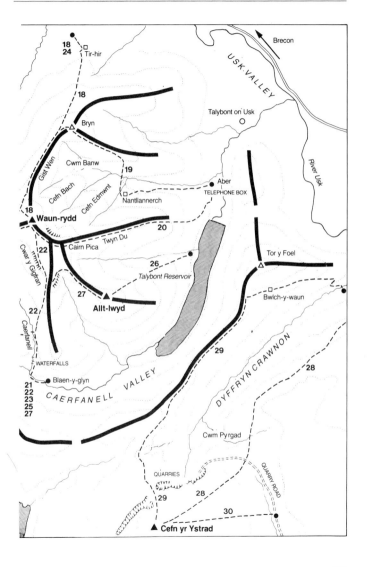

which they themselves are part of. There is more than a hint of the Pennines or the High Peak about these E Beacons.

The fifth ridge, mirroring the first, is less dramatic and shuns the higher ground. It offers a choice; either to the desolate windswept plateau of Waun-rydd, or round the edge of Cwm Oergwm to the almost imperceptible tops of Craig Cwareli and Gwaen Cerrig-llwydion where the world of Pen y Fan and Cribin seems a million miles away.

We are not yet finished with these N approaches. If you tire of the ridges or the Roman road there is a route through the delectable Cwm Llech; a real charmer that evokes the very quintessence of the Beacons. This is where you will find the Beacons' only tarn, snugly cradled beneath the cliffs of Corn Du, gazing into space like some primeval eye.

There are two other trails which start near Cwm Sere and Cwm Cynwyn, both of them lovely walks, as rewarding for their insights into the valleys as for their lead-ins to the high fells. These cwms are havens of mellow woodlands and sparkling brooks, immune from the worst excesses of the wind, the perfect foil to the stark simplicity of the tops. However, take care to keep to established paths when exploring them as the woods are dense and impenetrable, the slopes severe.

Despite the wooded foothills that bound the Beacons S, the only route in regular use from that direction, apart from the Roman road, is along the edge that extends from Craig Fan-ddu, near the Neuadd reservoirs, over Craig Gwaun-taf to Corn Du. As a peak Craig Gwaun-taf is an insignificant little hump, but the route itself, backed by the greens of the Tal Fechan Forest and the blue of the reservoir, is quite splendid. In contrast the nearby ridges that fall away on either side of Nant Crew lack character, facing the equally barren fells bordering Fforest Fawr with dull grassy slopes.

Why the lovely walk from the Blaen-y-glyn Falls to the exposed promontory of Craig Fan-ddu is not more popular is a mystery. Combine it with Waun-rydd and you have a pearl of a day; beauty and solitude in close alliance with waves of gently swelling hills and shaggy moors S, the fertile meadows of the Usk N, the high Beacons W and the Black Mountains E.

Two more routes climb Waun-rydd from the E. One crosses Allt-lwyd, guardian of the Beacons' E flank; the other follows the Twyn-du ridge to join the plateau at the ancient Cairn Pica. Either can be combined with a foray into Cwm Banw and an ascent of Bryn to give a perfect introduction to this most relaxed and intimate corner of the Beacons. A land of tight little cwms, bracken slopes and coppices, parkland and old world charm.

Finally there is Cefn yr Ystrad, alone and forgotten in a sea of undulating heather between the unjustly neglected Dyffryn Crawnon and the Pontsticilli reservoir.

Y GYRN
Few folk dawdle on this bleak moorland plateau preferring to treat it as an hors d'oeuvre for Corn Du, whose commanding presence fills the E skyline. Most never visit it at all, for there is no way of tackling it without a sizeable diversion from the main ridge. Y Gyrn is not all innocence and in mist you should be careful not to stray over its craggy W face. This is totally unsuspected on the ground but shows up clearly from the road N of the Storey Arms.

Storey Arms route (BB1)
The quickest way to Y Gyrn follows a wide muddy path that climbs beside the N edge of the forestry plantation near the Storey Arms, starting at 982204. Higher up, where the slope eases, the path fades and it is hard to distinguish it from a miscellany of other sketchy tracks that criss-cross some rather dreary fells. Try to maintain a bearing of 25 until you hit a dilapidated stone wall where a small cairn marks the top.

Pen Milan route (BB2)
It is far better to follow BB4 until you reach more level ground half a mile or so beyond the quarry. Then strike out on a bearing of 205 making use of any tracks that go in the right direction until you spot the wall that crosses the top. Not a route for mist.

Looking N to Corn Du from Craig Fan-ddu

CORN DU

Pen y Fan and Corn Du are the two most popular peaks in the Brecon Beacons and it would be nice to be able to relate that their summits are worthy of that distinction. But it is not so. The flat, bald top of Corn Du is a morass of peaty mud, encrusted with pink stones and speckled with tired grass and struggling heather. In a word, a scruffy top, the victim of its own popularity. Even the cairn lacks style despite being adorned with red, black and navy-blue stones in true Black Mountains tradition.

At least the view makes amends! Close to hand Pen y Fan, Cribin and the E Beacons stand arrayed in line abreast, while beneath the bold insistent sweep of Corn Du's N slopes are the sylvan charms of Cwm Llwch and its shy elliptical tarn. To the S glints of blue reveal the Neuadd reservoirs, with the S Wales foothills beyond. As the eye roams W it is Fforest Fawr that commands attention with the long profile of Mynydd Ddu peeping over its shoulder. N lies the lush vale of the Usk backed, on a clear day, by glimpses of the far-off Cwmdeuddwr hills and the Radnor Forest.

Cwm Llwch route (BB3)

Despite a tiresome and ugly last 20 minutes, this is one of the most rewarding walks in the Beacons and graded gently enough to be within the compass of all ages and capabilities. Park by Pont Rhydybetws and walk S down the leafy lane from 012253 with the wooded glen of Nant Cwm Llwch L, and a dazzle of wild flowers in spring. After a gate the lane runs alongside the brook before continuing across a bridge/ford and by-passing the dwelling of Cwm-llwch L. It then rises through pastures and bracken with Corn Du and Pen y Fan coming into view ahead.

After crossing a stile the atmosphere grows wilder. Pastures yield to coarse grass that contrasts strongly with the gently wooded slopes either side while the sparkling falls L are well worth a short detour. The path, pink and grooved now, curls round the hillside above Llyn Cwm Llwch to put you on the skyline near the memorial to the unfortunate Tommy Jones. Tommy, a child aged five, became separated from his father on a walk to Cwm-llwch Farm, lost his way and, quite incredibly, made his way alone up to this exposed and distant spot where his body was only found a month later, after he had died of exposure.

The final 600ft haul up the slope is tedious. There are wonderful views from the edge, but in its higher reaches the path is a churned-up mess of glutinous mud, greasy when wet and requiring great care in snow.

Pen Milan route (BB4)

Of all the N ridges this is the gentlest. There are lovely views of Cwm Llwch and the peace to enjoy them; no crowds or crocodiles on this route!

Leave the road at 002249 and walk down a lane to the cottage of Clwydwaunhir. Across the stream a stile signals a footpath to Cwm Llwch, a welcome shortcut if you plan to return through the cwm on BB3.

Carry on across a ford and pass a clump of holly bushes until you reach a gate giving access to open county. Then aim half-R for a path that snakes up a hillside attractively clothed in bracken, hawthorn and gorse. Before long you join a grooved mining track that leads to the spoil heap of a disused quarry. The track keeps just below the ridge for a while, affording shelter from the inevitable wind. Eventually, as you reach more level ground (a tilted plateau of shaggy heather dappled with peat hags) it degenerates to a narrow trail that meanders along the edge overlooking Cwm Llwch before joining up with the well-used path from Cwm Llwch described in BB3.

Storey Arms route (BB5)

If your aim is to get to Corn Du and back as easily as possible, this is the way. However speed, plus a safe way down in mist, is about all it does have to offer. The path, almost a minor road now, starts at 988198 from the S extremity of the car park by the Storey Arms. It enters the conifer plantations but after only a few paces, at a kissing-gate, leaves them R to ford a stream. Soon after this a plaque commemorates the Eagle Star Insurance Company's gift of this land to the National Trust. Thereafter the track slants steadily up the featureless slopes with none of the lovely views you get in Cwm Llwch or from Pen Milan. You are enclosed by the barren slopes of Y Gyrn and Cefn Crew all the way.

When the slope eases at Bwlch Duwynt bear L up a small rise for Corn Du; the well-worn track half-R leads to Pen y Fan (BB9) while a faint grassy trail R crosses Craig Gwaun-taf (BB7).

Neuadd reservoirs route (BB6)

It would be pedantic not to mention one of the finest routes to Corn Du just because it happens to cross the minor top of Craig Gwaun-taf on the way and is therefore not a direct approach. Refer to Craig Gwaun-taf for the route that far, after which a simple ten-minute stroll via Bwlch Duwynt gives you Corn Du as well.

CRAIG GWAUN-TAF

Few of the walkers who cross Craig Gwaun-taf's unmarked grassy top probably have any inkling that it is a 2000 footer at all. Its sole distinction is being the highest point of the long escarpment that rises from near the Neuadd reservoirs before reaching its climax in Corn Du.

Neuadd reservoirs route (BB6)

Enter the reservoir grounds at 032179, having parked outside. Turn L over a green iron bridge and then stride on past scatterings of rhododendrons to a path that climbs beside the forest boundary fence. This peters out where the forest turns S, but keep going to breast the ridge near the trig point on Twyn Mwyalchod, 022177. Alternatively (BB6,1) slants across from the foot of the woods towards a pink, crumbly track that scales the escarpment by a narrow gully half a mile N of the trig point, close to where three prominent furrows scar the edge. A cairn, the only one for miles, marks the head of the gully for descent.

A path along the edge gives a pleasant walk despite mud churned up by armies of walkers. On a sunny day the Neuadd reservoirs shine like jewels, transforming an otherwise desolate valley, but the vast grassy uplands bounding Cwm Crew W are too plain for a place in the hillwalker's repertoire. Not that the scene lacks interest! Witness the outcrops of Craig y Byllfa as you cross the narrow neck of Rhiw yr Ysgyfarnog, while the chiselled contours of the Big Three (Corn Du, Pen y Fan, Cribin) are every bit as stirring from this angle as from the N.

Storey Arms route (BB7)

See BB5.

PEN Y FAN

Pen y Fan is the highest peak in S Wales; indeed the highest S of Cader Idris or the Arans. With its precipitous N face, elegantly ribbed and massively riven, it is also among the most spectacular. Because of this and the easy ascent from the Storey Arms, it shares with Corn Du the dubious distinction of being the most heavily trodden hill in the range. Regretfully a price has to be paid and that price is serious erosion on the main paths and a flat rocky top that is a hostage to mud and litter. The N ridge and the onward path to Cribin are especially badly scarred; slippery and muddy when wet, treacherous in snow or ice.

Fortunately the view is eternal and no less electrifying here than from Corn Du. Though the bulk of Corn Du constrains the outlook

Corn Du from Pen y Fan with Fforest Fawr in the background

W, there is ample compensation in the graceful lines of the Black Mountains E. So, despite its wounds, Pen y Fan is still a peak to treasure.

N ridge (Cefn Cwm Llwch) (BB8)

For once in the Beacons there is no parking problem. There is ample space by the old Army training centre at 025248. Step over the stile where the tarmac road ends and cross the pastures on 220 to pick up a grooved track that climbs above the Nant Gwdi amidst clusters of blackthorns. It levels off near the disused mine-workings of Cwar Mawr at 018237 but then climbs again to a further level stretch that reveals Corn Du - not unlike Ingleborough from this angle - Pen y Fan itself, and the shapely cone of Cribin. The path is atrociously worn near the top and the final 500ft is a tedious slither of loose scree and oozy mud.

Alternatively (BB8,1) walk on 270 from the stile, aiming for a cleavage in the bracken that cloaks the slopes of Twyn-cil-rhew. A faint track rambles on to join the main route near the old mines. For another variation (BB8,2) bear L before the stile, as directed by a footpath sign, and cross the Nant Gwdi to join a green path crossing the W flank of Allt Ddu to join BB8 near the head of Cwm Gwdi.

Storey Arms path (BB9)
Follow BB5 to Bwlch Duwynt, then bear half-R along the popular path that heads straight for Pen y Fan. You can judge its popularity from its width - 50ft at one point!

CRIBIN
Cribin deserves the kudos of being one of the Beacons' Big Three. Less popular than the over-tramped Corn Du and Pen y Fan with their decapitated tops, it yields to neither in shapeliness. Whether you see it as a beautifully rounded cone from the N (reminiscent of Elidir Fawr in the Glyders) or, like Cadair Bronwen in the Berwyns, seemingly sprouting a shark's fin for the benefit of walkers from Neuadd, it is a striking sight. Mind you, it is no easy touch and you will certainly be panting as you struggle up the final grassy pyramid, no matter which way you tackle it.

N ridge (Bryn Teg) (BB10)
Bryn Teg may be the shortest of the Beacons' N ridges, but it is unrivalled for variety and drama. As you tramp down the cobbled Roman road from near the entrance to Cwmcynwyn Farm at 036235 (with space to park a couple of cars on the grass verge) the atmosphere exudes a quiet rustic charm. Tucked between the wooded gorge of Cwm Sere and the bracken-clad slopes of Cefn Cyff, the high fells seem a far cry away. But not for long. After 200/300 paces a gate ushers in a marked change.

The Roman road now sidles off L, keeping the shelter of the valley all the way to The Gap at 032206. As for the ridge, it rises through bleak moorland where the abiding memory is of scurrying clouds, billowing mist, raw wind, and white-topped pools whose peaty shores are lashed by tiny waves.

Battling on, a two-headed panorama builds up. R the face of Pen y Fan, its furrowed ramparts seamed with plunging gullies, and

Cribin fron Cwm Sere

ahead the massive pyramid of Cribin - an inspiring, if not frightening, sight at all times but never more so than when powdered with snow or teased by swirling mist. At the foot of the pyramid a 'sporting' path traverses across to the col between Cribin and Pen y Fan. This is dangerous in snow, and no place for vertigo sufferers. However it does offer an alternative approach from the W (BB10,1) if you wish to avoid the badly eroded path that a direct frontal attack entails.

Cwm Sere route (BB11)

Most walkers in the Beacons focus their minds firmly on the ridges; for every hundred that tramp the tops you will be lucky to find one exploring the cwms. But why not enjoy both? Leave the junction at 032252 and walk down the road towards Plas-y-gaer. However, after 200 paces where the road swings L, abandon it for a stile and follow a dark leafy lane a similar distance to reach open pastures. Cross these SE to a tree-lined bank, all that remains of an Iron Age settlement. Follow the fence round the E flanks of Allt Ddu on an improving path that skirts the woodlands of Coed y Croftau. The deep cleft of Cwm Sere beckons enticingly, the whites of a succession of falls sparkling against the sunless backdrop of the cirque moulded by Cribin and Pen y Fan.

The slopes of Pen y Fan are daunting in their severity, those of Cribin across the cwm merely formidable! So ramble on beyond the falls to the heart of this wild and lovely vale. Then, when the stream rises up to meet you, cross over and scrabble up the Bryn Teg ridge to join BB10.

Roman road N (BB12)

From the map you might well be put off what looks like a dull low-level plod. However that would be an injustice for the Roman road has much to commend it, especially on a cold blustery day or for tired legs homeward bound. The upper reaches are wild and remote and the vast sweeping slopes of wedge-shaped Fan y Big yield nothing in splendour to Cribin across the vale. See BB10 for the start.

Cwm Cynwyn route (BB13)

Set out on BB15 for Fan y Big, but instead of pulling up to the ridge (Cefn Cyff) bear R along a track above the woods fringing Cwm

Cynwyn. Follow it for the next one and a half miles in a parkland setting where thickets of bracken and gorse and mature twisted trees enhance the feeling of a bygone age. Pen y Fan's mighty wedge soars aggressively, the perfect foil to Cribin's slender, more feminine profile. Later on, as the track swings S, Fan y Big takes over the mantle and you can distinguish the 'notch' where the Roman road cleaves the skyline. As you near the vale head - a wild place of overpowering seclusion - cross the brook and snake up the fellside to join the Roman road and BB12.

Roman road S (BB14)

Park near the entrance to the Filter House at 032180 and make your way along either bank of the Nant y Gloesydd to the Roman road. Alternatively use one of the Forestry Commission's official parking areas at 037171 and join the Roman road just beyond. The route is obvious and easy, the main interest being the craggy ramparts of Craig Fan-ddu and the ever-changing lines of Cribin and Pen y Fan. Reaching The Gap at the head of Cwm Cynwyn scarcely raises a sweat, but now is the time to discard surplus clothing! The slog up Cribin's E edge is relentless and it is just as well for proud folk that the exquisite views give plenty of excuses for rests.

Turning R at The Gap gives an equally demanding haul up to Fan y Big, BB17. However there are easier options for anyone tramping the ridge who is not averse to missing a couple of the tops. From The Gap a sly path, but a good one, temporarily abandons the edge. Going W it by-passes Cribin to rejoin the main ridge at the foot of Pen y Fan; E it ignores Fan y Big and heads directly for Craig Cwmoergwm.

FAN Y BIG

'Hill of the Beak' (a rough rendering of Fan y Big) is an apt name, for it takes little imagination as you tramp its N ridge to picture a beak in the rocky outcrop that crowns the top of this neglected hillock. Though it cannot match the charisma of the Big Three, Fan y Big is well worth a visit, the ridge being one of the best in the area.

N ridge (Cefn Cyff) (BB15)

Walk down the narrow lane past Rhiwiau and carry on to where the road ends by the farm at Pen-yr-heol, 057241. Turn R through a blue iron gate (the gate straight ahead leads into BB L5) and follow a rough stony track beneath an archway of trees until a second iron gate leads you on to the ridge. Continue along a green path that weaves up a slope of bracken and rushes. A level half-mile is the precursor to another rise and then a second level stretch where the ridge tapers to a slender crest. There are glorious views into Cwm Cynwyn and Cwm Oergwm, both exquisitely wooded and richly carpeted in a mosaic of browns, oranges and greens.

There is no cairn at the top, just a small knuckle of rock dizzily perched high above Cwm Cynwyn. How it manages to present such a sharply-pinnacled profile on the way up is a mystery.

Roman road N (BB16)
See BB12.

Roman road S (BB17)
See BB14. When you reach The Gap, bear R for Cribin, L for Fan y Big.

WAUN-RYDD
Waun-rydd is a wild windswept plateau, a, peninsula of high ground protruding from the Gist Wen ridge. It is carpeted with short stubby grass and heather that can be boggy when wet, though never unpleasantly so. The highest ground (but only by 20ft) is at 061208, half a mile NW of the spot at 067202 where some of the older maps show a trig point. Only a cairn remains there now and in gloom it is an eerie place, cut off like some lost world, the flat featureless moors denying all but the most fleeting glimpses of life outside. Without good compass work you would soon be lost. Yet on a sunny day, as with the Migneint, the very isolation that is such a menace in mist gives it an evanescent appeal which, once experienced, is never forgotten.

Note that a grooved, peaty path rambles round the perimeter edge, a wild gem of a walk revealing a landscape of green rolling hills and forgotten cwms (see BB H7). You should always stick to this when mist is about.

Gist Wen ridge (BB18)

Leave the junction at 072249 and make for the ford at 073238. Keep to the L of the field on the far side, following a line of trees, but bear R at the top, away from the abandoned farmstead of Tir-hir. Go through a gate into the woods (Coed Caer'-ebol) and walk along their L boundary fence to another gate at 075243. Bear half-R now, on 190, up a slope dotted with blackthorn to gain the emergent ridge. Various tracks cleave the gorse and bracken hereabouts; choose one with a bearing of about 210 and remember that the track you want skirts the W slopes of Bryn, the height L, without ever crossing it. The scenery is superb: the main Beacon ridge W, Cwm Banw E and behind you the colourful patchwork of the Usk.

Now comes the finale. The track shuns the higher ground, avoiding Waun-rydd and clinging instead to the hillside overlooking Cwm Cwareli until, where the angle relents, it finally becomes a wide stony path that hugs the rim of the cwm round to Fan y Big. That is a grand walk, but for Waun-rydd you must leave the path where it levels off and strike up the tussocky hillside on 90. This takes you to within sight of the cairn.

A few minutes along the rim path would have brought you to a spot at 057206, Bwlch y Ddwyallt, where several tracks meet. One meanders across the fells to where the Waun-rydd trig point used to be, 067202. A second track cuts across a shallow depression to join the W edge of the 'peninsula' (see BB H7) while a third shadows the Craig Fan-las escarpment edge (see BB21).

Cwm Banw route (BB19)

Leave Waun-rydd W and drop down to the Gist Wen path. Look out for a trail sidling away R to ascend the rounded slopes of Bryn. Bryn is a friendly, breezy top with a cluster of reedy pools and a cairn decorated with green and yellow stones. It is an excellent viewpoint where the eye can roam freely from the Usk across the lonely folds of Cefn Bach and Cefn Edmwnt to Allt-lwyd and Waun-rydd; from the shapely cone of Tor y Foel across the Talybont reservoir to Fan y Big, Cribin and the high Beacons.

Follow Bryn's SE ridge down. A bridleway soon appears, leading through gorse and rushes to a gate into the woods at 085221. Do not enter the forest. It may seem right at the time but several of the trails shown on the map no longer exist and unless you want to end up near Talybont-on-Usk (or thoroughly confused) the temptation is best resisted.

Instead turn R along the edge of the woods to pick up a bridleway at 084216. This is slightly exiguous at first but once you reach the farmstead at Nantllannerch it becomes a surfaced lane and all is well with pretty woodlands, open parkland, meadows and the noisy chattering of the stream. Nature at her most ebullient. The telephone box at Aber, 106214, brings you back to earth.

Cairn Pica route (BB20)
Another approach from Aber starts from the bend in the lane at 103208, just short of Berth-lwyd-fawr Farm, where there is a stile and a yellow waymark sign. Climb the stile and proceed beneath an avenue of trees that gradually merges into a wood that rises steadily beside a stream. Before long you reach open bracken country where the woods are bounded R by a wall. The path breaks away L here to snake up to the crest of the broad Twyn-du ridge. Cairn Pica, an ancient landmark, is directly ahead on the lip of the plateau. So seductive is the calm of the hills and meadows bordering the Usk that it is quite a surprise to find the haul up so energy-sapping. You will be glad of a flop by the cairn with its pink, disc-shaped stones. For Waun-rydd follow the edge for a time before proceeding 'inland' on an E bearing.

For a hybrid that combines Cairn Pica with Cwm Banw (BB19,1) stroll up to Nantllannerch as in BB19 and cut across to the Twyn-du ridge from there.

Blaen-y-glyn route (BB21)
I imagine there must be many walkers who pride themselves on knowing the Beacons pretty well, yet who have never tried this lovely walk. (I used to be one of them.) It starts from Blaen-y-glyn amidst some of the prettiest woodlands and waterfalls in the whole of S Wales. Park at 064169 and walk down to the rushing Caerfanell to join a well-trodden track along its S bank. The track trends N and climbs beside mature woods and moss-encrusted walls while a succession of falls burble merrily below.

The track fades higher up and patience is required as it hops capriciously in and out of the woods. It is rather overgrown in places too. Perseverance is well rewarded, however, for on reaching the NE tip of the woods and crossing a stile you are greeted by a scene of massive splendour, the vast amphitheatre cupped by the escarpments of Craig y Fan-ddu and Cwar y Gigfran towering aloft. Follow the N boundary of the woods until it turns sharply S at 056182, then strike out direct for the crest of Craig y Fan-ddu. You will meet a well-worn path coming up from a car park at 054175. This provides a shorter easier routing (BB21,1) but at the cost of missing out the falls.

A grooved path hugs the edge, first of Craig y Fan-ddu and then of Craig Fan-las, before intersecting the main escarpment at Bwlch y Ddwyallt, 057206. This is an inspiring walk. Pen y Fan is seen from an unusual angle, Waun-rydd fills the skyline E, while S the eye jumps the Caerfanell Valley to lose itself in the seas of heather girdling Cefn yr Ystrad. There is a particularly memorable moment when the emerald-green of the Wye Valley suddenly springs into view to irradiate the scene. From Bwlch y Ddwyallt the top is a short half-mile away across stubby moors on 80.

Cwar y Gigfran route (BB22)

For a way back to Blaen-y-glyn that can be coupled with BB21 for a short but memorable day, make your way to the S tip of Cwar y Gigfran, either direct across the plateau or, better, round the escarpment edge. A toe-burning descent into Cerrig Edmwnt leads onto a faint path to the corner of the woods above Blaen-y-glyn at 062183. It is not easy to cross the stream here, and it is in any case best to stay on the E bank on a narrow path that rambles high above the stream until, at 061174, a wooden bridge by the largest of the falls enables you to cross over to rejoin BB21.

CRAIG CWARELI

The two upright stone stakes are all that rescue this minor top from oblivion. Even so it gets its fair share of visitors (though not all of them may recognise it) because the hike from Fan y Big round to Waun-rydd, which crosses Craig Cwareli en-route, is one of the finest rim walks in Wales, above the primeval grandeur of the vast amphitheatre enclosed by Cwm Oergwm and Cwm Cwareli.

Blaen-y-glyn route (BB23)

Follow BB21 along Craig Fan-las then, at about 053197, strike out W or slightly N of W across the shaggy moorland to achieve (depending on your navigational skills) either a bull's-eye or, at worst, a hit on the escarpment edge close by the top.

GWAEN CERRIG-LLWYDION

Gwaen Cerrig-llwydion is such a featureless little mound that it takes a dab hand with the map to know when you have got there. No one is likely to make it a prime objective and you are most likely to visit it as part of the excellent rim walk round the heads of Cwm Oergwm and Cwm Cwareli.

Gist Wen ridge (BB24)

Follow BB18, but instead of abandoning the rim path for Waun-rydd as indicated there, stay with it for about another half a mile until your eye judges you have reached the slightly elevated hump that is Gwaen Cerrig-llwydion.

Blaen-y-glyn route (BB25)

Follow BB21 to the escarpment edge at Bwlch y Ddwyallt, 057206, when Gwaen Cerrig-llwydion is along the rim to your L.

ALLT-LWYD

Anyone seeking a change from the treadmill could do a lot worse than sample the Beacons' E foothills. They are softer and lonelier than the over-trodden trails N and W. Allt-lwyd is a worthy gateway, with a narrow wisp of a ridge to entice you on to the Waun-rydd plateau thrown in for good measure. It is an unexceptional enough top in itself, yet to stride its copper-tinted turf, and to gaze upon the verdant green hills and vales that surround it, with the rounded dome of Tor y Foel pre-eminent, always engenders a sense of well-being.

Ascending Allt-lwyd: looking over Tor y Foel to the Black Mountains

Talybont reservoir route (BB26)

Go through the gate opposite the car park at 100198, cross a stile with a blue waymark sign and follow a green path between an avenue of trees. Before long the path veers L to join the edge of some woods. Stay with the woods until they turn S at 088195 and then make your own way up the hillside on 225. Gentle plodding for half a mile wins you a top cloaked in luxuriant golden-brown grass. No cairn, not even one solitary stone atop another, defiles the purity of the scene; just a lonely little tarn.

Blaen-y-glyn route (BB27)

From the top follow a faint path that crosses the narrow neck to Craig y Fan at the S tip of the Waun-rydd plateau. Slopes sheltering green wooded valleys and a delightful little climb up to the plateau looming ahead make this, for all its innocence, the very archetype of what a ridge walk should be. If only it were twice as high and twice as long; and with a bit of rock thrown in! Follow the edge round to Cwar y Gigfran to finish at the Blaen-y-glyn waterfalls as in BB22.

CEFN YR YSTRAD

Cefn yr Ystrad is too remote to attract much attention, but an enjoyable day in fresh unfamiliar terrain awaits anyone combining the two Crawnon Valley routes given below. The routes are described in sequence starting with the more S, but you could just as easily proceed the other way round.

Dyffryn Crawnon S route (BB28)

Start from the farm at Llwyn-deri and follow a track which proceeds SW from the farm buildings. Pass through a gate and then make a sharp L turn along the side of a wood towards the isolated homestead of Tyle Bach. Go through an enclosure at the front of this cottage, step over a stile, cross a field and then another stile, all on a bearing of 225. The path fades hereabouts, but if you strike out for a corner of a wood in the L foreground at 139184 it reappears firmer than ever.

It is now level going, with a stone wall R, and you need to decide whether to stay on the path for the next two miles or to strike out L for higher ground. Although there is no path the latter is preferable with cropped grass, widening views, and a succession of spiky outcrops.

Aim next for the head of Cwm Pyrgad, 111152, where a bridleway comes up from the valley to meet you (BB28, 1). You will now see a hollow ahead (ie looking W or SW) with a new quarry road. This is not marked on all the maps and it can be confusing if the first intimation you get is when it suddenly emerges from the mist. Over the road follow a bearing of 225 across an undulating heathery plateau. There are no tracks but it is firm underfoot and the only problem is locating the top in the midst of a featureless waste reminiscent of Kinder Scout.

Dyffryn Crawnon N route (BB29)

From the trig point thread a way as best you can through the desolation of quarries that despoil the foreground and aim for one of several tracks round the head of Dyffryn Crawnon. This means walking on an average bearing of 10. Near Bryn Cefnog, 088159, you will come upon a prominent bridleway. This extends the length of the fine ridge dividing Dyffryn Crawnon from the Caerfanell Valley;

a lovely walk with unusual views of the Beacons.

To recover your car leave the ridge where a surfaced road is met, 110188, and follow a bridleway down through the farmstead of Bwlch-y-waun and on to meet the road by a public footpath sign at 133192. Turn R for 200 paces until another footpath goes off L. This leads to a footbridge over the Afon Crawnon, thus completing the circle.

Quarry road route (BB30)

If you are just out to bag Cefn yr Ystrad as easily as possible, the way to do it is to drive up the quarry road mentioned in BB28, leaving the A465 in Tredegar, and then stalk your objective on a compass bearing. Quick, painless (provided there is no mist), but with little else to recommend it.

HIGH-LEVEL WALKS
N Horseshoes (BB H1)

A host of horseshoes can be constructed from the many trails that approach the Beacons from the N. All you have to do is to link them using the maze of lanes that crosses the toes of the hills. This sounds simple but take heed; distances are greater than they seem, especially after a hard day, and with all the bends you would not be the first rambler who, after impeccable compass work on the fells, faltered down these leafy lanes!

However, an exception needs to be made for the Cefn Cyff and Gist Wen ridges because linking them along the roads would entail a major diversion. Also it is a popular combination because it takes in the great rim walk round Cwm Cwareli and Cwm Oergwm. Fortunately a shortcut is available.

From the foot of the Cefn Cyff ridge near Rhiwiau (BB15) go to the junction at 058247 and follow the farm road towards Pentwyn. Leave this L just prior to the farm and follow a narrow overgrown trail, hedged either side, to a footbridge at 065244. Over the stream the path wends through woods to meet the road at 065240, opposite Cwm Oergwm Isaf Farm, whence a short walk returns you to the start of the Gist Wen route at 072249 (BB18).

*The Big Three - Corn Du, Pen y Fan and Cribin - from the head of
Cwm Oergwm; the ridge in the foreground leads to Fan y Big*

Neuadd horseshoe (BB H2)

The distance involved in the N horseshoes mean that few people do
more than combine adjoining ridges. This limits how much of the
main ridge you can cover. That is where this S horseshoe scores.
Joining the ridge where it intersects the Roman road on BB14 you
follow it over Cribin, Pen y Fan, Corn Du, and Craig Gwaun-taf
before wending homeward over Craig y Fan-ddu for a glorious
finale in the afternoon sun. A superb day that enables you to scalp
the Big Three rather more easily than you might have thought.

Cerrig Edmwnt horseshoe (BB H3)

This is a combination of two routes on Waun-rydd, out via the
Blaen-y-glyn Falls and back over Cwar y Gigfran (BB21 and 22). The
scenery is so splendid - matured woodlands, tumbling waterfalls,
rugged escarpments, a wild windswept plateau - that it would be
remiss of me not to give it special mention. A half-day should suffice
for a strong walker; try it after early rain has freshened the air to give

a sunny afternoon.

E horseshoe (BB H4)

If I were asked for an introduction to the calm of the E Beacons I would answer something like this. Park by the Talybont reservoir; climb Allt-lwyd (BB26); cross the neck to Craig y Fan; follow the edge round to Cairn Pica and Waun-rydd and then make a leisurely return over Bryn and Cwm Banw (BB19). If the weather clamps down, shorten the walk by dropping down from Cairn Pica (BB20). This would be a lonely day with shy wisp-like tracks supplanting the scarred peaty paths of the W Beacons. Apart from the giants on the distant skyline the scenery is pretty rather than dramatic; sheltered bracken-clad cwms and wooded foothills.

W horseshoe (BB H5)

Climb Y Gyrn on BB1, carry on NE to claim Corn Du along the edge above Llyn Cwm Llwch, then return to the Storey Arms on BB5. This does not compare with the other horseshoes, but for walkers based on the Storey Arms it is at least preferable to a simple there-and-back trip.

W to E traverse (BB H6)

The complete traverse of the Beacons from the Storey Arms to the Talybont reservoir, crossing 10 of the 11 tops en-route (Cefn yr Ystrad is too remote to be included) is a grand experience - though a tough one! It makes little difference which way you tackle it.

The plod up Y Gyrn (BB1) is not the most inspiring of starts, but the subsequent edge walk above Llyn Cwm Llwch soon makes amends as the vibrant greens of Cwm Llwch and the Usk Valley come into view. There is a sting in the tail, though, for the grooved path along the edge offers no hint of the final greasy slither it demands in all but the driest conditions.

Peak-baggers may make a short diversion from Corn Du to capture Craig Gwaun-taf. Otherwise it is but a short step on to Pen y Fan along an almost flat, gravelly path which, with its obscene width and litter, would not be out of place in a city park! However, as if to atone, the views are now approaching their best: the majestic sweep of the N escarpment; lush green valleys extending to Brecon;

barren moors S, rescued from oblivion by the glint of sunlight on the Neuadd reservoirs; and Cribin, Fan y Big and the whalebacked Bryn tempting you on E.

Beyond Pen y Fan the crowds gradually diminish. Care is needed on the 750ft descent to the col, first over a rock face shattered beyond redemption, then over steep muddy slopes that can be treacherous after rain or snow. Cribin poses a test of your fitness, a pitiless grind up being followed by an equally knee-jarring descent down to The Gap.

Whoever said that history does not repeat itself had obviously missed out on this walk because the haul up to Fan y Big is the Cribin medicine all over again. But then comes blessed relief. From Fan y Big an almost level path hugs the edge of the vast amphitheatre of Oergwm and Cwareli. Landmarks come and go in quick succession: a group of derelict mine workings (037199) where there is a rough shelter if a squall blows up; a small rise to the two stone stakes that are the sole clue to Craig Cwareli; the unmarked and unremarkable top of Gwaen Cerrig-llwydion which, unless you concentrate hard, you will cross without noticing!

(Short cuts are possible. You could cut the corner at 050205 by crossing a lunar-like area of peat hags, dried up tarn beds and stone-strewn flats. Cribin can be by-passed by a track that leaves the edge at the foot of Pen y Fan and contours round to rejoin it at The Gap. Indeed the same track also enables you to miss out Fan y Big by making straight for Craig Cwareli.)

Soon after Gwaen Cerrig-llwydion, at about 057206, you must desert the rim and cross the Waun-rydd plateau on a bearing of about 90 (see the Waun-rydd entry for details of this desolate plateau). Make for the E edge and follow it round to the S tip of Craig y Fan at 071195. From there it is all downhill, crossing a playful little neck to Allt-lwyd whence BB26 leads to the Talybont car park and the joy of boot removal.

Waun-rydd perimeter walk (BB H7)

This short but exhilarating walk 'on top of the world' has already been mentioned under Waun-rydd. It is a bit of an oddity in that it begins and ends at over 2000ft and must therefore be tackled as an addition. From the summit cairn on Waun-rydd walk along, or parallel to the edge, aiming for Cairn Pica. Cairn Pica is a good spot for lunch with plenty to engage the eye. Cwm Banw takes pride of place, Allt-lwyd looks tempting SE and over the reservoir Tor y Foel apes the Sugar Loaf in the Black Mountains.

After the break continue along the tip of Craig y Fan, 071195, and note the sharp little arête leading to Allt-lwyd. When you 'turn the corner' the delicate charms of Cwm Banw are replaced by weathered escarpments in a scene of almost Arizona-like desolation and splendour.

You are now on the homeward half. Look out L a little way down the slope, at 062200, for a memorial cairn close to two piles of aircraft wreckage. This commemorates a Wellington bomber that crashed on a cross-country training flight during the war. Shortly afterwards you have a choice of tracks, all of which slant across the upper reaches of Cerrig Edmwnt (plenty of peat-hags) to join the Cwm Oergwm rim track at 057206.

LOWER-LEVEL WALKS/EASIER DAYS
Llyn Cwm Llwch (BB L1)
For an easy day nothing conveys the spirit of the Beacons better than this. Leafy glades flanked by bracken-clad ridges, a gentle pull up to open fells, then a picnic by the lake with the mighty Corn Du and Pen y Fan in close attendance - what more could you ask for? (BB3 refers)

Blaen-y-glyn waterfalls (BB L2)
Stroll beside the waterfalls, the best in the area. There are plenty of soft spots for a leisurely lunch and pools for paddling too. Better still, climb up beyond the tree-line to view the gaunt cliffs enclosing Cerrig Edmwnt. (BB21 and BB22 refer)

Cwm Banw (BB L3)
Start from the telephone kiosk at 106214 and stroll along the narrow farm road to Nantllannerch. You might then continue on the bridleway towards Bryn's SE slopes as in BB19. Good for blowing the cobwebs away when time or the elements rule out anything more adventurous.

The Roman road (BB L4)

No matter from which direction you set out, BB12 or 14, this provides an excellent entrée to the wild with the bonus of a good firm track all the way to The Gap. Starting from sheltered valleys and woodlands it is hard to credit that you are only just below 2000ft when you reach The Gap, so easy is the going. But with Cribin and Fan y Big towering imposingly on either side, there is no doubting the sense of occasion!

Nant Menasgin horseshoe (BB L5)

I spent many years tramping the Beacons' tops before I discovered the delicate beauty of the cwms. Here is a walk that reveals it to the full in an easy half-day. It starts down the narrow lane that leaves the road from Llanfrynach to Pencilli at 075256. Park in the village as there is nowhere along the lane.

Soon after Caerau Farm the metalled road yields to a bridleway that wends through one and a half miles of old world parkland, mature woodlands and new plantations. As the woods thin out the skyline reveals the familiar outlines of Fan y Big and Waun-rydd, their stark austerity of line the perfect foil to the rustic charm of the valley. There is one particularly idyllic spot at 053223 where the path crosses Cwm Cwareli. Should you pause for a picnic on a summer day .... On resuming, a tumbledown wall leads to a crossing over the Nant Menasgin at 048216.

Once across aim for a rickety gate at 049221 and follow a track that re-enters the woods to cleave through dense bracken-clad slopes above the brook. This is narrower and less well defined than the bridleway and for that reason the walk is best done this way round - otherwise you could have a problem getting started. You eventually emerge at Pen-yr-hoel, near the start of BB15. For a quick way back to base see BB H1.

CADER IDRIS
OS maps 1:25,000 - Sheet 23 1:50,000 - Sheets 124

Peaks	Height (ft)	Map Ref	Page
Penygadair	2928	711131	162
Mynydd Moel	2804	727137	170
Cyfrwy	2646	703133	168
Craig y Cau*	2595	710122	169
Gau Craig	2230	745142	171
Craig Las**	2168	676136	172
Craig-y-llyn	2040	665120	173
Bryn Brith	1200	664150	175

* sometimes known as Craig Cwm Amarch or Mynydd Pencoed
** sometimes known as Tyrrau Mawr

Mountain Lakes

Aran	1580	734139
Cau	1540	715124
Cyri	1150	657118
Nameless	2053	706112
Y Gadair	1820	708136
Y Gafr	1325	711141

CADER IDRIS

Little is known of the legendary Idris. Old bardic writings variously
refer to him as giant, astronomer, philosopher and poet. At other
times he is depicted as a warrior killed fighting the Saxon foe. But
one thing is certain, to have chosen the gigantic hollow cradling
Llyn y Gadair for his chair (for Cader Idris means Chair of Idris) he
must have been a superb judge of mountains. Of all the Welsh peaks
only Snowdon can compare in architectural splendour.

Llyn y Gadair and the N escarpment from Cyfrwy

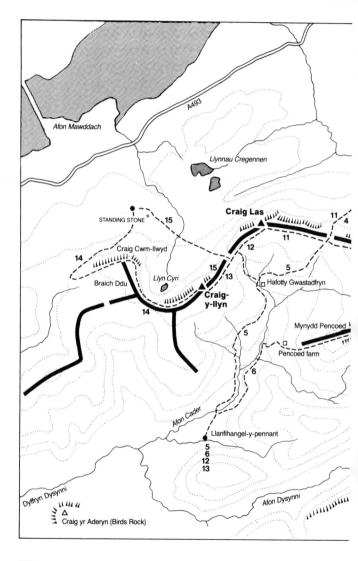

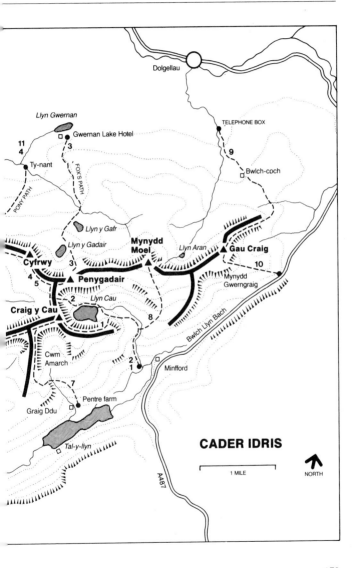

CADER IDRIS

1 MILE

NORTH

The great glory of Cader Idris is the long N escarpment that extends over seven miles from the rocky shoulder of Gau Craig above Dolgellau to the sea-girt ramparts of Craig Cwm-llwyd in the W. Only sporadically does the precipice yield to gentler slopes and, apart from the approaches at either end over Gau Craig and Braich Ddu (neither of which is well used) there are but three breaches in its defences: Fox's Path leading directly to Penygadair; the popular Pony Path and the col between Craig Las and Craig-y-llyn.

Below the massive cliffs nestle four glittering lakes: Y Gadair (supreme, cold, sombre, awe-inspiring corrie and guardian of The Chair); Y Gafr (serene but overshadowed by its loftier companion); Aran and Cyri (elusive, lonely, forgotten). Below the lakes the land ripples away to the sands of the Mawddach Estuary in a fantasia of tinkling streams, leafy glens, green meadows and wooded foothills. There are no finer lowlands than these and no finer introduction to their charms than the placid Llynnau Cregennen.

The SE slopes are no less spectacular. Giant turrets of rock knobbly and gnarled, frown down imperiously over the narrow defile of Bwlch Llyn-bach, the final S surge of the Bala Gap. Demonic in mist, a dazzle of sparkling pinnacles in snow, the whole mountainside becomes a brilliant blaze of mauves and coppery red as winter approaches. Framed in the pass and surrounded by the hills, Tal-y-llyn shines like a jewel, one of the loveliest roadside lakes in Wales. High above its N shore is a wooded vale, Amarch, and above the vale a hanging valley, the epitome of solitude and one of only two ways onto the hills from this side. The other one starts from the parkland and rhododendrons of Minffordd and is rapidly becoming a highway. It leads via Llyn Cau, another impressive deeply-gouged corrie, where the hills all but enclose you in their spartan grip.

Only along its S soft underbelly, where it declines in smooth grassy slopes, is Cader Idris crag-free. This is where the Afon Dysynni and its tributary, the Afon Cader, burrow deeply into the fastness of the hills to give access to all but the two most E of the tops

Out of the seven peaks, over 2,000 foot six lie along the N edge. The seventh, Craig y Cau, rises just to the S over Llyn Cau. Apart from Penygadair (which commands the high ground between Llyn y Gadair and Llyn Cau), the tops have two faces - dizzy precipice one side, easy grass the other. Yet despite the angular grandeur of Craig y Cau's E face, the razor-sharp arêtes of Cyfrwy and the classic triangle Mynydd Moel unveils to Gau Craig, it is not for its curvaceous peaks that you will remember Cader Idris. There are none of the shapely profiles of a Hebog, a Cnicht, an Aran Fawddwy or even a Rhobell Fawr to ingrain themselves upon the memory. Cader's appeal is more subtle, relying partly on the uncluttered flowing line of its great N cliffs, but above all on the interplay of cwm and corrie and the intriguing twist of the ridges that gravitate from Penygadair like the arms of some distant spiral nebula.

Cader is generous to dedicated and occasional walker alike. Access is easy, tracks firm and clear, gradients modest (for the most part). From almost anywhere on the N rim the views are breathtaking in their breadth and majesty. Plynlimon, Rhinogs, Arans, Arenigs, Tarrens and the Dovey hills are the staple fare; a timeless symphony of hills and dales. Even Snowdonia can be glimpsed through the translucent haze. All are embellished by the calming, mellowing spell of the sea, the tree-lined drift of the estuary and its golden sands, as well as the woodlands of many hues.

Cader Idris is a popular mountain, the romance of the name alone guarantees that. Yet a liberating sense of height and isolation is always present. Even on the main tableland 'highway' between Penygadair and Mynydd Moel the magic persists and, fortunately, crowds are easily left behind. Climb Cyfrwy or Gau Craig, grand vantage points both of them, and you are likely to be alone. Even on Mynydd Moel, a simple stroll from Penygadair, you can usually reckon on having the cairn to yourself, while over towards Craig Las or Craig-y-llyn the only sound is likely to be the rustling of the wind.

Cader bestows one more gift - enticing mornings and evenings replete with rustic charm. No other hills in Wales flow quite so easily and naturally out of gentle pastures, thriving farmsteads and leafy lanes. There is no need to despair if the tops sulk in mist or glitter in unmanageable ice or snow, a wealth of lowland walks are there for the taking. True the Carneddau rise from the green of Conway; Hebog from Pennant and the Beddgelert Forest; while the approaches to the Brecon Beacons and the Black Mountains have an ethereal charm all of their own. But none of these offers the riches that Cader expends on its admirers. The lanes and byways from Dolgellau to Gau Craig blaze with flowers in early summer and twisting bracken-clad dips and hillocks fringe the Fox's Path, the Pony Path and cradle Llyn Gwernan and the lovely Llynnau Cregennen. Add to these the peaceful shore of Tal-y-llyn, the rhododendron-dappled gates to the Minffordd trail, and you will see that Cader is above all a joyful, friendly mountain. There is none of the sense of melancholy, of tragedy even, that is never quite dispelled on Snowdon on even the balmiest of days. If Snowdon is the king of the Welsh hills, Cader Idris is surely the prince.

PENYGADAIR

Penygadair was popular way back in Victorian times. That was the heyday of the old refreshment hut whose crumbling remains on the edge of the cliffs still provide shelter from the wind though the tea, alas, is no more. The nearby trig point is the focal point nowadays. Mounted on a little rocky platform that sets it apart from the bouldery waste all around, and with the added luxury of steps up one side, it is a worthy vantage point for the premier peak of the range.

The ridge unfurls on either side. A sparse, stony sub-Arctic tundra covers the tableland that stretches away to Mynydd Moel the quintessence of mountain walking, while beyond the splintered cliffs of Cyfrwy a series of gentle undulations winds away to Craig y-llyn and the blue of Cardigan Bay. To the S the ground falls away sharply before rising with renewed vigour to the ferocious precipice of Craig y Cau. On a clear day you will also discern Plynlimon and its cohorts.

Memorable though these scenes are, they are totally eclipsed by a N prospect that is at once heroic and serene. Only a few steps from the cairn is the plunge to Llyn y Gadair and the awesome grandeur of The Chair. Lift your eyes and a single glance encompasses the blue-black ribbon of the Mawddach, fringed by the yellow-brown sands of the estuary, and the tapering line of the Rhinogs leading to Snowdonia itself. Across the green tapestry of the Coed y Brenin Forest lie Rhobell Fawr, the Arenigs, the Arans and Lake Bala.

There is no problem locating the edge path to Mynydd Moel o

Penygadair and Mynydd Moel from Cyfrwy

the Pony Path, even in the thickest mist, but it is a little more tricky
if your objective is Craig y Cau. You should then start as if for the
Pony Path but be sure to spot L, after a minute or two, the cairned
path sidling away SW.

The Minffordd trail (CI1)

Romantic and dramatic, a walk of sustained beauty and variety.
That, in a nutshell, is the Minffordd trail, one of the great walks of
Wales. It used to start through the iron gates of the old Idris Estate
at 730114, but it is more convenient nowadays to begin from a new
car park a couple of hundred yards up the road at 732116. A kissing-
gate at the rear leads to a tunnel of trees and a clearing where
flowering shrubs and rhododendrons, set against the backdrop of
craggy heather slopes and a shady glen, convey a hint of Arcady. A
series of steps - the price of erosion and popularity - lead into the
glen and on to a track that climbs between the conifers high above
the rushing torrents of the Nant Cader. The angle eases as you leave

the woods and the flanks of Mynydd Moel come into view R.

The path swings round above the corrie basin of Llyn Cau, the enclosed lake. The cold, awesome splendour is dominated by the presence of Craig y Cau, a gigantic, heavily buttressed pyramid of raw rock. It is flanked L by the great gully and the Pencoed Pillar, R by the stone shoot - the sole breach in its defences.

The path bears S up easy screes before curling round the rim of the mighty cliffs cradling the lake. Thrills come quickly now in a purple patch that leads above the great gully, climbs Craig y Cau along the very edge of the stupendous precipice guarding the lake, then drops down to the col at the head of the stone shoot. As if that were not enough, the longer views are enthralling too: the Dysynni Valley and the far off Tarrens, the solitudes of forgotten Cwm Amarch, then across the abyss of Llyn Cau to Mynydd Moel and the spiky crown of Penygadair itself. From the col a well-cairned path ascends increasingly rocky terrain to the summit; a fitting finale to a walk that will tempt you again and again.

Note the following route-finding points. First you will see that the path splits either side of Craig y Cau. One arm continues over the top as described above, the other (easier) contours round to the W. Second you can capture Cyfrwy en-route to Penygadair by an obvious traverse N from the top of the stone shoot to gain the rim edge at about 708130.

The stone shoot (CI2)

As you climb the Minffordd trail the white, snaking thread of the stone shoot can be seen rising from the NW corner of Llyn Cau. Probably because of its name it has gained a reputation as a thankless grind to be avoided at all costs, when in fact, though undeniably steep, it is agreeably firm underfoot. A strong walker should have no problem in taming it in little more than half an hour. It is no place for families, or the 'one-weekend-a-year' rambler, but for the connoisseur it provides a beautifully wild and litter-free alternative to the more popular Minffordd routing. The approach along the N shoreline of Llyn Cau offers superb views of the Pencoed pillar and is a fine walk in itself.

The Fox's Path (CI3)

Was there ever such a Jekyll and Hyde route as this? It is heralded by an iron gate across the road from the Gwernan Lake Hotel and as far as Llyn y Gadair is sheer delight. Moss-capped stones and aged trees adorn a trail that dips and twists through meadows and coppices, moorland and tiny outcrops. The Rhinogs fill the N skyline; the sea and Llynnau Cregennen peep in from the W. What better entrée to the hills could there be? Llyn y Gafr passes uneventfully (though crossing the innocent-looking stream just before you reach it can pose a problem after heavy rain), but the real pièce de résistance comes when, after a short stony rise, the gigantic hollow cradling Llyn y Gadair - the chair of the legendary Idris - strikes you like a thunderclap.

Cyfrwy soars in wild, bristly abandon, challenging the sky with quivers of jagged pinnacles and sending rivers of scree down to the lake shores below. Massive buttresses bolster Penygadair's tilted terraces and only on the E flank is there so much as a glimmer of hope for the humble pedestrian. As if to atone for such excesses the lake is the very embodiment of tranquillity, sheltered from all but the strongest winds and with every stone and pebble shimmering like a jewel through its fresh, clear water. Harsh, rugged, desolate, cold, unforgiving; this wild place is all of these. Yet alone on a still day it conveys a sense of at-oneness with the hills that is almost overpowering.

*   *   *

If you are wise you will stop here. The Fox's Path screes are purgatory; long, excruciatingly steep and treacherously unstable, eroded so badly in parts that they border on the dangerous. My advice would be to let well alone and either settle for a simple there-and-back walk or, better still, switch across to the Pony Path. You can then choose between a short but rewarding round trip back to the car park near Ty-nant, or carrying on up the mountain on CI4. You can just discern the path you want crossing the screes near the NW corner of the lake. Scrappy at first it gradually grows in confidence and before long a keen eye can identify two paths. The higher meets the Pony Path just below the ridge; the other meets it at 696143, at a rusty brown gate in a stone wall shortly after passing a tumbledown shepherd's hut.

The Pony (Ty-nant) Path (CI4)

The Pony Path is probably the most popular route on Cader Idris nowadays. A footpath sign by the telephone box at 698152 marks the start, close to Ty-nant Farm and only a short step from a well laid-out car park with toilets. The walk starts beside a brook, canopied by trees, and is every bit as delightful as the Fox's Path until you reach the rusty brown gate in the wall where the track from Llyn y Gadair comes in (see CI3).

After the wall a series of well engineered zig-zags brings you to the col between Penygadair and Craig Las - Rhiw Gwredydd. (It is also the top of a pass linking Abergwynant and the Dysynni Valley.) A gate and a ladder-stile in a wire fence make it an easy spot to identify in mist. From there to the edge at 704131 is a mile-long plod up a badly eroded track. Peaty at first but turning to rock, it is cairned to excess and as wide as a tramway. Then the magic returns. Whether or not you divert along the edge to Cyfrwy, the views round the amphitheatre of Llyn y Gadair are sensational and the easy scramble up to the trig point is the perfect finale.

(A second line of cairns runs N of the main path and leads direct to Cyfrwy. However there is virtually no path, and anyone going that way must expect an ankle-twisting hike over boulders that are very slippery when wet.)

Llanfihangel-y-pennant route (CI5)

This long approach really needs something extra to bring it alive. One way is to combine it with a return over the Pencoed ridge. You then get a nicely varied day in country that is all but forgotten. Park at 672089 and walk up the road to the remains of Mary Jones' cottage, Tyn-y-ddol, just across a bridge. In 1800, while still in her late teens, Mary set out barefoot on a 25-mile trek to the Reverend Thomas Charles in Bala to obtain a Welsh Bible. None were left, but he was so impressed that he gave her his own. Not only that, but her example led him to set about forming what later became the British and Foreign Bible Society.

A Land-Rover track continues up a valley that is pleasantly wooded at first but soon becomes dull and barren. (The prominent hill behind you, looking as if it were about to topple over, is the Bird's Rock, Craig yr Aderyn.) When you reach Hafotty Gwastadfryn

- a messy, untidy corral - ignore the bulldozed road L and keep R along a path that climbs the hillside, greening up as it does so. At the top of the pass at Rhiw Gwredydd bear R for Penygadair or L for Craig Las on CI12, 1.

Pencoed ridge (CI6)

Only a faint shadow in the grass betrays the wisp-like track across the long finger of Mynydd Pencoed. This is a route that promises much and delivers it all: superb views, a glittering fledgling tarn down the slope at 706112, crisp, springy turf underfoot and the exhilaration of tramping 'on top of the world'. It is best in descent. The W slopes, ideal for unwinding in the afternoon sun, would be toilsome to climb in the morning. CI5 makes a good partner.

Drop down to Craig y Cau where a fence, rickety at first, straddles the ridge on 240. Rock-encrusted grass soon gives way to the striding-out variety. As the ridge declines aim R for Pencoed Farm to pick up a Land-Rover trail that leads to the car park at Llanfihangel-y-pennant. Alternatively cross the bridge at 677101 (signposted) and return by Mary Jones' cottage.

Cwm Amarch route (CI7)

Try this as a way home from Penygadair if you came up the Minffordd Path and want to break new ground. It brings you out by Pentre Farm on the N shoreline of Tal-y-llyn, leaving you with an easy 20-minute stroll back to the Minffordd car park. The scenery is superb. Why the hanging valley of Amarch is not better known is a mystery!

Walk the Pencoed ridge (CI6) until you can break away L round the rim of Cwm Amarch. Then follow a fence down grassy slopes to a tarn at 706112 with two tiny islets. Stay with the fence for awhile but then cross the cwm to the stream at the head of the falls. This is a perfect spot for bathing tired feet, with bouncy pillows of bilberries to lie on and the lush crag-hung slopes of Graig Ddu across the vale resplendent in the evening sun. A variety of narrow shepherd's tracks leads down to Pentre Farm 717104.

The start is a bit tricky to find in reverse. As you approach Pentre Farm keep the buildings well to your L and walk straight ahead into the SW tip of a plantation of fir trees. (Ignore the footpath sign. This

Cyfrwy and Llyn y Gadair from Penygadair

signals a path which zig-zags up the opposite side of the cwm before carrying on above the lake.) Among the fir trees a stony farm track leads to a ladder-stile at 716104. This gives access to a grooved track (almost overrun by foxgloves) that climbs up to the falls.

CYFRWY
Cyfrwy is airily perched at the tip of the W arm of the legendary Chair. Bare and stony, ignored by the crowds that throng Penygadair, it is an exciting top which gazes across the yawning chasm of Llyn y Gadair to the majestic, striated rock-face of Penygadair and the pitiless screes of the Fox's Path precariously clinging to the opposite arm. Further on the cliffs extend with undiminished vigour to Mynydd Moel, and only W, where the Pony Path can be seen winding up the slopes and the hills eventually subside to the sea, is there even a hint of a break in Cader's ramparts. Nearer to hand, beneath your feet, spiky gullies, loose and sunless, plummet to the lakeshore 800ft below. A narrow arête leads the eye to the slender obelisk capped by Idris' Table, over half-way down.

*The harsh precipice of Craig y Cau and Llyn Cau
with the Tarrens on the skyline*

In view of its proximity to Penygadair it would be pedantic to give separate routes for Cyfrwy. It is easily climbed as a minor variation from the Pony Path (CI4), by a simple traverse across a grassy saddle from the Minffordd trail (CI1), or direct from Penygadair along the edge.

CRAIG Y CAU

Craig y Cau's tiny cairn is poised on the topmost pinnacle of the immense triangle of rock that falls away to the cold, blue-black waters of Llyn Cau in an impregnable and chaotic array of terraces and buttresses. On a calm summer's day, with the lake shimmering in the sun, few scenes are more sublime. On a blustery day in winter, with the waters of the lake whipped into swirling waves and spray, few settings exhibit more forcibly Nature's sheer elemental power.

Behind you the eye is held by the jutting finger of Mynydd Pencoed, the hanging valley of Cwm Amarch and the undulating skyline of Craig Las and Craig-y-llyn. To the N the ridge carries on to the ultimate goal of Penygadair itself.

Yet when all is said and done, something is lacking. Craig y Cau, dramatic viewpoint though it is, is but a staging post to greater things. Despite the awesome splendour of this lofty eyrie there is no denying the magnetic presence of Penygadair less than half a mile away, higher up the same slopes.

There are three routes which cross Craig y Cau on their way to Penygadair; the Minffordd trail (CI1), the Pencoed ridge route (CI6) and the Cwm Amarch route (CI7).

MYNYDD MOEL

Penygadair is the first objective of every newcomer to Cader Idris. Hopefully it will only be a beginning. One of the finest encores is the high-level tongue to Gau Craig. The path tends to favour the scarped N edge so do try to fit in a brief safari S when you will be inspired by the surge of Craig y Cau, the massive Pencoed Pillar and the cold, deep aquamarine of the lake.

A short mile brings a slight rise capped with a large windshelter. This is Mynydd Moel, innocuous enough as a top but an ideal belvedere. Penygadair, Cyfrwy, Craig Las, Craig-y-llyn, the estuary and the sea stand in line abreast W, while to the E the cliffs continue in full spate to Gau Craig. One of my most memorable New Year's day lunches was eaten here, alone and content one bright frosty morning; far removed in spirit, if not in distance, from crowded Penygadair.

Innocuous did I say? From the W, yes, but approach it from Gau Craig and you will see a Mynydd Moel as shapely and imposing as any peak in the range. A great furrowed precipice it stands, riven with gullies and strewn with scree, the guardian of the secretive Llyn Aran.

The Minffordd route (CI8)

Follow the enchanting Minffordd trail (CI1) to the edge of the woods at 728121. Cross the brook and strike out on 40 along a faint track that starts in a little dip in front of a grassy ramp adjoining the woods. You soon meet a tumbledown wall/fence struggling up the S ridge with a shaly path alongside. The wall ends at about the 2000ft mark, but the path carries on to the main 'plateau' before it expires too. However you have only to keep going due N to meet the escarpment close to Mynydd Moel. This is also a good way to return home if you started from Minffordd, although you then need to judge carefully when to cross over to the woods. Following the wall too long would land you above the impassable crags of Moelfryn with no choice but the frustration of having to retrace your steps. So on the way down look out for another derelict wall coming in from the E at 732124. About 100yds before you reach it the track you want sidles away slightly S of E.

GAU CRAIG

Gau Craig is the lone height at the NE tip of the Cader Idris massif. From Dolgellau and the N it is completely overshadowed by Mynydd Moel, it only does itself justice as you drive over Bwlch Llyn-bach when its giant crags frown down on the pass with a striking malevolence. It is a sparkling viewpoint and its NE ridge is a little gem of a walk, offering all the delights of hillwalking in miniature.

It is a fresh, 'top-of-the-world' sort of walk on to Mynydd Moel with firm springy turf to speed you along; flat at first followed by a short rise. The near rectangular Llyn Aran comes into view half-way along, cupped in a hollow beneath Mynydd Moel's rugged E face. To visit it makes an interesting side trip from CI9 if the weather clamps down.

NE ridge (CI9)

The best place to start is the junction by the telephone box at 738166. You are then well placed for a circuit of the ridge, coming down on the Pony Path (CI H2). The quiet country lane to Bwlch-coch is a flame of yellows, pinks and blues in early summer and there are few lovelier sights on a sunny morning than the meadows blending so beautifully into the surrounding hills. The lane ends at 744159 with a footpath sign. The path is little-used and long stretches have all but disappeared, although just when you despair it tends to turn up again. The best plan is to stay on an average bearing of 160 and aim for one of the grassy rakes leading up to the ridge. The scenery is superb, Mynydd Moel being the main focus of attention with the bristles of Cyfrwy peeping over its shoulder.

A playful track hugs the crest of the ridge, dodging boulders, splicing tussocks of bilberries, yet never far from the fearsome crags and the characteristic white quartz streak that is so prominent from the valley below. If only it were twice as long! But no, all too soon the cairn is yours and with it a view to relish.

Across the pass the Dovey hills look bare and uninteresting - which shows how looks can sometimes deceive! N a gently wooded landscape, speckled in greens of many hues, leads the eye to the grey tops of the Arans, the Arenigs and the gentle curve of Rhobell Fawr. Further W are the Rhinogs and the riveting pass of Bwlch Drws Arduddwy with Snowdonia in the haze beyond. The circle is completed by the estuary and the towering presence of Mynydd Moel; nowhere else as noble as this.

The ridge can also be gained from the E by following a boggy path that leaves the road by a footpath sign at 756140 (CI9, 1).

Mynydd Gwerngraig route (CI10)

You could also climb Gau Craig direct from 756140 by struggling directly up the hillside beside a wall. However, why anyone should wish to subject themselves to such unadulterated purgatory when the delectable NE ridge is so near and inviting is quite beyond me.

CRAIG LAS

Only a handful of walkers venture beyond the Pony Path to the two lonely outliers in the W, and even then the majority only see Craig Las side-on as they tramp the N escarpment. Pleasant walk though that is, to see Craig Las in its full glory you must travel to the Cregennen lakes. Massive green slopes, flecked with crags and soaring to an elongated band of rock, put its mountainly status beyond any shadow of a doubt! The highest point lies on the very edge of the abyss and is marked by a small cairn. The view takes in the Mawddach Estuary right round to Penygadair.

Ty-nant route (CI11)

Follow the Pony Path (CI4) to the col at Rhiw Gwredydd and then turn R for an uneventful walk along the fence. (Strictly speak̶ʼ ̶ ʼhe path keeps some distance 'inland' from the edge and just by-passes the cairn.) On the way you cross the stony outcrop of Carnedd Lwyd, noteworthy only because it stands out like a pimple on the skyline from almost any viewpoint of Cader from the N. It is thus a useful landmark.

Llanfihangel-y-pennant route (CI12)

Stay with CI5 as far as Hafotty Gwastadfryn, then take the new bulldozed trail that branches off L. Follow this until you come to a gate in a fence, just before the road bears E at 673131. (Ignore another bulldozed road off L at 674122.) A couple of minutes along the fence brings you to the escarpment edge at 672131 from where both Craig Las and Craig-y-llyn are within easy reach.

CRAIG-Y-LLYN

Craig-y-llyn (the Crag of the Lake) is the most W of the Cader hills. Its small, slaty cairn, supporting an upright wooden stake, rests on the edge of the dark cliffs in the bosom of which nestles lonely, sunless Llyn Cyri from which it takes its name.

Craig-y-llyn has a piquancy and freshness, enlivened by solitude and its sea views, which creates an atmosphere not unlike that of the N Carneddau. It deserves to be better known. Try it on a rain-shortened day when CI14/15 in tandem will blow the cobwebs away.

Llanfihangel-y-pennant route (CI13)

See CI12.

Braich Ddu route (CI14)

Park near the kink in the road at 648134 and advance down the bridleway that slants across the N flanks of Braich Ddu to a gate at 637137, just before some new forestry plantations. Pull up to the ridge beside a fence and follow it above the cliffs of Craig Cwm-llwyd, round the hollow cradling Llyn Cyri, up to the subsidiary top at 659115 with its ancient mound of stones - Twll yr Ogof, then on to the main top. The glorious seaward views stretch to Lleyn and Bardsey Island on a clear day. The Bird's Rock stands out dramatically

S against the flats of Dyffryn Dysynni, while E is a fine view of the N cliffs presided over by the great wedge of Penygadair.

The standing stone route (CI15)
For an attractive half-day with a difference try CI14 followed by a descent from the col between Craig-y-llyn and Craig Las at about 669127. The slope is ideal for trotting down, the ground less boggy than it looks and you can make a bee-line to inspect the standing stone at 654133, or even to Llyn Cyri if you don't mind wet feet!

HIGH-LEVEL WALKS
N edge traverse (CI H1)
Not to be missed provided you can cope with the logistics. You cross six of Cader's seven tops (and Craig y Cau, the seventh, involves but a small diversion), the views are magnificent all day long and the walk is nothing like as demanding as it looks, with friendly tracks ensuring firm and pleasant going throughout. Start with Gau Craig (CI9) and finish with Braich Ddu (CI14). You get the harder work over first and face the sea, hopefully shining like burnished gold, as the day wears on. Fortunately this great walk can be taken in two separate rounds if you cannot arrange transport, albeit at the cost of a little road work.

N edge: Gau Craig Pony path (CI H2)
This tackles the wilder, more rugged half, combining an ascent of Gau Craig (CI9) with a return down the Pony Path (CI4) and a longish but beautifully relaxing walk along quiet roads past Llyn Gwernan.

N edge: Pony Path to Braich Ddu (CI H3)
This time you start with the Pony Path (CI4) and come down over Braich Ddu (CI14).

Llyn Cau circular (CI H4)
Climb Penygadair on the Minffordd trail (CI1), follow the edge along to Mynydd Moel and then descend on CI8. If I had to suggest just one walk to convey the essence of Cader Idris, this would be it. CI1 says it all.

Cwm Amarch circular (CI H5)
Up the Minffordd trail on CI1; home via Cwm Amarch on CI7 having first backtracked down to Craig y Cau. In appeal this is second only to CI H4 for a walk of comparable length, and much more remote.

Penygadair/Gau Craig from the SE (CI H6)
Once again the Minffordd trail starts you off. Next you walk along the N edge to Gau Craig before descending on CI9, 1 to Bwlch Llynbach. This would be a first rate expedition were it not for the noisy bustle of the A487 back to Minffordd.

Llanfihangel-y-pennant/Pencoed circular (CI H7)
For a novel day away from the crowds without sacrificing the sights try driving to Llanfihangel-y-pennant and combining CI5 and 6.

Cwm Amarch/Pencoed circular (CI H8)
For an even more unusual day start with the Cwm Amarch route to Penygadair (see CI7). Then return to Craig y Cau and join the Pencoed ridge route. However instead of aiming for the farmstead of Pencoed as directed in CI6, stay with the wall/fence until you pick up a faint path that runs almost due E parallel to, but above, the Nant Pencoed. Some easy freelancing is called for before you reach the vicinity of Rhiwogof Farm, 709100, and hence your base.

LOWER-LEVEL WALKS/EASIER DAYS
Cregennen lakes (CI L1)
Few lakes are more immediately appealing than the lovely Llynnau Cregennen, peacefully nestling in Cader's N foothills. (I am ignoring the garish Plas Cregennen; this is too grand a spot to let one insensitive monstrosity spoil it.) Watched over by Craig-y-llyn and Craig Las to the S - never seen to better advantage than from here - and with Cyfrwy and Penygadair (in all probability) swathed in cloud, it is however the diminutive Bryn Brith that steals the show.

There are walks aplenty; directions would be superfluous. The stile behind Plas Cregennen at 659145 will get you going on a firm green track beside the shores of the more N of the two lakes. On no account miss Bryn Brith, a pocket mountain if ever there was one. A short easy scramble brings instant reward. The heather-clad top is a maze of twists and hollows, with outcroppings everywhere, a tiny tarn thrown in for good measure, and evocative views of the Rhinogs, the sea, and Cader itself. Perfect for a lazy day.

Dysynni Valley (CI L2)
For a varied day try exploring the Dysynni Valley. Mary Jones' cottage, 674096, the well preserved hill-fort built by Llewelyn the Great in the 13th century at Castell y Bere, 668086, and Craig yr Aderyn (the Bird's Rock) at 645067 are three places of interest that should get you out of the car with your boots on!

Llyn Cau (CI L3)
If you don't feel like the full haul to Penygadair, why not follow the Minffordd trail just as far as Llyn Cau? You can still have an exceptional day. Indeed, if you grasp the opportunity of a more leisurely tempo to wander round the shores of this most dramatic of Welsh lakes, instead of rushing up to the ridge as most folk do, you will experience every bit as much the call of the wild as the more energetic 1200ft above.

Llyn y Gadair (CI L4)
Take the Fox's Path to Llyn y Gadair and admire one of Nature's colossal masterpieces. The walk is delightful, the atmosphere awe-inspiring. You can either return the same way or contour across to return down the Pony Path beneath Cyfrwy's lowering crags (see CI3).

Mawddach Estuary (CI L5)
For an evocative day with a different style (particularly if you are fond of birdlife) and with no ascent and descent for tired legs absolutely guaranteed, you could do worse than follow the old railway track along the Mawddach Estuary. The George III Hotel at Penmaenpool is a good place to start and it is a pleasant tramp all the way to the sea.

Carneddau

THE CARNEDDAU
OS map 1:25,000 - Sheet 16/17 1:50,000 - Sheets 124

Peaks	Height (ft)	Map Ref	Page
Carnedd Llewelyn	3490	684644	197
Carnedd Dafydd	3425	663631	189
Pen yr Ole Wen	3211	656619	186
Foel Grach	3196	689659	201
Yr Elen	3152	673651	199
Foel Fras	3092	696682	205
Llwytmor	2785	689692	210
Penyrhelgi-du	2733	698630	191
Bera Bach	2647	672678	211
Pen Llithrig-y-wrach	2622	716623	194
Bera Mawr	2604	675683	211
Drum	2529	708696	206
Drosgl	2484	664680	212
Craig Eigiau	2390	714656	196
Creigiau Gleision	2224	729615	213
Gyrn Wigau	2109	654676	212
Pen y Castell	2043	721688	208
Tal-y-fan	2001	729727	217
Mountain Lakes			
Anafon	1625	698698	
Cowlyd	1200	727624	
Dulyn	1750	700667	
Eigiau	1225	720650	
Ffynnon Caseg	2460	679650	
Ffynnon Lloer	2165	662622	
Ffynnon Llugwy	1800	693628	
Ffynnon Llyffant	2800	688646	
Melynllyn	2100	702657	
Y Coryn	1300	731591	

THE CARNEDDAU

Of the 14 peaks in Wales that exceed 3000ft no fewer than six have their roots in the Carneddau, the largest concentration of sustained high ground in the whole of Wales. You can walk from Drum in the NE to Pen yr Ole Wen in the SW eight miles as the crow flies - without ever dropping below 2000ft or crossing a road. Gyrn Wigau to Pen Llithrig-y-wrach, a NW to SE expedition this time, is another long hike that stays above the 2000ft level; Gyrn Wigau in the W to Pen y Castell in the E another. No other hills in Wales can compare with this.

The Carneddau are bounded W by Nant Ffrancon, N by the sea, E by the Conwy Valley, and S by the A5 from Ogwen to Betws-y-coed. What these bare facts do not reveal is that if they had been designed to order, the outcome could not have been more pleasing. The juxtaposition of ridges and valleys, saddles and peaks, is a hillwalker's delight with walks to suit all tastes.

No one can stride the Carneddau without experiencing a distinct sense of spaciousness. Ridges are long, wide and often whalebacked too. Rolling open moors and grassland blend into uncluttered skylines and far horizons. Short crisp turf dissolves the miles as skyline after skyline succumbs to the tread. On the other hand there is little of the rugged grandeur of the neighbouring Glyders; few of the sharp sinuous sorts of ridges you find on Snowdon or Nantlle, and no hidden valleys or twisted cwms to explore. Despite the appeal of Ffynnon Lloer and the fleeting charms of Ffynnon Caseg and Ffynnon Llyffant, there is little of the intimacy of the Moelwyns or the Rhinogs with their rock-engirdled tarns either. No, this is simple, open country, reminiscent in many ways of the S Wales hills.

Simple country it may be but simplicity can be deceptive, glossing over the imprint of true greatness. To roam the Carneddau is to experience the timelessness born of profound peace and solitude, while to survey the Olympian breadth and spaciousness of these most expansive of Welsh highlands from on high is to be cast a pygmy in a land of giants!

Views are on the grand scale. Anglesey and the Irish Sea (the Isle of Man on a good day), the emerald green of the Conway Valley and the blue haze of the Denbigh hills, Snowdon, the Glyders, Moel

Siabod and blue waves of hills beyond - this is the staple diet. From Carnedd Llewelyn the panorama extends from Foel Fras to Cader Idris, while from Pen Llithrig-y-wrach it includes the Moelwyns, Arenigs and Arans. Further S the long views persist but the sea and the lowlands are less dominant. Pride of place now goes to the splendour of the Glyders, the lakes and cwms of Y Garn and Foel Goch, Y Gribin and the Devil's Kitchen, Bochlwyd, Idwal and Tryfan. One of my most abiding memories of the Welsh hills is the spectacle of Tryfan from Carnedd Dafydd, a dark jewel in the clear air of a blue summer dawn.

S of Carnedd Llewelyn subtle changes occur. No longer will you see the wild horses that roam the N grasslands. Ridges are narrower, slopes steeper. The terrain is stonier, more broken. The smooth grassy hillsides of Drum yield to the boulder-strewn slopes above Ffynnon Llugwy. Heather, patchy and thin in the N, cloaks the S hills in glorious pinks and mauves, especially around Pen yr Ole Wen and the saddle beneath Penyrhelgi-du. The place to find good bilberry pickings is between Drum and Pen y Castell where the whole hillside is a mass of succulent fruit in season.

The most spectacular terrain - and the finest walks - are all in the S: the high-level tramp from Pen yr Ole Wen to Carnedd Llewelyn; the sombre cliffs of Ysgolion Duon (the Black Ladders); the precipice of Llech Du and the narrow arête of Crib Lem; the climber's playground of Craig yr Ysfa; the all-too-brief ridge linking Yr Elen to the main massif and the twisty tracks that climb from Ffynnon Llugwy and Cwm Eigiau to the saddle beneath Penyrhelgi-du. Whereas in the N one tends to talk of hills and sea views, the further S one wanders the more likely one is to speak of peaks and mountains, crags and cwms.

Apart from two outliers the peaks form a series of ridges like the branches of a tree. The exceptions are Tal-y-fan and Creigiau Gleision, lying NE and SE of the main 'trunk' respectively. (Creigiau Gleision, a real charmer, stands aloof across Llyn Cowlyd, the deepest lake in Snowdonia, while to the E it shelters peaceful Llyn Crafnant, one of the loveliest lakes in Wales.) Both are playful, undulating, heathery tops where many a happy hour can be whiled away.

These apart, the actual tops lack style, tending to be big and flat,

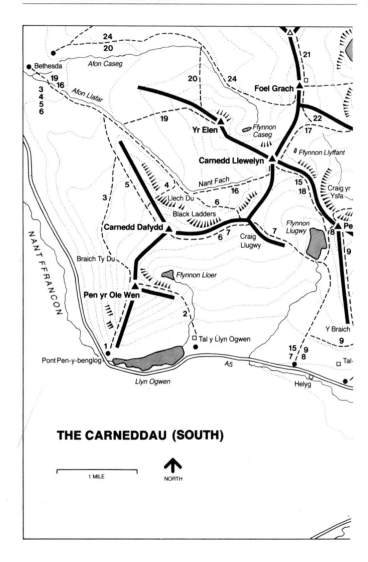

THE CARNEDDAU (SOUTH)

1 MILE

↑ NORTH

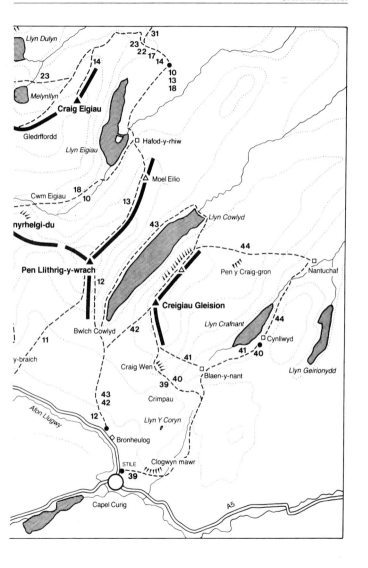

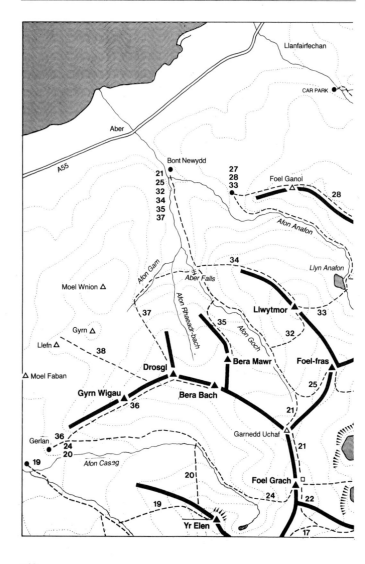

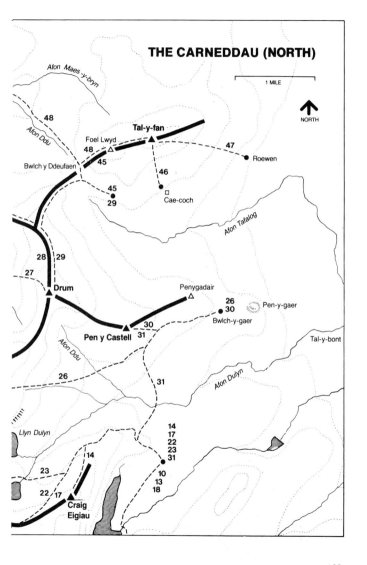

THE CARNEDDAU (NORTH)

lumpy rather than shapely and grassy rather than rocky. There is no characteristic Carnedd skyline as there is an instantly recognisable Snowdon, Nantlle or Hebog skyline. Yet, that said, few sights are more imposing than Pen yr Ole Wen brooding over Nant Ffrancon, or more menacing than Yr Elen as it towers ominously over Bethesda. The castellated monoliths of Bera Mawr and Bera Bach in their turn cast as eerie a spell as any when seen in swirling mist or fading light.

The most popular routes in the Carneddau all start from the S, using Capel Curig or Ogwen as a base. For every ten hikers you meet in the Carneddau, it is a fair bet that eight set out from the S where there are at least six approaches. Of these, two of the best are the rough scramble up the SW ridge of Pen yr Ole Wen, and the reservoir road to Ffynnon Llugwy. The ridge is among the toughest hikes in Wales but tremendously rewarding nonetheless. Ffynnon Llugwy starts with a dull first 20 minutes but then suddenly comes alive as the track twists and turns up to a luscious saddle to reveal the very heart of the Carneddau - Penyrhelgi-du, Cwm Eigiau, the awesome cliffs of Craig yr Ysfa and Carnedd Llewelyn itself.

Enticing though the S routes may be, there is no shortage of fine alternatives. Take Bethesda for example, where you can choose between a slow amble up Carnedd Dafydd's gently expansive NW ridge, an airy scramble over Llech Du, a direct assault on Yr Elen (with 'assault' being the operative word for it is very stiff), or an easy ramble on the long grassy arm that reaches out beyond the 'tors' of Bera Mawr and Bera Bach to the tiny outpost of Gyrn Wigau. On the other hand you can keep low initially and follow one of two streams, the Llafar or the Caseg, both of which burrow into the central massif to leave you with a bit of rough walking before you get on to the tops.

There are two more routes which start near Aber, the Carneddau's N gateway, famous for its 200ft falls and a perennial favourite with day-trippers. One climbs up behind the falls where the hanging valley of the Afon Goch thrusts deeply towards Foel Grach and the very centre of the range. The other follows the vivacious Afon Anafon to its source. Either way your only company is likely to be a noisy stream and the sheep, for these are lonely by-ways far off the beaten track.

The Conway Valley routes are more cunning. From just N of the

Entering Cwm Eigiau; Craig yr Ysfa directly ahead

bridge over the Afon Dulyn, near the tiny hamlet of Tal-y-bont, a mountain road sidles surreptitiously up to the 1300ft contour line to leave you on the site of the old Roman road that once crossed Bwlch y Ddeufaen. From here you are well placed for Drum, Foel Fras and all points S. And if that were not enough, on the other side of the bridge a second road, equally sly, climbs to 1200ft near Llyn Eigiau to offer you another bumper choice: across the broad uplands of Gledrffordd to Foel Grach or Carnedd Llewelyn; S into Cwm Eigiau to gain the ridge airily, though safely, atop Craig yr Ysfa; or maybe over Moel Eilio to capture Pen Llithrig-y-wrach from the N.

Roaming the Carneddau on a warm sunny day it is hard to imagine the dangers that lie in wait in less favourable weather. Yet these giant whalebacked hills can be harsh antagonists. By dint of their very openness they offer little shelter from wind or rain. The calm geniality of a fine day can be replaced in a flash by near Arctic and potentially lethal conditions. In a blizzard, or even under a light powdering of snow, lack of contrasts can lead to white-outs and disorientation and help could be a long way off. Your average distance from a road is probably greater in the Carneddau than almost anywhere else in Wales.

Mist, too, requires more than usual care. However adept you may be with a compass, the small and gradual variations in height on many of the routes make it difficult to judge whether any variation is just part of the dip to the next col, or inadvertent straying off the ridge. Just a small error in compass work can send you badly astray. The environs of Garnedd Uchaf and Carnedd Llewelyn are particularly tricky. Even if you *are* able to follow the compass line accurately, the inevitable straight line will often take you over slithery rocks or tiring dips and humps which you would never dream of negotiating in clear weather.

The message is simple. Enjoy the Carneddau when it is fine and they will reward you with wonderful sport, but never forget that distances are great and help far away. Above all never be deceived by their illusion of innocence; if you tackle them in mist or winter be fully equipped for the worst and abort as necessary.

PEN YR OLE WEN

Pen yr Ole Wen is the supreme manifestation of the power of the Carneddau - no smooth, rounded flanks here. As you survey the shattered crags and massive grey rockfalls of the long ridge that looms so threateningly over Ogwen, it is almost as if the full might of the vast rolling uplands that stretch from Aber and Conway had been coiled up to be released in this one immense wave of elemental energy that sought to leap the narrow pass dividing Carneddau from Glyders.

To scale the SW ridge is as tough a test of fitness as you will find in many a long day. The gain in height, 2200ft in under a mile, is not the only problem. For unlike (say) the N ridge of Tryfan where leverage for tired legs is provided by a succession of rocky steps and giant boulders, and where there is the occasional shelf for respite, here the angle is unremittingly steep and without such support.

Yet climbing Pen yr Ole Wen (Hill of the White Light) is an experience to relish. The poetry of the name is matched by the air which, after the rigours of the climb, always seems to have a special purity and freshness. The view alone is worth the effort. Pride of place goes to the Glyders; Tryfan, Cwm Idwal and the Devil's Kitchen, Y Garn, Foel Goch and the rounded cone of Elidir Fawr. Beyond the Glyders are Snowdon, Crib Goch and Moel Eilio with distant glimpses of Mynydd Mawr and the Nantlle ridge. The N skyline belongs to Anglesey and the sea; if recent rain has lightened the atmosphere you may even glimpse the Isle of Man.

Stretching away NE is the connecting ridge to Carnedd Dafydd, grassy at first but soon becoming a sea of boulders, and a doddle after the long haul up from Ogwen. On the way it curls round the hollow cradling the romantically named Ffynnon Lloer (Fountain of the Moon). The circle is completed E by the tapering slopes of Penyrhelgi-du and Pen Llithrig-y-wrach and the heathery knobbles of Creigiau Gleision.

SW ridge (CA1)

Cross the memorial stile just N of Pont Pen-y-benglog at 649605 and scramble over a jumble of huge boulders until you spot the path (never in doubt once you have found it) that twists steeply up the crest of the ridge, with only the tiniest of terraces for relief. Hard work it may be, but exhilarating too, particularly in summer when thickets of heather cloak the whole mountainside in a glorious splash of purples and pinks. Such is the angle of attack and the grandeur of the view that the sense of achievement must be experienced to be believed!

About half-way up you come to a scree slope; two steps up and almost two back! Follow it round to the R towards a skyline that raises hopes. Hopes, alas, that are soon dashed, for only a long tilted band of stony grass is revealed. Worse, once you have conquered that, another takes its place. Only the glorious views maintain morale until, as you break the skyline yet again, a large cairn and windshelter appear only minutes away on the verge of a grassy plateau big enough to stage a cricket match. It may not be until you have rested a few moments that it dawns on you that even this is not quite the highest point. That is still a little further on across the grass.

You should use this route for climbing the mountain in the morning when you are fresh. It is pitiless on tired knees and aching feet at the end of a hard day when CA2 is by far the better bet.

Tal y Llyn Ogwen route (CA2)

This little-used route deserves to be more popular. It is much easier than the SW ridge, just as attractive (though lacking the high drama) and infinitely more enjoyable in descent. It begins as a stony path

Ffynnon Lloer and the Ogwen Valley from Pen yr Ole Wen

that leaves the summit cairn on 110, hugging the edge of the heather-clad crags overlooking the lovely triangular-shaped Ffynnon Lloer. Later on it bears S, then E again, down a gully with a little easy scrambling to the foot of the mountain's E spur at 665618. Soon after this it fades, near a patch of marshy ground, and you must aim for a ladder-stile near 667617 that crosses the only wall in the vicinity. From here it is plain sailing as a springy green path leads down gentle slopes of gorse and bracken, with the music of the tumbling Afon Lloer to serenade you. You eventually join the A5 at 668605 by Glan Dena, having passed the farm of Tal y Llyn Ogwen to your R.

This route is equally pleasant in ascent apart from a slight problem where the path temporarily disappears after you cross the wall. You must then strike out half-L for the foot of the E spur and hope to pick it up again there.

Bethesda approach (CA3)

Start off along Carnedd Dafydd's NW ridge (CA5). Sooner or later you must break away S or SE for a long trackless grind across to Bwlch yr Ole Wen, 655620, and the summit plateau. It hardly matters where you do this, though the sooner you cut across towards Braich Ty Du the sooner you will enjoy the fine views of the N Glyders across Nant Ffrancon.

188

CARNEDD DAFYDD

Sandwiched between two peaks of the calibre of Pen yr Ole Wen and Carnedd Llewelyn, and with the poetically named Ffynnon Lloer (Fountain of the Moon) to one side and the spectacular Black Ladders to the other, Carnedd Dafydd is certainly not starved of visitors! Indeed when combined with its two neighbours you have, mile for mile, the finest walk in the whole of the Carneddau. Add to that the Llech Du cliffs and the Crib Lem ridge, which together give as exciting an approach as you could wish for, and you have a peak that has more going for it than is often supposed. The top itself is a vast sea of stones and boulders of little intrinsic interest. It is a stirring viewpoint however (see CA6 below), and surprisingly visible from below as a tiny but unmistakable blip on the skyline leading N from Pen yr Ole Wen.

Llech Du/Crib Lem ridge (CA4)

As a scramble this is the best in the entire Carneddau; a bit like the Bristly Ridge but shorter. Any doubts about Carnedd Dafydd's mountainly stature are soon dispelled, for what the ridge reveals is a savage wilderness of rocky hollows, broken precipices and jagged pinnacles.

Follow the road that leads through Gerlan to the entrance to the waterworks at 638659 (ignoring the 'Private' sign just beyond the bridge across the Llafar). Climb a stile into a field to the R of the waterworks entrance and follow the edge of the field to another stile near its top left-hand corner. The way ahead from there is none too clear for a while, with a scrappy carpet of grass, thistles, bracken and pebbles underfoot. But the general direction is clear enough and you soon come to a field of bog cotton where an ancient iron gate ushers in a friendly green path.

Prior to writing this book I had not walked the Llafar Valley (the Valley of Voices) for many years and was not particularly looking forward to it, which just shows how wrong you can be! A mountainly aura, a delightful all-pervading camaraderie with the hills, grows with every step. The narrow streets of Gerlan are less than a mile away but it seems like light years. The long, humped brow of Yr Elen links with Dafydd's twisty ridge across the dark head-wall of the Black Ladders to enclose a valley of dappled greens and monumental emptiness. Most gripping of all is the cruel, spiky comb of Llech Du, even now casting its spell.

A pleasant walk brings you to the foot of the Llech Du cliffs at 665639. They justify their grim name (Black Slab) and are clearly out of bounds to non-climbers. Fortunately they are easily by-passed on their NW flank where a rough, toilsome scrabble beneath the cliffs before bearing L brings you into a gully. From here the crest of the ridge above the cliffs can be gained along an obvious grassy rake. Once on the arête - Crib Lem - keep on top. A succession of rocky turrets and lichenous knolls requires the use of hands but there is no exposure and it is a disappointment when, all too soon, the dazzling exhilaration of the ridge quietly succumbs to the summit scree.

NW ridge (CA5)

Begin along CA4 but break away R to the ridge as soon as it starts to swell. There is no path but none is needed as easy grass gives way first to boulders and then to scree. A quiet plodding sort of a walk, not to be compared for thrills and excitement with Llech Du, but a safer bet if you suffer from vertigo or want a less taxing day.

Cwm Llafar route (CA6)

Follow CA4 to the foot of Llech Du but then continue up the valley to gain the saddle (Bwlch Cyfryw-drum) linking Carnedd Llewelyn to the E arm of Carnedd Dafydd at 679635. The pull up to the saddle is trackless and a bit tedious on a muggy day, or when wearing waterproofs, but the rewards are

Carnedd Dafydd across the Black Ladders

immediate in the form of a rousing tramp along the tops of the Black Ladders (Ysgolion Duon). These famous cliffs are aptly named for they are dark and forbidding, seldom enjoying the warmth of the sun. There was a time when they were a popular haunt of the climbing fraternity but nowadays they tend to be neglected.

The view from the tops of these gaunt sentinels is as magnificent as it is extensive. Across the Llafar Valley the foreground is dominated by the huge bulk of Yr Elen and Carnedd Llewelyn. Behind lies the tor country of Bera Bach and Drosgl while further afield again, if the day is fine, you can distinguish the spiky crest of Llwytmor and the rounded dome of Foel Fras, all of them framed by Anglesey, Puffin Island and the sea. The S skyline belongs to Snowdon and the Glyders, yet such is its charisma that nothing can compare with Tryfan. This gigantic triangle of naked rock, revelling in its isolation, seems to challenge the sky itself! Beyond the Black Ladders the path climbs uneventfully to the vast bouldery waste that is Carnedd Dafydd.

Craig Llugwy route (CA7)

Leave Carnedd Dafydd and follow CA6 in reverse along the tops of the Black Ladders until you reach the spot where the saddle to Carnedd Llewelyn breaks away N, 678633. Next follow a faint path that meanders away SE. This keeps Craig Llugwy L and heads towards the boulder-strewn slopes of Creigiau Hirion above Ffynnon Llugwy. Good navigation is needed as formidable crags guard the lake, so look out for a stone wall to the S that crosses the hillside almost due E and when you have found it let it do the route-finding for you. It is quite dependable and will lead you down a grassy rake to the shoreline of Ffynnon Llugwy near 693624.

PENYRHELGI-DU

Penyrhelgi-du (the Hill of the Black Hound) looks decidedly prosaic from the A5; a simple grassy dome. As far as the actual top goes, this is true, but tops are not everything and that is nowhere better exemplified than by Penyrhelgi-du. All around are treasures in abundance: the sharply serrated NW arête; the soft luscious saddle beneath; the wild ascents from Ffynnon Llugwy and Cwm Eigiau;

the dramatic cliffs of Craig yr Ysfa and splendid views of the Glyders and the heart of the Carneddau.

Many walkers combine Penyrhelgi-du with its near neighbour, Pen Llithrig-y-wrach. Simply follow the E ridge down to Bwlch Trimarchog (the Pass of the Three Horsemen) when an almost identical pull up the other side gives you the second top. All on easy grass with spacious views of Cwm Eigiau as you pause for breath.

Helyg/Ffynnon Llugwy route (CA8)

This fine walk begins inauspiciously with what looks like a dull one and a half miles up the insensitive reservoir road that leaves the A5 at 687602 to penetrate the fastnesses of the Carneddau. In practice it is better than that. You cannot help but be gripped by the raw primeval desolation that pervades Cwm Llugwy, a desolation that not even the few visible signs of reservoir activity can dispel. Just before the road finally bears L for Ffynnon Llugwy, leave it R to join a well-trodden stony track that climbs above the shores of the lake before commencing a series of steep zig-zags to reach the narrow saddle linking Penyrhelgi-du with the minor hump of Penywaunwen.

What a delightful perch this is! Juicy bilberries and bouncy cushions of heather provide the ideal excuse for lazing in the sun. Cwm Eigiau and the central Carneddau stretch before you with a twisty little path straight ahead to tempt you down into the cwm. Turn L and you have an exhilarating climb to Carnedd Llewelyn with spectacular views of Craig yr Ysfa's massive ramparts. R is Penyrhelgi-du itself. So follow the saddle along to the foot of a rocky tower where you will find a cairn. This marks the start of a trail that sidles across to the S ridge (CA9), sneakily by-passing the summit altogether. Good news for tired walkers on their way home but not for now! The tower looks formidable, even perhaps a little frightening to mere walkers, but there are hand-holds in abundance and no exposure whatsoever in good conditions. In ice or snow it should be left strictly to experts.

After the scramble the ending is tame; a short walk over scrappy grass to the scattered flaky stones that litter the flat top.

S ridge/Y Braich (CA9)

Walk up the reservoir road as in CA8 until you reach the leat linking the Afon Llugwy with Llyn Cowlyd. Either cross the leat and walk directly across damp moors to the ridge R or, better, follow a path along the S bank of the leat until you come to two bridges close together where, for good measure, a wall crosses your path as well, 695608. Cross the second bridge whereupon the dark peaty path that straddles the ridge comes clearly into view on a bearing of 80 beyond a patch of black glutinous bog. It is now plain sailing up an open whalebacked ridge of rolling grassland with the Glyders, as you glance back, the main focus of interest.

The route is most enjoyable in descent when it provides a quick and easy way down with the Glyders silhouetted in the evening sun. But you do need to be sure of your aim near the top if mist is about; the gap between Cwm Bychan E and the harsh slopes above Ffynnon Llugwy W is a narrow one!

The map shows a footpath leading to Tal-y-braich-uchaf Farm from the A5 at 691602 which looks as though it might provide an alternative routing. However it is of little interest as the path effectively peters out at the farm and you are then left to freelance N to pick up the leat as before.

Cwm Eigiau route (CA10)

Eigiau is silent now. The quarrymen have long since gone, leaving behind a sense of melancholy that not even the riveting presence of Craig yr Ysfa can fully dispel. Yet such is the grandeur of those lofty crags that I am sure it is only the remoteness of the start that prevents this from being as popular as the well-used Ffynnon Llugwy route.

The walk into the cwm is little more than a jaunt. Park where the mountain road from Tal-y-bont ends at 732663 and continue down the cart-track that skirts the reedy head of Llyn Eigiau before gently rising into the cwm, passing a standing stone and a cluster of derelict miners' huts on the way. The all-pervading solitude of the cwm is relieved only by the tiny blue/red specks of the climbers clinging to the awesome crags far above.

The jaunt is over; now for the muscle work. Cross to the foot of the twin buttresses of Craig yr Ysfa, spread like the wings of some giant eagle on either side of the river of scree that forces its way into the massive cleft which splits the cliffs asunder to form the famous amphitheatre. A keen eye is needed to spot the path that meanders up to the col close by the E 'wing'. The best way to locate it is to climb up the scree towards the crags until you see its gravelly line snaking steeply away L. A sporting scramble across the bilberry-clad slopes, with little rocky steps to add zest, gives you the col at a sprawling cairn exactly opposite the top of the Ffynnon Llugwy approach (CA8). It is hard work and you will appreciate a good rest before pressing on.

PEN LLITHRIG-Y-WRACH

Watching benignly over Capel Curig, with a face that is sometimes pleasantly rounded, at other times curiously hunched, Pen Llithrig-y-wrach (the Slippery Hill of the Witch) is one of the last outposts of the Carneddau, the end of a long ridge that starts from Bwlch y Ddeufaen and Foel Fras in the far N. It is a worthy finale, for though it boasts no more than a bare stone-studded grassy top, its cairn is dizzily poised over the deepest lake in Snowdonia - Llyn Cowlyd - and calls for a cautious step in thick weather.

The panorama from this lofty eminence is electrifying in its breadth and intensity: the E Carneddau from Llyn Eigiau and Foel Fras, across Carnedd Llewelyn and round to Penyrhelgi-du; Tryfan and the Glyders; Moel Siabod; Cnicht and the Moelwyns. Across the lake Creigiau Gleision shows a gnarled and rugged face, with the Conway Valley beyond leading the eye to the Irish Sea. On a clear day you may also glimpse the Black Rock Sands near Portmadog, the purple-green moors of the Migneint, the long tapering lines of the Arenigs, the Arans and Cader Idris.

A curious feature of Pen Llithrig-y-wrach is the man-made ditch, or 'leat' to use the local word, that crosses its S slopes to link the Afon Llugwy with Llyn Cowlyd. Apart from the three routes below, Pen Llithrig-y-wrach is often climbed by its W ridge from Bwlch Trimarchog (the Pass of the Three Horsemen) as part of a longer round including Penyrhelgi-du. The ridge is an easy walk and probably the safest way off in mist, though you then have a boggy plod down the cwm to the Tal-y-braich path.

Tal-y-braich route (CA11)

Leave the A5 at 699599 and walk up the stony road to Tal-y-braich-isaf farm. Pass through the farm and stay with a track that winds slightly E of N through a shallow, rather dull, depression. Ignore the dark boggy looking trail (shown on the map) that heads off E towards Llyn Cowlyd. As you stride along beneath the slopes of Penyrhelgi-du the mound of Pen Llithrig-y-wrach grows steadily in stature. Before long you find yourself walking parallel to the leat, eventually crossing it over a bridge at 704616. The track fizzles out there and you are left to your own devices for the long 1200ft plod up the featureless hillside. Not that it matters; the only problem is boredom! The best plan is to aim slightly N of E when you should pick up the higher reaches of CA12 with a good track and dramatic views of Llyn Cowlyd.

Bronheulog route (CA12)

Leave the A5 at 719589 at the footpath sign just NW of Bronheulog. A path that used to be obscure years ago, except where it followed a line of power poles, is now well-trodden though the poles have long since disappeared leaving only a few isolated stumps. The mud remains, however, in what is a notoriously wet and boggy stretch of barren moorland, saved from oblivion only by the majestic views of the Ogwen Valley and Tryfan that gradually unfold.

At 717609 you cross a bridge over a leat. You must ignore the friendly-looking path through Bwlch Cowlyd (except perhaps for a brief foray to inspect this deepest of Snowdonia's lakes) and instead gird your loins for the long 1200ft haul up the slopes ahead. Fortunately this is not the struggle it looks. The path is well-graded, offers plenty of bilberry cushions to rest on, and rewards you with a wonderful sense of achievement as a vast panorama of peaks gradually appears to mollify the harsh insistence of the precipitous slopes guarding Llyn Cowlyd.

NE ridge (CA13)

Drive up the mountain road S of Tal-y-bont to the parking area at 732663. Walk down the stony track that leads to the dwelling of Hafod-y-rhiw and then select one of several tracks that cleave a way up the hillside to mount the ridge. You have the chance to bag the

S top of Moel Eilio, 727640, after which it is an easy walk, high and breezy, with intimate glimpses into Cwm Eigiau, and helped by sporadic traces of a trail beside the relics of an ancient wall. It is a lonely walk too. A loneliness born not simply of the absence of fellow walkers but even more of the deep solitude of Cwm Eigiau; quiet and peaceful now where once it echoed to the tune of industry.

CRAIG EIGIAU

Craig Eigiau does not appear on most lists of Welsh peaks. Why, I do not know. It is suitably remote from its fellows and encircled by a contour ring at the 2375ft level. Most important of all it looks the part, a lonely rocky eyrie perched high above Llyn Eigiau, overlooking a corner of the Carneddau that seldom resounds to the walkers' tramp. So here it is.

N ridge (CA14)

A narrow mountain road, steep and twisty, leaves the B5106 just S of the bridge at the village of Tal-y-bont. It is one of several that penetrate the fastnesses of the E Carneddau to give a flying start to a day in the hills. This one ends at 732663. After parking, cross a stile to a Land-Rover track that leads round the NE spur of Craig Eigiau. At its foot, 726666, by a gate, a brief diversion L reveals a beautiful view of Llyn Eigiau cupped in the V of Penyrhelgi-du and Pen Llithrig-y-wrach. Look out also for a rambling rustic path that comes in from the N, half-lost in a jungle of bracken. On another day it may take you to Pen y Castell (CA31).

The track contours round the spur to reveal a landscape of poignant sadness. Empty grasslands - treeless, sodden, and forgotten - rise to the very tops of the 3000ft giants across the valley, while at their feet forbidding black cliffs lead the eye to the deep sun-starved hollows where Llyn Dulyn and Llyn Melynllyn lie. Cheerless indeed on a gloomy day but when the sun shines ....

Leave the track when you see a wall L and follow the faint path that struggles up the fellside alongside it, swathing through the rough moorland grass to bring you safely to the summit ridge. 'Ridge'? Not quite; rather a line of giant, tilted slabs of rock (not unlike those that cap Moel Siabod) that effectively divides Craig

Eigiau's malicious, craggy E face from the gentle grasslands extending W to the Carneddau's main central axis. The highest point, a fine smooth slab that rises to a tiny pinnacle, is some way S along this 'ridge'. Whether the cairn will be there I cannot say. I have rebuilt it several times only to find it gone again by my next visit.

To the W the eye is held by the patchwork of the Conway Valley meadows and the wrinkles of Creigiau Gleision; S by Pen Llithrig-y-wrach, displaying an unusually shapely line, and its neighbour Penyrhelgi-du, with Moel Siabod some way behind. The high Carneddau themselves fill the W horizon, a long flowing line from Foel Fras to Carnedd Llewelyn. Then there are the Glyders. Faint usually, but capable of creating a magical effect when the main range is wreathed in mist and only Tryfan is visible to the fore, a lone black pyramid seemingly suspended in the air!

CARNEDD LLEWELYN

After Snowdon and her nearby consort, Crib y Ddysgl, Carnedd Llewelyn is the highest mountain in England and Wales, and at 3485ft only 75ft lower than Snowdon herself. Its capture poses quite a challenge as it is a good two and a half miles from the nearest road. However its conquest is obligatory for anyone seeking to savour the true spirit of the Carneddau. Not only is Llewelyn the senior peak in terms of height, more significantly it is also where four of the main ridges meet.

As all of these ridges begin some distance from the summit cairn, and as the top itself is an immense convex-shaped stony plateau littered with clusters of boulders and cairns of all shapes and sizes, it is very easy to get disorientated. Believe me, this can happen in fine weather, let alone in mist! So be warned and take a compass bearing before setting off again. It is also worth spending half-an-hour strolling round the perimeter of the summit plateau. Not only will you get a better feel for the lie of the land, it is also the only way, because of the scale, to appreciate the full splendour of the scene.

Virtually all the Carneddau are on display; an array of epic proportions with none more splendid than Yr Elen and Carnedd Dafydd. W and N, beyond Foel Fras, the land falls away to the calm of Anglesey and the distant sea. E the elongated rocky cap of Craig

Eigiau leads the eye to the lush Conway pastures, the purple of the Denbigh moors beyond. As you turn S harsher climes prevail. The skyline is now pierced by the restless, jagged tops of the Glyders with the towering presence of Snowdon peeping over their shoulder. But even a scene as tempestuous as this must eventually be quelled and, sure enough, on a clear day peace is restored as the distant horizon reveals the long tapering line of Cader Idris.

As for the ridges, taking them clockwise, a bearing of 180 takes you down a shaly path to the saddle of Bwlch Cyfryw-drum en-route to Craig Llugwy or Carnedd Dafydd above the Black Ladders; 290 links up with a twisty path that hugs the cliff edge above Ffynnon Caseg on its way to Yr Elen; 25 leads to a cairned track that threads through seas of boulders on the broad ridge to Foel Grach; while 150 puts you on a well-used path that follows the rim of Cwm Eigiau over the top of Craig yr Ysfa and on to Penyrhelgi-du.

Helyg/Ffynnon Llugwy route (CA15)

Few walkers would dispute that this is the finest of all ways to Carnedd Llewelyn, indeed one of the best tramps in the entire Carneddau. It starts in great form with the exhilarating climb to the delectable saddle NW of Penyrhelgi-du (CA8). After resting awhile on soft cushions of heather and bilberries turn L along the ridge. A formidable-looking rocky bluff faces you with deep cleaving gullies either side and you may have a few qualms if you suffer from vertigo! Luckily the hand-holds are massive and a sporting scramble lands you on the minor top of Penywaun-wen almost before you know it. (Great care is needed in snow or ice, however.)

Penywaun-wen lacks the presence to be listed as a peak in its own right but is a good spot from which to survey Cwm Eigiau and the plunging buttresses of Craig yr Ysfa. An easy spell on grass comes next, offering plenty of opportunity to admire the Glyders and the shy Ffynnon Llyffant snugly tucked beneath Carnedd Llewelyn's E face. The last stage follows a loose, gravelly track that leads directly to the top.

Nant Fach approach (CA16)

Follow the Afon Llafar to Llech Du as in CA4. Now carry on a short distance until the Nant Fach joins you L, pointing almost directly to

Carnedd Llewelyn's rounded dome. Follow it to its source and then press on up steep stone-encrusted grass to gain the saddle of Bwlch Cyfryw-drum at about 682638. There you will meet the gritty ridge path that traverses the Carneddau without a break from Ogwen in the S to Bwlch y Ddeufaen in the far N. Carnedd Llewelyn is the next port of call. With so much else to do, this is a route best kept in mind as a possible quick way down.

Tal-y-bont route (CA17)

See CA22; keep near the S rim of the Gledrffordd tableland if you want the best views of Cwm Eigiau and Ffynnon Llyffant.

Cwm Eigiau route (CA18)

This excellent walk is a combination of CA10 to the saddle beneath Penyrhelgi-du, followed by CA15 thereafter. It is everything you would expect from such a combination. However, experienced walkers seeking solitude who are not averse to a spell of trackless walking have yet another option, namely to proceed over the head of Cwm Eigiau from the foot of Craig yr Ysfa to gain the saddle from Foel Grach about half a mile N of Carnedd Llewelyn at 690654 (CA18, 1). Having got that far, why not gild the lily and break off to visit Ffynnon Llyffant too? Rough, wild, magnificent!

YR ELEN

Yr Elen has always held a fascination for hillwalkers. Part of the appeal is its commanding position, aloof like some sentinel at the tip of a twisty scarped ridge that would be a classic if only it were longer. Its breezy green top with its twin cairns - spacious enough for a game of rounders - has an enviable freshness and the views are everything you would expect from a thin, high neck encroaching over the barren wastes of Llafar and Caseg. Away N the tor country of Bera Bach is backed by the bare scalps of Llwytmor and Foel Fras. Nearer to home the double-humped nose rising to Foel Grach leads the eye to the immense bulk of Carnedd Llewelyn, completely dominating the E skyline. Grander still is the massive triangle of Carnedd Dafydd, where a dotted line of quartz reveals the cliffs of Llech Du and the Crib Lem ridge. Finally, alone in a secluded bowl of mottled green, is perhaps the loneliest lake of them all, the teardrop-shaped Ffynnon Caseg (Mare's Fountain).

Yr Elen lacks a satisfying direct route. Both approaches to the NW ridge involve tedious spells of bog-bashing and soon degenerate into a pitiless grind up the final 500ft. There could conceivably be a way up the NE ridge from Ffynnon Caseg, but if there is (and I have not attempted it!) it would clearly be a brute. That leaves the spur ridge from Llewelyn, a pearl of a walk whose only shortcoming, as I have said earlier, is its brevity. To pick it up from Llewelyn (where care is needed in mist) set out on 290. You will then meet a shaly path that curls delightfully round the lip of Cwm Caseg with the diminutive lake dramatically framed in the arms of the giant, splintered gullies that rend the mountain's E face.

(Peak-baggers should note that having visited Yr Elen from Carnedd Llewelyn there is no need to retrace your steps. You can contour across to pick up the main Carnedd 'highway' either N to Foel Grach or S to Carnedd Dafydd.)

NW ridge from the Llafar Valley (CA19)

Start on CA4 but stay with it only as long as it takes you to plot a course over to Yr Elen's NW ridge. The intervening ground is wet and boggy so it pays to aim for the drier rocky slabs a little higher up the valley. The ridge is cloaked in thick grass at first and throws up a couple of interesting outcrops along the way. So far

Carnedd Llewelyn from high up on Yr Elen

so good. Unhappily there is a sting in the tail as the looming dome ahead spells out all too clearly. Sure enough the final 400/500ft is a grind severe enough to test the fittest on a gravelly, slithery track that winds aloft with excruciating steepness.

NW ridge from the Caseg Valley (CA20)
Begin with CA L5 but then choose your moment to cross the Afon Caseg to the ridge to finish as in CA19. Unless you have any particular reason for choosing this route, you should note that CA19 from Cwm Llafar gives an easier, shorter and much more picturesque approach.

FOEL GRACH
Foel Grach is a slightly elevated outcrop on an otherwise flat and grassy stretch of the Carneddau's main N/S spine. It offers superb views of Yr Elen and the upper reaches of Cwm Caseg (if you walk a short distance SW of the cairn), but otherwise it is the least distinguished of all the Welsh 3000 footers. However, what it lacks in charisma it makes up for in creature comforts, sporting a stone refuge hut beneath a rocky knoll just N of the cairn. Dirty and unkempt this may be, but no Hilton was ever more welcome when the alternative was a cold wet night on the open fells!

A short diversion takes you to the grim cliffs overlooking Llynnau Dulyn and Melynllyn, two of the loneliest lakes in Wales as they huddle in the dark seclusion of their cold crater-like hollows. Dulyn is reputed to attain a depth of 50ft within 3ft of the shore!

Afon Goch route (CA21)
Any approach to Foel Grach means a long day and this is no exception. However it has the advantage that if energy flags (or the weather clamps down) you can peel off at any of several points to tackle Bera Mawr, Llwytmor or Foel Fras instead. The starting point is Bont Newydd, 663720, where cars can be parked after driving up the glen from Aber.

Go through a vintage iron gate and follow the Afon Rhaeadr-fawr through the woods. Stay with the path as it continues up the vale, with gnarled trees and gently wooded slopes either side and the drama of the highest falls in Snowdonia building up inexorably before you. The falls are some 200ft high and their plunging white ribbons are a thrilling spectacle when in full spate. However you should not leave this epic scene and its roaring torrents without first sparing a glance for the neglected Rhaeadr-bach falls off R. Were it not for the misfortune of being cast in the shadow of a greater neighbour they too would enjoy the limelight.

Now to more serious matters. It is necessary to join a path that slants across the screes E of the falls. The screes are very loose so it is advisable to backtrack a little to scramble up to the path beside the edge of the woods, around 200yds back. You then meet it where it leaves the woods over a stile at 669704. (Alternatively you could leave the valley trail at 666710, shortly after passing a cottage, where a tumbledown wall leads to the edge of the woods and a yellow waymark sign indicating the path. This skims the edge of the woods initially but then glides over a carpet of pine needles to reach the stile at 669704 as before.)

Crossing the screes calls for a cautious step, especially in snow or ice when a slip could be nasty. There is a particularly awkward-looking moment where a runnel has to be crossed and the path seems to disappear. However a minor deflection into the runnel quickly solves the problem.

Above the falls the path roughly follows the hanging valley of the Afon Goch. I say 'roughly' because it is flirtatious in the extreme, now disappearing in soggy bog, now twisting round little rocky knolls, now leaving the stream to cavort up the hillside and so on. When it is wet it is very, very wet and will test your stamina and patience to the full if tackled at the end of a tiring day!

Only seaward are there long views and the main interest lies in the teeming ravines of the Afon Goch. After a wet spell these atone for a lot of aggravation. One fearsome gash in the stream bed follows another, each host to white foaming falls, their rocky sides bedecked, as often as not, with red-berried rowan trees dizzily perched above the raging cataracts below.

Before long you come to a cluster of sheepfolds and it is about here that you should contemplate a crossing if your objective is Bera Mawr. A short crisp pull up gives you the peak's NW ridge for a simple approach on grass until you reach the final rocky tor, CA35.

The cliffs of Llynnau Dulyn and Foel Grach

Here are two tips: first make sure you go far enough W to reach the NW ridge (otherwise you could easily find yourself struggling up a steeper slope from the NE that has unpleasant slippery boulders); second, remember that crossing the Afon Goch is not a trivial task (except in dry conditions) and it could well be prudent to move higher up the valley. I once experienced a very unhappy 20 minutes, one damp winter's evening as dusk was falling, when trying to cross on the way down from Bera Mawr. I might still be there were it not for a slip on a rock, as I was examining a possible crossing place, making any further contemplation on my part purely academic!

If you do decline the earlier challenge, the best place to cross the Afon Goch for Bera Mawr is probably at about 683682 when you can stalk your prey from the E (CA35, 1). Llwytmor can also be tackled from here (CA32). Either way involves a tiring grind up tussocky, energy-sapping slopes that are liberally embellished with copper-tinted grass and a smattering of peat hags.

Otherwise continue on a bearing of 140 to meet the main Carnedd 'highway' between Foel Fras and Garnedd Uchaf. Next either bear NE for Foel Fras along a trail that is nowadays sadly eroded and oozy (CA25), or proceed SW for Garnedd Uchaf, where a cairned path leads unerringly up a gentle rise to Foel Grach (passing the refuge hut on the way).

No one can pretend that the upper reaches of the Afon Goch are other than bleak and barren, but at least they provide shelter from the prevailing wind and there are days enough when that alone can be a blessing!

Tal-y-bont route (CA22)

Begin as in CA14. You can either bag Craig Eigiau en-route or stay with the Land-Rover track to pull up to the Gledrffordd plateau further along.

The plateau, a broad grassy saddle really, is fine striding-out country with a couple of shallow tarns and views that extend from N of Foel Fras to Craig yr Ysfa and the heights curling round Cwm Eigiau from the S. As you approach the skyline veer R for Foel Grach, L for Carnedd Llewelyn. Either way you soon pick up a well-used path through short-cropped grass that becomes progressively stonier as it approaches the two tops. The views are wide and magnificent, typical Carnedd 'top of the world' stuff; the soft green mosaic of the Conway Valley E, the Snowdonia massif S, Yr Elen and the sea W and N.

Dulyn/Melynllyn route (CA23)

Start from 732663 and follow the Land-Rover track described in CA14 until it peters out by the shores of Llyn Melynllyn. Then pull up onto the grassy tongue between the two lakes when a bearing of 270 will give you a bull's eye on Foel Grach. There are fragments of track here and there, but even when there are not it is still a pleasant walk over grassland that you will probably have all to yourself.

Note the contrasting characters of the two lakes. Melynllyn is light, open and friendly; Dulyn is dark and sombre, dominated by evil-looking cliffs, black squat pillars and a great triangle of rock high above the lake that seems to be waiting for its opportunity to plunge like a giant dagger into the icy depths below.

Afon Caseg route (CA24)

Follow CA L5 until, having entered the 'defile', you meet a stream tumbling down from Cwm Bychan L at about 678656. You should then clamber up onto the steep grassy nose that rises directly ahead, exploiting a temporary break in the crags. This will put you astride

The vast rolling uplands of the N Carneddau;
Foel Fras from Foel Grach

the main Carnedd 'highway', almost midway between Carnedd Llewelyn and Foel Grach.

FOEL FRAS

Were it not the starting or finishing point (depending on which way you tackle it) for those hardy souls who attempt to visit all 14 of the Welsh 3000 footers in the course of a single 24-hour period, it is unlikely that Foel Fras would be the well-known peak it is. Apart from a dense and chaotic cap of boulders that almost obscures the trig point, and a high stone wall that crosses the long wedge-shaped summit plateau (providing some, but not much, shelter for anyone sleeping out prior to attempting the 3000's N to S), it is a barren, cheerless place.

Foel Fras is frequently approached from Drum in the NE, a long trudge on grass, boggy in places, with only the sea and Anglesey for inspiration. The path follows a wire fence nearly all the way until, just before the end, a stone wall takes over.

If you are continuing on to Garnedd Uchaf and all points S, the path, which gets buried near the top in the proliferation of boulders, restarts on 220 at the S tip of the summit plateau, near where the wall reverts to a wire fence again. This path is fast becoming an ugly scar;

a glutinous peaty morass where, a mere ten years ago, the fells still retained their pristine freshness.

Afon Goch route (CA25)
See CA21.

Afon Garreg-wen route (CA26)
I give this route without recommendation. It is wild, lonely and trackless and only likely to appeal to dedicated walkers for whom it might provide a link that enables a longer round to be constructed. Start from Bwlch-y-gaer, 744693, as in CA30 and follow the routing for Pen y Castell. However, instead of turning R through a gate for the latter peak, stay with the cart-track until, after crossing the Afon Ddu, you should abandon it and walk on a bearing of 260 until you meet the Afon Garreg-wen. Then it is largely a matter of freelancing in the same general direction with the stream as a guide, dodging outcrops and bog as best you can, and steering a course directly for the top as soon as the slope eases sufficiently to permit it.

DRUM
Seekers after inspiration will have little luck on Drum. There are pleasing views across the Conway Valley and seaward to Anglesey and the Great Orme, but little else graces its bald grassy top. Little, that is, save a junction of disintegrating wire fences and a robust windshelter that sheltered me one foul December day while the rain lashed the sodden fells and the wind roared its displeasure like an express train.

Not surprisingly, Drum is rarely a prime objective but more usually a transit stop on the long ridge S to Foel Fras. It is also pleasant to link Drum with Pen y Castell. A wire fence leads down the SE ridge (the other carries on to Foel Fras), passing first over Foel Lwyd and then down the most prolific bilberry slope in Snowdonia before a gentle rise puts you on Pen y Castell's playful little battlements.

Oddly enough Drum's N flanks were probably trodden more in olden times than today. The pass that crosses them, Bwlch y Ddeufaen (Pass of the Two Stones), was in regular use in prehistoric times to by-pass the coastal hills around Penmaenmawr and later on the Romans drove one of their famous roads across it. Nowadays the stony track that remains is handily placed for hillwalkers, but little else.

Llyn Anafon approach (CA27)

Provided you can face the final 1000ft slog up its W slopes this is the best of all routes to Drum. Surprisingly it is virtually unknown. It begins from the roadhead at 677716, a point reached either by driving down the wooded vale from Aber to Bont Newydd, parking there and walking up the hill; or by motoring up to the roadhead itself (in a setting mildly reminiscent of Switzerland) where there is also space to park a couple of cars. Go through a gate, ignoring the stony track that doubles back on itself to wind up the hillside, and carry on S beside a wall until you reach the verdant green banks of the Afon Anafon. This happy little stream will accompany you for the next two miles, charming you with a succession of tumbling falls. The path runs you a merry dance though; sometimes following the stream, then hugging gorse-clad slopes, now on turf as fine as many a lawn, then cleaving its way through dense bracken.

After a while a stony track which links up with the Roman road that crosses Bwlch y Ddeufaen comes in L (you could have joined it at the start by a short pull up the hillside on 90 but that would have meant missing the best of the brook), and shortly afterwards you come to what must surely be one of the largest networks of sheepfolds in the whole of Wales. Sadly all good things come to an end, and sure enough the noisy clatter of the stream eventually subsides to be replaced by the quiet calm of lonely Llyn Anafon from where the only escape is R up the slopes to Llwytmor (CA33), or L up equally steep grass to Drum. Aim due E and you should breast the ridge slightly N of the top.

Bwlch y Ddeufaen route W (CA28)

Start from 677716 as in CA27 and go through the gate as before, but this time follow the stony track that doubles back up the hillside. Stay with it as it curls round Foel Ganol, first N then E (where it becomes the old Roman road), but leave it R as you approach a couple of power pylons near 693723 to join a similar stony track that slants SE, veering to S, across the hillside. This new track meanders away for a couple of miles with impressive views of Tal-y-fan and the Drosgl ridge of Drum, but not much else in the way of excitement. However it does provide shelter from the prevailing wind, courtesy of Foel Ganol, a gift not lightly turned down in winter. The track eventually degenerates into an ugly, gravelly scar that runs parallel to the last stages of CA29 before fizzling out a few feet short of the top.

Bwlch y Ddeufaen route E (CA29)

Now for the other end of the Roman road with a start from the small parking area at 721715 where the tarmac road from just N of the bridge at Tal-y-bont ends. This can be quite crowded on long summer evenings since it is one of the regular starting points for walkers tackling the Welsh 3000 footers N to S. The usual routine is to climb Drum and then press on as dusk is falling to snatch a few hours sleep beneath the wall that straddles Foel Fras' stony top. Then at first light (3.30a.m. or thereabouts) it's off on the long trek to Snowdon. Quite a day!

The plod up the pass between the barren slopes of Drum and the surprisingly virile crags of Tal-y-fan is unremarkable, even when the dull greys of the crags are festooned with brilliant yellow gorse. Unfortunately nothing can atone for the power lines that now deface this ancient highway. Even these cannot completely blot out history, however, and near the top of the bwlch are the two monoliths after which it is named (Pass of the Two Stones), though their authenticity is by no means certain! Just beyond, where a stone wall with a ladder-stile crosses the pass, you have a choice: R for Tal-y-fan's W ridge (CA45); L for the Drosgl spur of Drum.

The 800ft climb up Drosgl's grassy slope is a hard, boring grind and it is a relief, as you turn L at the top to be faced with a similar looking slope along a wire fence, to find that the gradient has by then moderated to a more acceptable angle.

PEN Y CASTELL

'Castell' means 'castle' and there is undoubtedly something about the spiky outcrops that litter Pen y Castell's rambling crown that brings medieval battlements to mind. None more so than Craig Cefn-coch, a rocky eminence SE of the main top. A cairn overlooks the saddle separating Pen y Castell from Drum, but the highest point is slightly E by a quiver of tiny coppery-brown pinnacles. As a vantage point Pen y Castell suffers from being in the shadow of Drum and Foel Fras. The best views are N and E encompassing Bwlch y Ddeufaen, the long crinkled ridge of Tal-y-fan, the Conway Valley and Craig Eigiau.

Bwlch-y-gaer route (CA30)

Few walkers are sorry to have the occasional high start; here is one to fit the bill. Drive up the mountain road that leaves the B5106 just N of Tal-y-bont (not to be confused with the equally hilly road to the S) and look out carefully for the L fork at 749699. Follow this and park at 744693 where the road degenerates to two stony tracks. You are now at 1200ft and if the ramble to Pen y Castell does not seem challenging enough, you can always fill in with a side trip to Pen-y-gaer, 750694, a prehistoric hill-fort with stone circles, and Penygadair, 739694, a local vantage point.

For Pen y Castell take the more N of the two tracks, a sunken cart-track, and follow it through three gates, the fells aglow with the yellow of gorse in summer. A few hundred yards further along you come to a gate embedded in the wire fence to your R. Go through this and climb the diminutive ramparts of Craig Cefn-coch to complete an easy conquest of Pen y Castell and its gently undulating plateau.

Llyn Eigiau route (CA31)

Start along CA14 as if bound for Craig Eigiau, but just after passing the gate at 726666 look out R for a narrow, overgrown, track that is garlanded with hawthorn blossom in early summer. Follow this as it winds wistfully round the NE spur of Craig Eigiau amidst thickets of gorse and bracken, scattered boulders and twisted old trees, until you come to a weir at 725676. Cross the weir and then, almost at once, a narrow leat. Next strike out N over half a mile of rough scrappy ground to join the cart-track referred to in CA30 that straddles Pen y Castell's S slopes. Turn R to the gate to finish as before. (It is useful to note that a track runs along the S bank of the leat. This eventually meets the cart-track at 741691, quite near to the first gate mentioned in CA30.)

LLWYTMOR

I have never met a fellow walker on Llwytmor. No doubt this is partly because it lies slightly off the main Carnedd ridges which makes it difficult to fit into a satisfying day's round. But it also has to be confessed that all three of the routes given below involve a degree of hard labour. Not that Llwytmor is without appeal. Its huge summit plateau conjures up visions of some lost world in its sheer abandon and isolation, rather like Waun-rydd in the Brecon Beacons. The illusion is especially compelling in mist when the scattered, spiky castellations of rock that fringe the top are magnified by the gloom and rear up like ghostly apparitions. On a clear day, on the other hand, Llwytmor is as good as gold with superb views of the Drum/Foel Fras ridge, Bera Mawr and the sea.

Afon Goch route (CA32)
See CA21.

Llyn Anafon route (CA33)
Follow CA27 to Llyn Anafon, then press on to the vicinity of the stream at 697698 where a tough trackless slog up the hillside leads to the shallow col between Foel Fras and Llwytmor. The worst is over then, with firmer ground and a more accommodating angle when you change course to NW for the final assault.

Aber Falls route (CA34)
This is the shortest and most direct route to Llwytmor; it is also the most gruelling. Unremittingly severe on wind and limb going up, it is equally merciless on toes and knees coming down. However, purely for masochists, here it is.

Start from 669704 where the Afon Goch path leaves the woods before crossing the screes above the falls. (The two ways of reaching this point are outlined in CA21.) You will have gleaned an inkling of what lies in store during the stroll from Bont Newydd when Llwytmor reveals its most dramatic face: a colossal, towering triangle embedded with scattered islands of rock garlanded in heather. Obviously excruciatingly steep! The route calls for little description. From 669704 it is simply(!) a matter of crawling your way up to the corner of the woods at 673703 when you should bear R (the going is

Wild ponies in 'tor' country; Bera Mawr and Bera Bach

merely steep by this time) on 110 for the windshelter on Llwytmor
Bach. Then continue on 120 past a cluster of peaty pools for what is,
at last, a pleasant walk to the main top.

BERA MAWR/BERA BACH

The sight of these giant tors with their huge citadels of jagged, naked
rock thrusting aggressively skyward from the pale yellow uniformity
of the surrounding moors always reminds me of Dartmoor. Lightly
capped with snow, or with wreaths of mist adding a touch of
mystery, or simply as you approach them over Drosgl from Gyrn
Wigau, they have the same riveting but slightly sinister presence.
For once the 'Mawr' and 'Bach' are misplaced. Surveys show that
Bera Bach is actually the higher by 40ft. Both peaks demand a little
easy scrambling before they yield their topmost secrets, but Bera
Mawr is architecturally on a grander scale altogether.

A mere half-mile of flat, spongy moorland separates the two tops
and, with the lie of the land permitting easy (but maybe damp)
walking almost anywhere, it would be pedantic to describe routes
for both - hence this combined entry. CA21 below leaves you on

Bera Mawr. For Bera Bach carry on SW across the open fells with little tracks here and there if you can find them, but nothing to worry about if you can't.

Afon Goch/NW ridge route (CA35)
See CA21.

GYRN WIGAU/DROSGL

The NW tip of the Carneddau is a seldom-trod region of coarse, stubbly moorland where gentle slopes, a minimum of bog and a network of minor tracks ensure rapid progress. As with Bera Mawr and Bera Bach it makes little sense in such conditions to give separate routes for two hills as close together as these, especially when Gyrn Wigau is often regarded more as a hump on Drosgl's SW spur than as a top in its own right.

I have given Gyrn Wigau the benefit of the doubt. It is a jolly little hill where two tiny rocky spurs and a band of bright green turf break the monotony of the surrounding fells to create, more in imagination than in reality perhaps, a 'mini ridge.' Drosgl is sterner stuff, though only in relative terms; a grassy mound for the most part, capped with a stony top and a huge circular pyre of stones reputed to be Bronze Age in origin.

Gerlan route (CA36)

Park where the road ends at 639663 but stay with the cart-track into which it degenerates until you reach a gate at 639665. Go through the gate and then maintain a bearing of 60 to gain the crest of the shallow ridge ahead, aiming initially for a ladder-stile on the skyline. Bracken and gorse give way to bleak open grassland, but any hint of boredom is soon dispelled by the immense vista that quickly unfolds.

It is Carnedd Dafydd's mighty NW ridge that first commands attention, bare and open but compelling by its sheer scale, as it leads the eye to the aptly named Black Ladders and the spacious yet wild Llafar Valley. Yr Elen, aloof as usual, rises giant-like across the valley while the E skyline is scarred by the spiky tors of Foel Grach and Yr Aryg. A scene of power, but power tinged with a solitude bordering on sadness.

What a pleasant surprise when, after a few false promises, Gyrn

Wigau's tiny outcrops suddenly break the skyline. Moreover, once you are there you will see that Drosgl is but a simple stroll across a shallow heathery dip. Then, as you near Drosgl, comes the biggest surprise of all, the twin castles of Bera Mawr and Bera Bach; great shattered piles of rock, resplendent in their pinnacled glory, oases of grandeur in a moorland wilderness. Another 20/30 minutes of easy walking and they could be yours too.

Afon Gam route (CA37)

I mention this lonely route with some diffidence because its practicality all depends on whether you can cross the stream at the foot of the Aber Falls at 668701, having started out on CA21. There is no problem in dry weather, but when the falls are in full spate - a common enough occurrence given the Welsh climate! - it takes a cool head and a steady step. Once across proceed W for about half a mile beside a wall, keeping beneath the slopes enclosing the vivacious Afon Rhaeadr-bach. Next spy out a green path that follows the true L bank of the next stream, the Afon Gam, and stay with this to gain the high moors at about 657694. From here on it is plain sailing, trackless but easy, with only the sheep for company.

You could avoid crossing the Afon Goch by starting from somewhere like Henffordd, 652723, and following one of the footpaths shown on the map. However, this takes you further afield than is probably justified with so much else to do.

NW approaches (CA38)

You can make a variety of approaches to Gyrn Wigau and Drosgl from the NW, although none is of any great interest. They all cross the minor line of hills ranging from Moel Faban, 635680, to Moel Wnion, 649698. Some, but not all of the paths are shown on the map. All are easy. One line of approach skirts the S slopes of Moel Faban; a second uses Bwlch ym Mhwll-le between Moel Faban and Llefn; a third passes between Llefn and Gyrn and a fourth between Gyrn and Moel Wnion.

CREIGIAU GLEISION

Creigiau Gleision (the Blue-green Rocks) shares with Tal-y-fan the distinction of being the most E of the Carneddau. It is a beautiful peak rising between the cold austerity of Llyn Cowlyd and the calm serenity of Llyn Crafnant. Separated from its fellows physically, it is even more detached in spirit. In place of the open grassland of the high Carneddau, Nature has furnished gentle hillocks, shaggy moorland and knuckles of rock, all generously cloaked with heather and bilberries in a setting reminiscent of the N Rhinogs. If some malevolent fate confined me henceforth to roaming just one of the Carnedd peaks, the one I would choose would be Creigiau Gleision.

The top is a breezy eyrie, perched high above the cliffs that sweep down to Cowlyd. Across the lake are the sheer slopes that sustain Pen Llithrig-y-wrach and a Glyders skyline dominated by Tryfan and Gallt yr Ogof. N and E the drama of the high peaks is balanced by the colourful mosaic of fields and pastures bordering on the Conway Valley and the Irish Sea, and by an occasional, tantalising glimpse of Crafnant itself.

Although many walker do not realise it, Creigiau Gleision has two tops. The second is at 734623, half a mile NE of the main top along a delightfully undulating ridge. Try to visit both, and while at the second do not overlook the pretty tarn nestling on a nearby shelf (see CA43).

The very features that make Creigiau Gleision such a joy in clear weather - fantasies of hillocks and hollows, broken ground abounding in tiny outcrops - are the very same that cause problems in thick weather. So avoid it then, if you can. The safest course if you are unavoidably caught out is to follow the Bronheulog route, CA42.

Capel Curig route (CA39)

Climb the ladder-stile across the road from the post office at Capel Curig and join the well-trodden path that wends E for the next half-mile. After passing through a charming little glen beneath Clogwyn-mawr be sure to bear L where the path crosses a stream by a bridge at 732582. With such peace and beauty all around it is hard to credit that the A5 is less than half a mile away! Everything is here in miniature - richly wooded tors, marshy flats, slopes dappled with gnarled rocks, heather, bracken and colourful mosses. The firm, flat boulders make for pleasant walking underfoot.

The path climbs slowly. Where it levels-off at a gap in a wall just before descending to Llyn Crafnant, 738597, bear L through another tumbledown wall and follow the S rim of the Crafnant Valley. Rest awhile by the fine cairn on Crimpiau, 733595. On a sunny day the view from here can hold its own with the best. Llyn Crafnant takes pride of place; nothing, even in the Lake District is lovelier as it nestles amidst the greens of meadows and woods with the rugged purple slopes of Creigiau Gleision the perfect backdrop. When you turn your back old friends are waiting too; Snowdon and Lliwedd, the Glyders, Moel Siabod, Moel Hebog, the Moelwyns, the E Carneddau and, further afield, Arenig Fach, the Berwyns and the Conway Valley.

Alas, it is time to leave. So drop down to a little hollow where a path (CA40, 1) comes in from the valley R and then pull up to the bouldery waste of Craig Wen. You can then see that a succession of rocky hummocks lies ahead, a bit like Crinkle Crags except that here it is only necessary to climb the last 'crinkle'. So cross over to the fells well to the W of the 'crinkles' (with striking views of the Ogwen Valley and Tryfan) until a stony path appears to lead you up the final hump.

A shorter but equally enchanting route (CA39, 1) climbs up behind Clogwyn-mawr and then heads N to skirt Llyn y Coryn, 731591, before joining CA39 either on Crimpiau or in the depression between Crimpiau and Craig Wen. After mounting the stile opposite the post office at Capel Curig, cross a field as before but then turn L at a gap in the first stone wall you come to. Proceed N for a couple of minutes, go through a gate, then strike out NE for the crest of the shallow ridge ahead. The view is truly majestic, even this early in the day, with the Snowdon horseshoe, Glyders, Ogwen Valley and the Carneddau all vying for attention. The diminutive Llyn y Coryn, when you reach it, is well worthy of such an auspicious start. Set in a hollow, surrounded by islands of rock and thickets of heather, it s the very embodiment of what a mountain tarn should be.

Llyn Crafnant route (CA40)

Another lovely route starts from the lakeside by the café at Cynllwyd, where refreshments are available and boats may be hired on a lazy day. Stroll up the valley until the road divides at a gate at 740603. Then bear L up a bank of fine green turf. After passing through an iron gate in a wall the path climbs to the top of the pass and the gap in the wall at 738597, referred to in CA39.

Alternatively (CA40, 1), for a rougher and wilder approach, continue on to Blaen-y-nant and then aim for the vale-head between Crimpiau and Craig Wen at 731598 to finish once again as in CA39.

E face direct (CA41)

For an ascent that is short and sharp, walk up the road from Llyn Crafnant to Blaen-y-nant and then scramble up the steep slope of grass and scree that lies between the forestry plantations and the crags higher up the valley. A rough, gruelling climb brings you to a gap in the rocky undulations (Bwlch Mignog) where you can break through to the open fells to the W and join CA39.

Bronheulog route (CA42)

Follow CA12. When you reach the footbridge at 717609, or slightly before, take to the open hillside for an oozy plod up to the rocky hummocks of Creigiau Gleision. This is a dull route whose only merit is to offer a safe way down in mist - provided you avoid the steep slopes directly above Llyn Cowlyd.

Llyn Cowlyd route (CA43)

Here is an unusual way back to Capel Curig to complement CA39. Leave the main top and follow the summit ridge, with its wee heathery pools, to the subsidiary top at 734623, crossing a conspicuous band of limestone en-route and with stupendous views across the abyss to Pen Llithrig-y-wrach. Then aim for a corner in a wire fence, slightly NE at 737624. On the way try and spot a pretty little tarn cupped on a heathery ledge R. Bear L at the fence and follow it down to Llyn Cowlyd. There is a faint track but some rough going with deep tussocky heather and patches of bog is unavoidable. Cross to the W shore of Llyn Cowlyd where a stony road leads to the footbridge at 717609 and hence by CA12 back to Capel Curig.

NE ridge (CA44)

Combine this with one of the routes from Llyn Crafnant, say CA40, and you have a pearl of a day that unites the best of Creigiau

Gleision with a high-level circuit of the lake. Unless you are already familiar with it, the NE ridge is easier to navigate in descent. So leave the N top and start by following CA43 to the corner of the wire fence at 737624. Then, instead of bearing L, stay with the fence first SE, and later as it veers NE round the flanks of Pen y Craig-gron, until in just under a mile you come to a remote spot in the midst of the open moors at 746627 where two fences intersect at a twisted old iron gate.

The narrow trail that has chaperoned you thus far, paralleling the fence on its N side, now blossoms into a firm stony track. However it deserts the fence to maintain a predominantly E course. Ploughing through seas of heather - this is an ideal romp for a breezy autumn day with the clouds racing overhead - it eventually merges into a forest road which, after the usual zig-zags, meets the road to Crafnant by the guest-house of Nantuchaf at 763624. If you ever follow this route the other way ignore the signs for Llyn Cowlyd, keeping L where they indicate R.

TAL-Y-FAN

Tal-y-fan is a loner, tucked away to the NE of the main Carneddau range and separated from its colleagues by Bwlch y Ddeufaen and the old Roman road. It only just qualifies for the exclusive 2000ft club and, despite the attractive undulating profile it shows the Conway Valley, it is one of those hills that can be climbed from almost any point of the compass. However do not be put off. Tal-y-fan has plenty of interest and is ideal for a lazy day. Its soft heathery top, a rarity in the Carneddau, is made for picnicking and there are lovely sea views over Anglesey and the Great Orme, not to mention the Carneddau giants to the S.

Bwlch y Ddeufaen route (CA45)

Walk up the pass as in CA29. Cross over the stile at the top and then climb alongside the wall up steep grassy slopes to Foel Lwyd. The angle eases there and a peaty path meanders through fields of pale mauve heather with glorious views of the coast and the Afon Ddu N. Then comes a minor col after which a step up a little rocky bluff leads to the trig point just beyond.

Cae Coch route (CA46)

Cross the stile at 731715 to join a faint track that swathes through a field of bracken and scattered boulders. Continue slightly W of N through a gap in a wall. After a while, with the occasional waymark sign for comfort, you come to a second stile at 728723. This crosses a wall R near where another wall comes in from the E. Either head N for the col as in CA45 or slant across the hillside NE over broken ground for a direct approach (CA46, 1).

Roewen route (CA47)

Walk through the sleepy little village of Roewen, where there literally are roses round the cottage doors, until you come to open country beyond the woods at about 748722. From there an easy cross-country walk gives you the E tip of Tal-y-fan's tapering ridge.

Afon Ddu route (CA48)

This lonely route is all but unknown, no doubt because it starts from Llanfairfechan and is thus difficult to fit into a satisfying round. However, it is worth a try on a rain-shortened day, especially if you combine it with a return over Cefn-coch and Moelfre.

Turn SE at the traffic-lights in the middle of Llanfairfechan and drive down Valley Road. Go R at the bridge over the Afon Ddu and then straightaway L down a leafy lane until you reach a little car park where the road ends at 695738. A kissing-gate leads into a cart-track that bears L over the Afon Ddu just before its confluence with the Afon Maes-y-bryn. Already, barely a couple of minutes from the road, you are in a new world with Dinas, green but grandly rugged, towering above you L, and Anglesey with its tiny consort, Puffin Island, peeping through the trees to your rear.

When you reach open country either stay with the Afon Ddu to reach the top of Bwlch y Ddeufaen, or aim across the moors for the col between Foel Lwyd and Tal-y-fan (CA48, 1). Either way you finish as in CA45.

HIGH-LEVEL WALKS
S to N traverse: Ogwen to Aber (CA H1)

A classic, this, with insights into each of the Carneddau's many faces. Not a walk to be tackled lightly. The distance is long, about 14 miles, five 3000 footers are crossed and transport has to be arranged for the other end. Fine weather is essential - it would be a crime to risk spoiling such a magnificent expedition in anything less.

The hardest work comes first with that supreme test, the SW ridge of Pen yr Ole Wen (CA1). Once that is in the bag, follow the grassy path that curves round the rim of the hollow cradling Ffynnon Lloer, pass over the rocky monolith of Carnedd Fach and thread your way through rivers of boulders to mount Carnedd Dafydd, a top so chaotic that its scattered cairns are barely distinguishable from the stony waste all around. Next continue on grass along the tops of the Black Ladders before bearing L across the spiky saddle of Bwlch Cyfryw-drum. Easy and safe as houses, this nevertheless manages to convey a pleasant sense of airiness with views down the Llafar Valley to Bethesda one side and over Ffynnon Llugwy to Penyrhelgi-du's long, tapering ridge on the other.

The saddle leads into a gritty path, tedious on a hot day, that snakes up Carnedd Llewelyn. It is about here that the scenery starts to change. So far it is Snowdon, the Glyders and the Ogwen Valley that have been pre-eminent. Increasingly now the emphasis shifts to the Irish Sea, to the meadows of the Conway Valley, the whalebacked hills of the N Carneddau, the tors of Bera Mawr and Bera Bach and the pyramid of Yr Elen.

Indeed strong walkers may be tempted to bag Yr Elen en-route for it is a splendid vantage point at the tip of a slender spur. Regretfully there is no easy way. Its capture inevitably involves an undulating there-and-back trip along a narrow, shaly track that straddles the top of the cliffs that almost enclose the teardrop-shaped Ffynnon Caseg. Unless you are already familiar with the lie of the land it is best to set a bearing of 290 before you leave Llewelyn's premier cairn. You will then pick up the Yr Elen track with minimum height loss. (Tigers should note that you can cut corners by contouring across to the Yr Elen track from both N and S of Llewelyn's main cairn.)

Back at Llewelyn proceed N, initially through rivers of stones and boulders, then over short-cropped grass. Spare a moment for a brief foray E to glimpse the elusive Ffynnon Llyffant, a tiny tarn that somehow manages to irradiate the whole of Cwm Eigiau when it catches the sun's rays. Foel Grach, with its refuge hut and stony top, comes uneventfully next, followed by a shallow descent to Garnedd Uchaf and a near level mile to Foel Fras. It is easy going now, across what is more a grassy plateau than a grassy ridge, though the path to Foel Fras is unfortunately close to becoming a peaty quagmire these days.

Follow the stone wall crossing Foel Fras' stony top and then let the wire fence that replaces it lead you on to Drum. You now have a choice of endings. One possibility is to drop down from Drum to the Anafon Valley (CA27) to end up in Aber, with plenty of opportunities for bathing tired feet en-route. Alternatively you could make for the Roman road that follows Bwlch y Ddeufaen (either end) on CA28 or 29. Other options are to leave Foel Fras down the Afon Goch (CA25), or to make an easy crossing of the fells from Foel Fras to Llwytmor for a steep descent on CA34, in both instances ending the day with the drama of the Aber Falls. You could also vary the start. For example you could set out from Pen Llithrig-y-wrach or Penyrhelgi-du, trading off the Penyrhelgi-du saddle and Craig yr Ysfa against the Black Ladders and Bwlch Cyfryw-drum; an unenviable choice! The permutations are virtually endless. All you can be sure of is weary feet and a memorable day, provided that the weather is kind.

W to E traverse: Bethesda to Conway (CA H2)

Another fine traverse crosses the Carneddau W to E, visiting the tors and prairie-like country of the N half of the range. It looks a long way but the going is surprisingly easy and less taxing than you might think from the map. The main problem, as with any traverse, is transport.

Start from Bethesda and follow CA36 over Gyrn Wigau, Drosgl, Bera Bach and/or Bera Mawr. Then press on to Yr Aryg, a monolith in the same tradition but too small to be rated a top in its own right. From Yr Aryg it is but a short step across the fells to Garnedd Uchaf where you should bear L for Foel Fras and Drum as in CA H1 before descending Drum's SE ridge to Pen y Castell. Either CA30 or CA31 then takes you down to the taverns of the Conway Valley.

Like the Ogwen/Aber walk the variations on this basic theme are almost endless. You could start by climbing Yr Elen or Carnedd Dafydd and finish on Craig Eigiau or Pen Llithrig-y-wrach. Almost any combination is possible (and rewarding) given the energy and suitable transport arrangements.

Pen yr Ole Wen/Carnedd Llewelyn (CA H3)

If you cannot manage the full Ogwen to Aber traverse this is the next best thing. Indeed, mile for mile, it is one of the two finest walks in the Carneddau (CA H4 being the other). Simply follow CA H1 as far as Carnedd Llewelyn and then turn round. Some folk seem to have an aversion to retracing their steps. Personally I have never shared that view - it is a never-ending source of wonder how fresh the hills look, and what new faces they present, when viewed from different angles and in varying lights. The truth of this is perfectly illustrated by this pearl of a walk with its abundance of riches - the SW ridge of Pen yr Ole Wen, Ffynnon Lloer, the Black Ladders and the saddle to Carnedd Llewelyn.

Despite what I have just said about retracing one's steps, I must mention one variation that I do strongly recommend for the homeward half. This uses the neglected but attractive Tal y Llyn Ogwen route (CA2) for coming down off Pen yr Ole Wen at the end of the day. You then have either a mile of road work beside Llyn Ogwen, or a quiet stroll along a track that follows the lake's N shoreline to recover your starting point. Both are infinitely preferable to a tortuous slither down Pen yr Ole Wen's SW ridge, the last place in the world for tired legs!

Pen yr Ole Wen/Craig yr Ysfa (CA H4)

This is the second of the outstanding walks mentioned above. Once again the outward half is CA H1 to Carnedd Llewelyn, but this time the return is over Craig yr Ysfa and the Penyrhelgi-du saddle and thence down past Ffynnon Llugwy (CA8). An expedition with even more variety than CA H3 at the cost of a tedious and noisy hike back along the road at the end of the day.

Caseg/Llafar horseshoe (CA H5)

Sheep are your most likely company in the lonely wastes of the Caseg and Llafar valleys. This is another easy round with plenty of variety - the barren tor country in the morning, then the high peaks and finally a long, relaxing descent with the Glyders at your elbow and the sea shimmering like burnished gold in the evening sun.

Follow CA36 round the N rim of the Caseg Valley, visiting Gryn Wigau, Drosgl, Bera Bach and the rocky outcrop, Yr Aryg. Then march on to the main spine of the Carneddau: Foel Grach, Carnedd Llewelyn, and across Bwlch Cyfryw-drum to Carnedd Dafydd before returning to base down Dafydd's NW ridge. Numerous variations are possible. For example the round could easily be split into two halves by coming down off Yr Elen. Or you could do it the other way round and start by challenging Llech Du (CA4).

Eigiau horseshoe (CA H6)

Another of the N Wales classics, and a circular one at that, thus avoiding any road bashing or transport problems. Start from 732663 near Llyn Eigiau and follow CA17 to Carnedd Llewelyn. You can add side-trips to Craig Eigiau and Foel Grach if you wish, but be sure to hug the edges of the Gledrffordd tableland first for views of Llynnau Dulyn and Llynnau Melynllyn, then later for views of Cwm Eigiau and Ffynnon Llyffant.

Descend Llewelyn's SE ridge (CA15). This is the highlight of the day, crossing over Craig yr Ysfa, Penyrhelgi-du and finally Pen Llithrig-y-wrach. The final stretch down Pen Llithrig-y-wrach's N ridge (CA13) provides a fitting finale, the easy turf and gentle slope giving you every opportunity to relax in the evening sun. The scenery is magnificent to the end; forgotten Cwm Eigiau on one side, the crinkled heather top and furrowed precipices of Creigiau Gleision on the other.

As usual many variations are possible. One would be to use CA23 for the outward half, taking in Llynnau Dulyn/Melynllyn. Another option would be to shorten the way home by dropping down to Cwm Eigiau on CA18.

E Carneddau circular walk (CA H7)

Here is another circular walk based on 732663, but this time encompassing the more N fells. Climb Foel Grach as in CA22 and then embark on a round that includes Garnedd Uchaf, Foel Fras, Drum and Pen y Castell, with CA31 to complete the circle.

NE Carneddau circular (CA H8)

Few people sample the solitude of the N Carneddau and the NE corner is the most neglected of all. Here is an unusual tour that brings it into the fold. You begin by climbing Tal-y-fan from Cae Coch (CA46). Thereafter the route is down to the head of Bwlch y Ddeufaen (CA45); up the opposite side of the pass to Drum (CA29); down Drum's SE ridge to Pen y Castell and then on to the roadhead at Bwlch-y-gaer (CA30). This leaves you with three miles of country lanes to get back to Cae Coch. Not full of high drama, but worth considering if you are looking for a quieter day or something different. (The road work could be reduced by steering a direct course from Pen y Castell to Cae Coch over Penygadair, provided you are prepared to put up with some damp, trackless and rather scrappy terrain en-route.)

Penyrhelgi-du/Pen Llithrig-y-wrach (CA H9)

A combination of Penyrhelgi-du via Ffynnon Llugwy (CA8) with a descent from Pen Llithrig-y-wrach on CA11 to Tal-y-braich, gives an easy but satisfying hike suitable for a shorter day. The descent and ascent into Bwlch Trimarchog is on easy grass and presents no problems apart from the 600ft height loss that has to be regained.

Creigiau Gleision/Pen Llithrig-y-wrach (CA H10)

These two peaks of very contrasting characters (one undulating, wreathed in heather and full of secrets; the other rounded, grassy and bare) feature in this high-level round of Llyn Cowlyd. The walk is based on Capel Curig and is essentially a combination of CA39 and CA43 on Creigiau Gleision plus an extra high-level section in the middle.

Assuming you start on CA39 and return along Llyn Cowlyd, the addition comes near the beginning of the return walk along Cowlyd's W shoreline. Look out for a place where a cluster of three trees to the L of the track are quickly followed by two more on the other side. There you will see a wall struggling up the hillside R, through a break in the otherwise steep and rocky slopes. Follow this to gain

Pen Llithrig-y-wrach's N ridge and hence the summit. The way home is then down the SE ridge to the bridge over the leat at 717609, and so via Bronheulog back to Capel Curig (CA12).

LOWER-LEVEL WALKS/EASIER DAYS
Llyn Crafnant (CA L1)

Snuggling beneath the colourful slopes of Creigiau Gleision, Crafnant is one of the prettiest lakes in Wales, its tranquillity and beauty unruffled by the narrow road along its E shoreline. A rustic café offers refreshments and rowing boats for hire in summer. The walk across the foothills from Capel Curig is easy and delightful (see CA39/40). You can also walk around the lake, though it is wet in places, or combine it with a tramp to neighbouring Llyn Geirionydd along footpaths marked on the 1:25,000 map.

Aber Falls (CA L2)

Aber Falls, the highest in Snowdonia, have always been a popular attraction, and justifiably so. In full spate the foaming white of the central downpour, flanked by countless scurrying rivulets, crashes with a mighty roar in the depths below. Spray billows far and wide, churning the otherwise peaceful Afon Rhaeadr-fawr into a mass of surging, twisting vortices as it begins its journey to the sea. What a contrast to the aura of calm cast by the engirdling hills as you stroll up to the falls through the meadows and woods from Bont Newydd! It is hard to believe that you are never more than two miles from a trunk road (CA21 refers).

Afon Anafon (CA L3)

A pleasant but lazy day can be spent sauntering beside the murmuring cascades of the Anafon with picnic, paddling and bathing opportunities galore (see CA27).

Llyn Cowlyd (CA L4)

Llyn Cowlyd maintains an air of austerity even on the brightest of days. Perhaps it is the openness of the valley to the N; or maybe it's because Creigiau Gleision exhibits its more forbidding W slopes. Whatever the reason Cowlyd is still a candidate for an easy day, although best kept for cool bracing weather (see CA12/43).

Caseg Valley (CA L5)

The Caseg Valley is dull at first, despite the enveloping hills, but this is a walk that improves the further you go. Foel Grach and Yr Elen gradually seem to coalesce leaving only the narrowest of defiles, backed by Carnedd Llewelyn, to penetrate the Carneddau's inner sanctum. There is no hint of the secretive twisty cwm that reaches its climax in Ffynnon Caseg.

Start where the tarmacked road ends at 639663 and a couple of cars can be parked. Carry on along a stony farm track to a gate at 639665. ((CA36) for Gyrn Wigau breaks away here.) Turn R along a green path which keeps above, but roughly parallel to, the Afon Caseg. This fizzles out as the hills converge and it is then best to follow the stream into the 'defile', whereupon a shadowy path reappears to take you up to the lake. The mountainly atmosphere grows increasingly overpowering until, at long last, the harsh severity of the slopes that bear down on either side finally dissolves in the clear sparkle of the lake.

Llafar Valley (CA L6)

It is hard to envisage a trail that leads into the wild as effortlessly as this. So gentle is the rise that I was amazed, on consulting the map, to find that the gain in height from Gerlan to Llech Du is nearly 900ft. However there is no denying the rewards, the rugged splendour of pinnacle and crag being matched only by the tranquillity of a lonely cwm and the happy chortle of the brook (see CA4).

Cwm Eigiau (CA L7)

This lonely cwm is well off the beaten track and ideal for a quiet picnic beneath the towering crags of Craig yr Ysfa (see CA10).

Llynnau Dulyn/Melynllyn (CA L8)

An easy walk into lonesome broken country, with the added advantage of a firm stony track all the way and a brace of sparkling lakes to relax by at the end (see CA23).

THE CWMDEUDDWR HILLS
OS map 1:50,000 - Sheets 147

Peaks	Height (ft)	Map Ref	Page
Drygarn Fawr	2103	863584	231
Gorllwyn	2011	918591	235
Bryn Garw*	2005	798771	237

* shown as Pen y Garn on the most recent maps.

Mountain Lakes

Carw	1750	856612
Cerrigllwydion Isaf	1650	844700
Cerrigllwydion Uchaf	1650	840693
Du	1755	800698
Egnant	1400	793670
Fyrddon Fach	1755	797701
Fyrddon Fawr	1755	800707
Gwngu	1450	839729
Gynon	1400	800647
Hir	1400	789676
Isaf	1600	803758
Nameless	1850	926603
Nameless	1800	809765
Nameless	1400	789669
Nameless	1350	779678
Teifi	1350	785675
Uchaf	1625	803762
Y Figyn	1600	812704
Y Gorlan	1400	787669

Note:

As the number of 2000 footers is so small in relation to the large expanse of the Cwmdeuddwr hills I have included more lakes than is strictly justified by my self-imposed limitation for lakes to be in the immediate vicinity of their mountain group. This gives the opportunity to include more walks in this largely unknown region.

THE CWMDEUDDWR HILLS

Nowhere else in Wales is quite like the Cwmdeuddwr hills. There are no soaring heights, no shapely lines, no precipices, few crags, in fact precious little rock of any kind at all. No walls cross the fells. Even the lakes are remote from the higher ground where the scene is one of windswept grassland stretching uninterruptedly to far horizons.

Yet despite a lack of the more obvious mountainly attributes, the Cwmdeuddwr hills have a strange ethereal charm that is none the less real for being at once ephemeral and enigmatic. One key to the puzzle is the quirk of geography whereby the uplands are all of similar height. It is as if Nature, in the act of creating what could have been one of the most extensive mountain ranges in the principality, tired of her efforts and sliced off the tops, leaving behind a vast and empty highland plateau.

It is this 'toplessness' that enables you to enjoy the uncluttered views that are such a delight of the Cwmdeuddwr hills. The narrowness of the valleys also helps. As you walk the high ground between Drygarn Fawr and Gorllwyn try picking out the reservoirs that are so prominent on the map. It is not easy. You will be lucky to get more than the odd tantalising glimpse as the eye sweeps across and on to the distant horizon. Thus, lacking the attractions of peaks and cols and crags, the Cwmdeuddwr hills bewitch you instead with vast panoramas and the freedom to roam (illusory though it may be) a lofty plateau, from where the eye is drawn down to the clefts that alone reveal the all but hidden valleys.

In a strange way it is reminiscent of sailing at sea - the smooth horizons; the softly undulating waves of hills, all of similar height, their troughs hidden; the level going, remoteness and solitude (for you will be unlikely to meet fellow walkers). Even the jolting from the giant grassy tussocks that have to be crossed from time to time evokes the rocking of a choppy sea!

Cwmdeuddwr is Welsh for 'Valley of the Two Waters', the

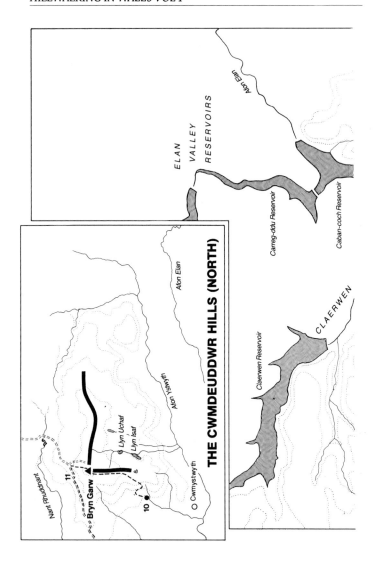

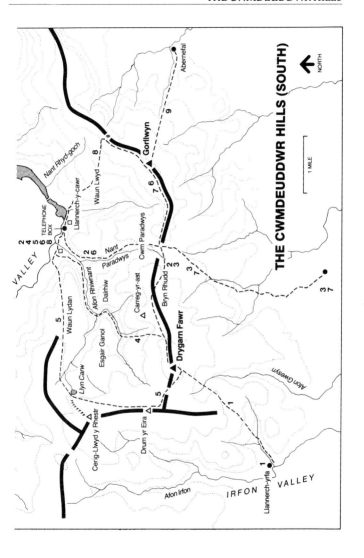

THE CWMDEUDDWR HILLS (SOUTH)

NORTH

1 MILE

*Looking SW from the trig point on Drygarn Fawr, with Cwm Gwesyn
in the middle-distance and the S Wales peaks on the skyline*

waters in question being the Ystwyth (source 855782) and the Elan
(source 819736) which, though they rise within a few miles of one
another and follow parallel courses for a time, flow in opposite
directions. The hills that bear this name lie mostly to the S, in a
quadrilateral bounded W by the upper reaches of the Afon Teifi (or
the B4343), S by the A482 and A483, and E by the Wye Valley - a vast
area. Nowhere else in Wales is there so large an expanse of empty
wilderness or such a sustained concentration of height. What a long
chapter this would be if 500m were the qualifying height for a peak
rather than 2000ft!

Drygarn Fawr and Gorllwyn are the only 2000 footers in this
area, and even then neither is more than a minor blip in the rambling
swell of bleak, shaggy moorland all around. Yet care is needed.
Tracks are few and far between, and those that do exist have a
distressing habit of petering out just when you least expect it. A
watchful eye is called for - a very watchful eye - because to walk
trackless here is no more fun than in the Rhinogs. The problem
arises from the grassy tussocks already referred to. A brilliant lush
green, they lie in wait all around the two main peaks and in the
absence of some sort of path (even a sheep track is like manna from
Heaven) soon reduce walking to a tiring, jolty tedium. Be warned!
Not even the best navigation in the world will save you from times
when you rue the very day you ever set foot on these demanding
hills.

The remaining peak, Bryn Garw, lies N of the two rivers in a remote region more akin to Plynlimon than Cwmdeuddwr. It is a nondescript area of coarse grass, man-made forests and peat hags, with little appeal except for out-and-out peak-baggers and lovers of solitude.

The Cwmdeuddwr hills are no place to be in mist. Sketchy tracks, virtually non existent landmarks, and spells of tussock-bashing or manoeuvring through peat hags make it hard to judge distance and easy to get lost. Individually the tops of the Cwmdeuddwr hills give meagre reward, and it is only in fair weather when enjoyed as part of the rolling open landscapes that surround them that their special magic comes alive, to seduce and enchant.

DRYGARN FAWR

Drygarn Fawr is the crowning height of the Cwmdeuddwr hills. A very pleasant place it is too; a long wedge-shaped oasis of springy heather and rocky knobs adrift in a sea of comfortless, tussocky grass. Its two enormous beehive cairns (W top being the higher) are a landmark for miles around when silhouetted on the skyline. Yet despite its pre-eminent position it is a solitary spot for who has heard of Cwmdeuddwr?

The view is the finest of any in the Cwmdeuddwr hills despite the dull rise of Drum yr Eira blocking the outlook W and its sister peak, Gorllwyn, monopolising the E skyline. N and S the eye can still roam on the grand scale, the vista extending from Bryn Garw and the Plynlimon hills in the N to the noble profile of the Black Mountains, the Brecon Beacons, Fforest Fawr and Mynydd Du in the S.

Should you ever be stranded in mist, the best course is either SW for the Irfon Valley or E for Cwm Paradwys, though in the latter case the all-pervading tussocks will test your patience and stamina to the full.

Irfon Valley route (CR1)

The enjoyment starts even before you lace your boots because you will surely be reminded of a Scottish glen as you drive up the picturesque Irfon Valley. Park near Llannerch-yrfa, 835557, where the valley opens out, and take the stony track by the stream that climbs through the forest. It twists and turns as all forest trails seem

Drygarn Fawr summit

to do, but eventually brings you above the tree-line by a gate with open country beyond.

The trail shadows the woods, so leave it here and strike out NE on a worn path through grass - easy walking provided you do not stray and attempt to take on the deep squirmy tussocks that lie in wait on every hand.

A giant beehive cairn comes into view and for a moment the top looks tantalisingly near. An illusion! There is still a way to go, including a small depression where you jump the infant Afon Gwesyn. Gradually grass gives way to scattered outcrops, bilberries and the occasional peat hag, and you can now see that Drygarn Fawr actually boasts two large beehive cairns, the more E capped with a white crown and a good place for lunch!

Cwm Paradwys N route (CR2)

Park near the telephone box at 901617. Cross the bridge and just before the farm at Llannerch-y-cawr follow the road round as it doubles back on itself W. However leave it almost at once, through a gate, to join a dirt track L. This climbs for almost a mile, high above Nant Paradwys, when it suddenly make a U-turn. Abandon it there and follow a faint track S into Cwm Paradwys. This gradually becomes more distinct as it rises, well to the E of the stream, to the shallow col on the skyline.

The cairns of both Drygarn Fawr and Gorllwyn are visible from the col, but the pièce de résistance is S; a glowing mosaic of pastures

Looking N up the Irfon Valley

and woodland all framed by the S Wales foothills. It is as well to rest a while because hard work lies ahead with little in the way of tracks. The best plan is to scrabble up the slopes towards Bryn Rhudd and then to skirt just S of the rocky knuckle of Carreg-yr-ast where, near some shallow peat hags, a track at last appears and all is well.

Alternatively (CR2, 1) stay with the dirt track until it ends high on the hillside above Llanerch-y-cawr. Then continue S to an ancient cairn (with a tree growing out of it!) way above Cwm Paradwys at 897599, from where you can drop down to the path in the cwm as before.

Cwm Paradwys S route (CR3)

Follow a mature green path into the forest at 888541. Where several tracks converge at a wire fence you stay with the fence L down a wide avenue with Drygarn Fawr's twin cairns peeping over the trees. Ignore the first forest road off R but turn down the second almost immediately afterwards, 881553. Gorllwyn is now visible NE while half-L is the deep-cut gill of Criegiau Duon. Where the road ends in a turning-circle continue over a frail log bridge and leave the forest through a gate at 883565, close by the Nant Gewyn. Lush, unbounded grassland lies ahead. Cross it on 30 to an ancient cairn at 889578. A short hike on 40 then leads into Cwm Paradwys and CR2 or 6.

For a more rustic alternative (CR3, 1) follow a path that zig-zags up through the forest behind the chapel at 893538. Cross the wide forest road at the top of the rise and descend into the lonely valley beyond, leaving it at the derelict farmstead of Pen-cae, 893556, where a path cleaves the bracken-clad hillside ahead to join CR3 by the cairn at 889578.

Rhiwnant Valley route (CR4)

Cwm Rhiwnant is a joy; an enchanting finger of crag-hung slopes and tiny gorges, swathed in bracken and heather, dotted with rowan trees and soothed by the music of a tumbling brook. Intimate and secluded, it burrows to the very heart of the empty grassland bordering Drygarn Fawr yet is a world unto itself; an enclave of fertility and peace amidst the barren yellows of the surrounding fells.

Follow CR2 until the stream R divides near a sprightly copse at 891610. Cross the stream and join a long since abandoned miners' track, green and firm, that heads up-valley W. Stay with the higher arm where the track splits above some spoil heaps, but leave it and drop down to a little path by the stream just as it begins to swing SW above a little ravine. The valley soon opens out again whereupon a tiny tarn heralds one of the highlights of the day - a mermaid's pool fed by the stream tumbling down from distant Llyn Carw. On a hot summer's day the temptation to linger in the shade of the rowans that gild this idyllic spot is well night irresistible. (The miners' track, meanwhile, continues high above the valley, finally ending near the old mine-workings at 875607. These are an easy scramble up from the pool and so offer an alternative routing for the more adventurous.)

Back to the main walk. Follow the stream through another 'gorge' that widens out to a shallow valley on a bearing of 240. The track has switched to the S bank now. After half a mile, at 872598 where the Rhiwnant divides, leave it and follow a faint track beside a tributary L until it peters out. Drygarn Fawr looks deceptively near R, but the price of a direct approach is horrendous tussocks and no path. Best avoided! Instead bear E of S - only tame tussocks this way - for level ground and a civilised track skirting just S of the rocky knoll of Carreg-yr-ast. Drygarn Fawr is then a simple 20-minute walk away.

The entrance to Cwm Rhiwnant from just above where
CR4 crosses the stream

Cerig-llwyd y Rhestr route (CR5)

Leave W top on 310, having first psyched yourself up for a rough stomp across virgin moor - peat hags, tussocks, bog, the lot! Eventually you meet a path sheltering in the dip just E of the shallow swell of Cerig-llwyd y Rhestr. This brings you to Llyn Carw, surely the squarest lake in Wales! Keep going to a sheepfold at 860617, in a little hollow by a stream. Next proceed E across the breast of Waun Lydan along a track that obligingly does not fade until you are safely descending the slopes above the farmstead of Rhiwnant. A descent beside the stream that feeds the mermaid's pool at 877605 also looks tempting from the map. I did it once - never again! No hint of a track, just tussocks and tussocks and tussocks.

GORLLWYN

Gorllwyn has few pretensions. It crowns a vast area of billowy moorland, overtopping its surroundings by a mere 200ft and sprawling aimlessly. For all that it is a jolly place with soft heather for a bed and heartwarming views of the Wye and Irfon valleys. From the map it looks tempting to combine Gorllwyn with Drygarn Fawr. Fine walk though that is, it is harder than it looks owing to the tussocky terrain en-route. So, unless you already know what you

The Caban Coch reservoir from the foot of Waun Lwyd; the entrance to Cwm Paradwys can just be seen in the middle distance

are letting yourself in for, it is wise to start by tackling Gorllwyn on its own.

In mist Gorllwyn is a navigator's nightmare. The best way off is SW for about quarter of a mile before bearing W for Cwm Paradwys and CR2. This slightly circuitous routing avoids the more difficult ground.

Cwm Paradwys N route (CR6)

Follow CR2 to the col at the head of Cwm Paradwys. Strike out E, aiming to make the final approach from the SW. In this way you will encounter fewer tussocks than a more direct N course entails. Alternatively a line of boundary stones crosses the high ground with a faint path nearby linking them together. Either way the nearer you get to Gorllwyn the easier the going becomes, with jolty tussocks gradually succumbing to cushions of heather and succulent bilberries.

Cwm Paradwys S route (CR7) See CR3.

Waun Lwyd route (CR8)

From Gorllwyn aim for the tarn at 926603. This is normally visible from the more N of Gorllwyn's two cairns; in murky conditions take a bearing of 40. Otherwise follow the boundary stones referred to in CR6. (They continue to the tarn and beyond.)

From the tarn proceed NW over the breast of Waun Lwyd and hope to pick up one of the several sheep tracks that lead down to the valley. The stream-beds either side are rough and enclosed and best avoided. However, if you should stray towards Nant Rhyd-goch look out for wild orchids growing in the fields just beyond the N tip of the copse at 915617. A farm track gives a delightful walk back along the shores of Caban Coch to Llannerch-y-cawr.

Abernefal route (CR9)

Descents E and SE of Gorllwyn are useful to have in the repertoire if you ever plan a traverse from the Irfon Valley over both Drygarn Fawr and Gorllwyn. The simplest route leaves the cairn on 105, aiming for the cottage at Abernefal, 949584; a lovely, relaxing end to a day.

BRYN GARW

It would be easy to dismiss Bryn Garw as dull, of interest only to dedicated peak-baggers. That would be unfair, for if your ascent includes a brief foray to the wild Rhuddnant Valley (by combining CR10 and 11 for example), an enjoyable day can be had in remote country that seldom resounds to the walkers' tread.

S ridge route (CR10)

Go through the rusty gate at 793754 (with ingenuity a few cars can be parked nearby) and follow a damp grassy lane through a copse and past a derelict cottage. Continue through a second rusty gate and then turn R and pull up to a stony road inclining SE up the hillside. This ends at a gate. Go through this and then walk on a bearing of 40, passing through more gates. There are fragments of a path but the top is soon in evidence N. It is then simply a matter of navigating by eye, dodging intermittent splodges of marsh.

The view from the top is wild and spacious. W a mesh of green, dappled foothills drifting to the sea; S countless waves of the

Cwmdeuddwr hills; E a waste of moors and peat-hags worthy of Bleaklow itself. To complete the circle stroll N from the cairn, through a fence. You are met by an epic of startling splendour and profound silence. The heavily wooded slopes of Rhuddnant, riddled with crags, convey an aura of mystery and power that reaches its headiest climax when trails of mist lend scale to the scene. How different it is on a sunny day with lonely Llynoedd Ieuan glittering from high on the tops beyond!

If you had followed the lane beyond the second rusty gate you would have come to two grey sheds where the stony road mentioned earlier begins, as does a bulldozed road. This gives an alternative line of ascent (CR10, 1). Simply follow it N to NE for about one and a half miles (avoiding side-shoots) until it turns sharply R. A short climb L by a fence then leads straight to the trig point. Not much excitement, but trustworthy in mist.

For a new route home (CR10, 2) drop down and walk E along the last vestiges of the bulldozed track. Where it ends turn R down the crest of a minor ridge. There is no path but the way is obvious on easy grass, and if you trend slightly E you can visit Llynnau Uchaf and Isaf and their nameless satellite, their shores a dazzle of cottony white in summer.

The forest route (CR11)

Start from the picnic site at 765756, near the arch erected in 1810 to mark George III's Golden Jubilee. Use the forest trails to emerge on Bryn Garw's N slopes around 801776 with a final grassy rise to the cairn.

HIGH-LEVEL WALKS

If I had to recommend just one walk in the Cwmdeuddwr hills, I would be hard pressed to choose between the two listed below. The circular is easier logistically and includes the delectable Rhiwnant Valley. The traverse lumbers you with a transport problem but, in exchange for this and the loss of Rhiwnant, includes the Irfon Valley and an eventide return along the leafy lanes round Abernefal.

Both expeditions are more demanding than you might think because, however expert you may be at route-finding, you will be lucky if you do not suffer at least a couple of spells of energy-sapping tussock-bashing. This is worst between peaks so let me repeat two tips to minimise the agony. First, when leaving Drygarn Fawr for Gorllwyn, remember that the best route is NE towards Carreg-yr-ast. Tracks that head more directly E soon leave you stranded (see CR1). Secondly, follow the track in Cwm Paradwys up to the head of the cwm before striking out for Gorllwyn (see CR6).

Drygarn Fawr/Gorllwyn circular (CR H1)

This combines the Rhiwnant Valley route to Drygarn Fawr (CR4) with the Waun Lwyd route from Gorllwyn (CR8) to bring you back home again.

Drygarn Fawr/Gorllwyn traverse (CR H2)

This pairs the Irfon Valley route to Drygarn Fawr (CR1) with the Abernefal route back from Gorllwyn (CR9).

LOWER-LEVEL WALKS
Llynnau Cerrigllwydion (CR L1)

The 'Ancient' road that takes to the fells at 897716 provides an ideal introduction to the Cwmdeuddwr hills. Gently graded and well-defined for the most part, it strikes directly to the heart of some of the loneliest moors in Wales. A solitary white cairn at 872710, Drygarn Fawr's twin cairns on the skyline, the Plynlimon hills N - these are the sole sights early on. Later they are to be joined by the prominent spiky top of spot height 546 and, if you are lucky, the glitter of Llyn Cerrigllwydion Isaf peeping through the hills. As ever there are rounded green hills and still more rounded green hills, as far as the eye can see; Cwmdeuddwr's staple diet!

The road fades in bog at a col at 848691 but soon reappears. You could stay with it and link up with CR L2 near Claerwen, but that means a very long day or transport to meet you. Otherwise pull up to spot height 546 and walk along its tiny rocky ridge - the only rock of the day - to view the two Cerrigllwydion lakes and the shuttered cabin at 842692 that shares their lonely vigil.

NW Lakes (CR L2)

The cluster of lakes NW of the Cwmdeuddwr hills offers a relaxing half-day in country that seldom sees a soul save the local shepherds. Leave the B4343 at Ffair-rhos and drive up a minor road until it degenerates into a Land-Rover track at about 795680 where you park.

You are in a shallow valley with higher ground either side. Stay with the track, bearing L almost at once, and after quarter of a mile where it turns sharp R, strike out N over easy grass. Cross the Afon Claerddu, keeping the derelict farm of the same name L, and work up bilberry-clad slopes to Llyn Du. Next freelance round Llynnau Fyrddon Fawr and Fyrddon Fach and on to the diminutive Llyn y Figyn a mile away E. Committed 'Llyn-baggers' could even march NE to Llyn Gwngu, using the high ground over Domen Milwyn and Geifas to avoid wet feet. A long tiring grind of little interest.

Aim next for the tip of the reservoir, dodging peat-hags as you go and trending R towards the end to rejoin the Land-Rover track you left earlier. Just before the farm at Claerwen recross the Afon Claerddu and climb the 'ridge' to the S. Follow the crest as far as the fancy takes you and then make your way through the Teifi lakes back to the road and your car.

EASIER DAYS
Rhiwnant Valley (CR E1)

Park by the telephone box at Llanerch-y-cawr, 901616, and follow CR4 into the Rhiwnant Valley. Within the hour you should be well and truly ensconced in one of Wales' most secluded vales. The best stretch is around 877606 where the Rhiwnant flows N for a while and is joined by a little stream from Llyn Carw. There is heather and bracken to laze in, the chatter of falls to lull you and a mermaid's pool to picnic by. The mildly energetic can explore the Rhiwnant 'gorge' just beyond, while a quick climb above the pool is rewarded with more enchanting falls and pools. If you did that you might make a high-level return along the miners' track as outlined in CR4. All the ingredients for a relaxing day.

Llyn Gynon (CR E2)

Not many walks in the Welsh hills take in old abbeys en-route; here is one that does. Drive down the road S of Pontrhydfendigaid, 730665, to Strata Florida. The abbey is of Norman origins, parts of it probably dating back to around 1160, and a number of Welsh princes are reputed to have been buried in its grounds. It was for many years a leading cultural centre and one of the greatest of Welsh medieval poets, Dafydd ap Gwilym is also buried there.

Having inspected the ruins, continue to the farmstead of Tyncwm, 771656, where the road ends and a couple of cars can be parked. Then it is boots on for a delightful tramp into the fastness of Cwm Mwyro beneath an awning of trees. This is a little gem where Nature has blended a wooded hillside, lightly flecked with rock and bracken, into a colourful patchwork of marshland and pasture. What a contrast Llyn Gynon is - the embodiment of windswept desolation with endless waves of equally bleak hills beyond! Dibyn Du's W ridge offers an alternative way back.

Cedni Valley (CR E3)

The Cedni Valley is full of surprises as it worms its way into the hills; and it's beautiful too. The lines of forestry plantations - usually so harsh - are tempered by stretches of open hillside mottled with bracken. Scattered woodlands fringe the chattering stream. Green pastures flecked with buttercups and foxgloves blend with shady glades while moss-capped relics of ancient walls bear witness to the resurgence of Nature.

Park near 926522. Follow a farm road, and the stony path into which it degenerates, past the farms of Cefn-hafdref and Gilwern and continue on up-valley. The path E of the stream peters out short of Carregronw at 895548, so cross the bridge at 905536 (before the deserted homestead of Llednant). You now have a path all the way to Pen-cae where open country lies ahead and CR3 carries on.

The Dovey Hills

THE DOVEY HILLS
OS maps 1:25,000 - Sheet 23 1:50,000 - Sheets 124

Peaks	Height (ft)	Map Ref	Page
Maesglasau	2213	823152	248
Waun-oer	2197	785148	243
Cribin	2132	794153	246
Mynydd Ceiswyn	1983	772139	245
Mynydd y Waun	1861	766133	245
Mountain Lakes			
Foel Dinas	1400	850146	

THE DOVEY HILLS

Few of the travellers who cross Bwlch Oerddrws every day en-route to Dolgellau, Cader Idris and all points W cast more than a passing glance at the shapely green hills that bear down from the S. Walkers may pause to admire the silver thread of the Maesglasau Falls or marvel at the solitudes of Cwm Cerist, thrusting so deeply into the heart of the hills, but are unlikely to don their boots. As the wisp-like tracks on the tops soon reveals, these are forgotten hills.

Three moorland peaks straddle the band of high ground that stretches from Dinas Mawddwy in the E to Craig y Llam and the towering bastions of Cader Idris in the W. In between lies a succession of high heathery plateaux linked by narrow necks and brooding crags that create the illusion of a broken ridge. To the S the land falls away in a convoluted network of twisting ridges and steep-sided cwms that could so easily have been a fellwalker's delight, similar to the Howgills. But no chance today as dense forest cloaks the land.

Luckily Maesglasau and Cribin save their most rugged faces for the N where Nature is still supreme. This is where you will find the

Cwm Cerist; Craig Portas directly ahead, Cribin Fawr R

best walking and the finest cwms. Cwm Maesglasau is rustic and serene while Cwm Cerist is barren, stern, but mightily impressive nonetheless. Waun-oer, the third top, is more retiring and best climbed from Craig y Llam in the W.

Once launched there is little in the crisp heather to break your rhythm and a network of shy trails is never far away to help you along. Despite the modest heights the views have an ethereal charm. Tarrens, Cader Idris, Rhinogs, Arenigs, Arans, Plynlimon, Snowdonia, the Mawddach Estuary, the sea: all combine in one of those mid-Wales pageants of loveliness where hills and dales ripple away in a glorious mosaic of yellows and browns, greens and blues.

WAUN-OER

I would not recommend Waun-oer's long SW ridge on a dull day when the tops are hidden in mist. Not unless you like gazing at barren moorland with one false crest following another in seemingly endless progression! How different it is on a sunny day with the massive splendour of Cader Idris commanding the Mawddach Estuary and the flat-topped Dovey hills urging you on above a placid sea of forest.

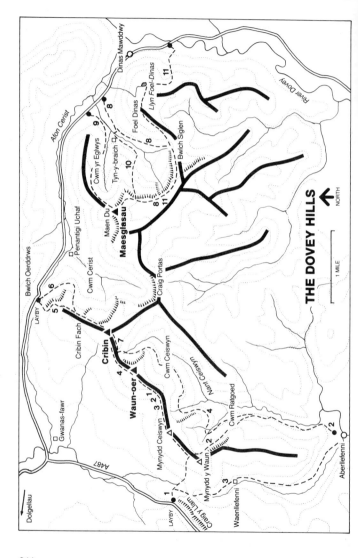

THE DOVEY HILLS

Having claimed Waun-oer it would be a pity not to carry on along the ridge as in DY H1. The descent to the col between Waun-oer and Cribin is a steep, shaly slither but thereafter the going could hardly be better; similarly with the views. Sadly change is in the air. Even as I write permission is being sought to erect a 60m radio mast complete with access road and outbuildings. Where will it all end?

Craig y Llam route (DY1)

A footpath sign at 757138, near the lay-by at the top of Bwlch Llyn-bach, points the way up a grey slaty path. This soon leaves the pass behind and veers SE before crossing a bulldozed trail that comes up from Aberllefenni. A grassy slope then looms ahead. It looks a bit of a grind - and it is! There is a path of sorts although it is by no means obvious (very often it doubles up as a watercourse), and the best tip is to keep about 300yds R of a decrepit old wall that eventually loses itself in some crags. You will not be sorry when you at last gain the ridge at 768135 where twin stiles cross the fence marking the forest boundary, a short distance from the hump of Mynydd y Waun. The rest is plain sailing, staying with the fence all the way and crossing the minor height of Mynydd Ceiswyn en-route.

Cwm Ratgoed Forest route (DY2)

For a day with a difference try climbing Waun-oer from Aberllefenni, using this for the outward half and DY3 for the return. A grassy lane leaves the road at 772100 near the junction at Aberllefenni and disappears into the depths of the forest beside a wall almost as mossy and green with age as the trail itself. Keep R and slightly downhill where the path forks by a slate tip, then L as you emerge from the woods onto a stony forest road with lonely Cwm Ratgoed below R. After roughly half a mile you will see three excavated cavities with their attendant spoil heaps on the hillside across the valley; like the three bears one is small, one medium and one large. This is your signal to look out for a yellow arrow at 777120 that points the way up a narrow trail which leaves the road to climb the wooded slopes L.

After crossing another forest road the trail slowly curves beneath the heather-clad cliffs of Mynydd y Waun with the long, winding ridge of Waun-oer filling the skyline ahead and countless hillocks, cloaked in the myriad greens of the forest, stretching as far as the eye can see. You join the ridge by the two stiles at 768135 to finish as in DY1.

Forest walks are a gamble. They are often dull and boring, not to say annoying at times as trails disappear or are ignored by the map. Suffice it to say that this walk is on a different plane. It is a beauty with plenty of interest and none of the closed-in feeling so many forest walks convey.

Waenllefenni route (DY3)

For a relaxing descent follow DY1 in reverse to the bulldozed trail at 760138. This merges into a stony farm track and then a country road to give a delightful and easy way back to Aberllefenni, the valley views being quite exquisite with more than a hint of Switzerland about them. A lovely way to end a day.

Cwm Ceiswyn route (DY4)

Begin as for DY2 but this time stay with the forest road at 777120 and only leave it at 790150, shortly before it terminates and just after passing beneath the harsh-looking crags of Waun-oer. A short scramble up to the col L, followed by a steep climb beside a fence on a badly eroded track that is slippery when wet, is then all that remains. The winding of the forest road makes this a very long approach and it would be wrong to pretend that the upper reaches of the cwm, with their restricted views and regimented plantations, are anything but monotonous.

CRIBIN

The map indicates both a Cribin Fach and a Cribin Fawr. Cribin Fach, at 798158, is easily dismissed, being merely an outcrop on the mountain's crag-studded N nose that looms over Bwlch Oerddrws. Cribin Fawr is sterner stuff. Its highest point, at 801151, is excitingly poised at the angle of a line of gaunt, damp, black cliffs that frown down upon the green wilderness of Cwm Cerist. However, despite its dominating presence and the epithet 'Fawr', it is not the highest ground. That is half a mile away at 794153 where a boundary stone laying flat on its back is the sole landmark in the otherwise ..distinguished fells.

Cribin Fawr from Bwlch Oerddrws

N spur variant 1 (DY5)

There are two tracks which attack Cribin from the N, both starting from a lay-by and ladder-stile off the A470 at 803170 near the top of Bwlch Oerddrws. However, these two approaches are so different in character that I shall treat them as separate routes. The first, an old quarry track still banked in places, twists up the boulder-strewn slopes on 220 until it reaches more level and open ground beside a fence that has also climbed up from the parking area - though not quite so warily. It is important to locate this spot accurately in descent, so I erected a small cairn the last time I was there.

It is now an easy but dullish tramp across the moors to the horizontal 1861 boundary marker that is Cribin's only adornment. The fence makes route-finding skills quite redundant. On the way DY6 comes in from the L, while just before the disused Cloddfa Gwanas Quarry another path joins you R. This is the culmination of a long, gradual approach from the A470 at 770168 that begins with a track leading to Gwanas-fawr Farm (DY5, 1). Beyond Cribin the fence leads down to a minor col where there is a ladder-stile followed by a short, sharp pull up to Waun-oer.

N spur variant 2 (DY6)

After a slightly toilsome start this is the more charismatic of the two N approaches. From the lay-by look out for a track that crosses the hillside on 150. There are actually two such tracks but the higher one, which is the one you want (the lower one gives up the ghost after a while), is all but hidden from the road. Never mind. Make for the track you can see and then after a few minutes scramble up the slope to the higher one, a narrow stony trail that just manages to cling to the hillside. Spiky crags aloft, and vehicles like toys in the pass below, soon create an aura which reminded me of Honister the last time I was there.

The best is held back until the track - a delightful green path by now - swings round Cribin's E spur to reveal a scene of wild open splendour. On display are the empty green amphitheatre of Cwm Cerist, the huge dome of Maesglasau atop the plunging screes of Craig Rhiw-erch, the dark angry face of Craig Portas to the S and the shattered black-green cliffs carrying the rocky crown of Cribin Fawr. You will have chances aplenty to savour this epic scene for the way up to the fence on the skyline (where you join DY5) is easy on both wind and limb.

An alternative start (DY6, 1) can be made from 815164. Take the upper of two paths that leave the A470; not the one that goes to Penantigi Uchaf Farm. Leave it after crossing a stream and pull up the hillside to meet the green path at 806161.

Cwm Ceiswyn route (DY7)
Follow DY4 to the col at 790151 and then turn R for a short easy climb beside the fence.

MAESGLASAU
Maesglasau is the highest and most interesting of the three Dovey hills. It is a vast rambling plateau of billowy moorland, rather like Kinder Scout in Derbyshire or Waun-rydd in the Beacons. To the NE the plateau is rimmed by a band of fearsome black cliffs, down which plunge the spectacular Maesglasau Falls. On second thoughts, 'plateau' is too tidy a word. The stream that feeds the falls creates such a large depression that the overall effect is rather like a cake that has sunk in the middle because it was taken out of the oven too quickly!

A network of pebbly, peaty tracks - mostly along the edges - makes for easy walking, but even if you leave the tracks and strike out on your own it is still crisp and pleasant underfoot. The highest ground lies on a little jutting promontory, Maen Du, facing the

Arans. Away W Cribin fills the skyline while on a sunny day you can just catch the sparkle of Llyn Foel Dinas in the E. No cairn marks the top. The only sign of civilisation is a wire fence. Otherwise you are alone in a bouncy wilderness of mosses, heathers and bilberries. It is best avoided in mist unless you are accompanied by a companion who has been there before.

Cwm Maesglasau route (DY8)

Stimulating though it can be to have your objective in sight right from the moment you lace your boots, there is no denying that it can also be rather daunting. For example when you march down the lane that leaves the A470 at 848154 towards Ty'n-y-braich Farm, Maesglasau soars aloft with intimidating vigour - a great wedge completely dominating the sylvan depths below! Luckily its conquest is nothing like as gruelling as it appears, which is just as well because no one should be denied what is arguably the best tramp in the region.

The vale is Arcadian in its freshness and innocence. Hemmed in by Maesglasau and its acolytes on three sides, it is no time at all before the Arans close the circle behind you to create a rustic hinterland. Young woods mingle with mellowed pastures while twisted old trunks fringe a sparkling brook. Purple screes and bands of golden bracken flow unhindered from heights buttressed by the awesome crags of Craig Maesglasau and ribboned by the white plume of the slender falls that tumble to the valley below.

Few directions are needed. Leave the lane at a footpath sign at 841152, just before the road starts to descend to the farm, and bear L through a gate into a field. Thereafter a well-worn path continues all the way to the top, curling above the crags near Bwlch Siglen, passing close by the rocky shelves over which the falls begin their plunge, then swathing through the luxuriant heather of the summit plateau round the edge to the cairnless top.

A more prosaic start (DY8, 1) can be made from 857150 where a footpath sign by a lay-by invites you to join a path (shown on the map) that passes through some woods prior to crossing the slopes of Ffridd Gulcwm to link up with DY8 near Bwlch Siglen.

Cwm yr Eglwys route (DY9)

This is a good route to take in tandem with DY8. From the top at 822152 follow the fence slightly E of N down steep grass. Next bear half-R for a trail that heads W slightly before, and below, the crest of the ridge marked on the map as Moel Cwm yr Eglwys. You by-pass Ty'n-y-celyn Farm to your L to reach the A470 at 844158. Pleasant, easy going all the way.

E face direct (DY10)

This route is not only direct, it is also relentless, steep, wild and lonely. Ideal for a day in pioneering mood. Proceed down the lane to Ty'n-y-braich as in DY8, but this time continue beyond the farm up the valley. Look out for a slim green track snaking down the fellside R and cross the meadows to join it around 832146. Now comes the challenge. Hot, sweaty work but magnificent too. You feel like a fly as you hug the massive slopes, forgotten to the world, the black pitiless crags but a stone's throw away. When you at last gain the plateau it is roughly midway between the falls and Maen Du.

Foel Dinas route (DY11)

I hold no brief for this route which will mostly be of interest to purists wishing to undertake a complete one-way traverse of the Dovey hills from Craig y Llam in the W. It begins in great style (treating it as a descent) with a rollicking moorland ramble from Maen Du to Bwlch Siglen followed by an equally enjoyable pull-up beside the woods to the minor top of Foel Dinas - soft cushions of mossy grass and heather all the way. It is then all downhill - in more senses than one! A half-mile of rough tangled heather brings you to Llyn Foel Dinas, one of the bleakest sheets of water in Wales. Then comes a drop down to the old quarry workings at 853140 with the devastated remains of the incompletely felled woods L, looking like the grotesque aftermath of some battle.

From the quarry a yellow (erratically) waymarked track that is an extension of an old tramway leads down between the woods L and a huge pile of waste slate R. After 200yds it joins the main forest trail at a hairpin bend at 857140 to bring you down to the A470 by the junction at 859141.

HIGH-LEVEL WALKS
The Dovey hills traverse (DY H1)

Whether you tackle it W to E or E to W the traverse of the Dovey hills guarantees a memorable day. Between Mynydd Ceiswyn and Craig Maesglasau, four miles as the crow flies but considerably more on the ground, the land never falls beneath 1800ft in a fellwalker's extravaganza of wild moors and deeply-scooped cwms, laced with dark N-facing cliffs and linked, here and there, by traces of a twisty ridge. Despite this surfeit of riches the going is always easy, so easy in fact that a moderately strong walker should have no difficulty in avoiding transport problems by covering the ground twice in the day, although in this case starting with a W to E crossing, as described below, is to be preferred.

Climb Waun-oer on DY1. Next follow the fence steeply down to a col that reveals the depressingly barren upper reaches of newly afforested Cwm Ceiswyn. The fence carries on over a ladder-stile to Cribin. Indeed you could follow it all the way to Maesglasau if you wished - or if mist intervenes. However, let me suggest a variation that gives more interesting views. Just before the fence up to Cribin makes a sharp L turn at 794151, bear R to join a track on 120. This curls round to reveal Cwm Ratgoed attractively framed by the distant Tarrens. Soon the fence you abandoned earlier comes in L. Cross it and wander over towards Cribin Fawr, following the edge down through a depression and then up to the heights of Craig Portas where only the white streaks of cascading brooks break the vast green expanse of Cwm Cerist in the depths below.

You are now back with the fence and the next half-hour, over Craig Portas and up the gentle rise to Maesglasau, is the highlight of the day. Memory recalls the Nantlle ridge (NH H1) as the path weaves above the crags on a carpet of mossy turf and heather. Craig Portas itself is the embodiment of grim inaccessibility, a malicious-looking face of shattered rock, seamed with tiny rivulets of scree and cloaked in dark, damp heathers and mosses. Across the vale the craggy triangle of Cribin Fawr looks equally forbidding. Fortunately the longer views more than atone: the Dovey foothills rolling away S in resplendent leafy finery, leading the eye over the Tarrens and Plynlimon to the sunlit sea. N are the Arans, backed by the Arenigs and the pyramid of Dduallt.

Maesglasau can be confusing in mist, but not on this walk. Turn L at the edge of the plateau where, at a ladder-stile, you meet another fence crossing your path. Let that guide you to the top. Now you must choose. To return the way you came, follow the edge to Craig Maesglasau and the falls at 827140. Then strike out due W for a fence that leads NW to the stile you met on the way up and retrace your steps from here. Otherwise you could use any of the four Maesglasau routes down to the road.

Cwm Cerist horseshoe (DY H2)
You can avoid transport problems by taking the Dovey hills traverse in two stages, though both halves entail a spell of road-bashing to get back to your starting point. The first is a grand walk in its own right; up Cribin on DY5 or 6, down off Maesglasau on DY8 or 9.

Cribin/Waun-oer circular (DY H3)
More artificial. Climb Cribin on DY5, 1; come off Waun-oer on DY1.

Aberllefenni horseshoe (DY H4)
Combining two routes on Waun-oer (DY2/3) may not seem very interesting, and if it's red-blooded excitement you're after then maybe this is not for you. However for a quiet varied day off the beaten track (taking in colourful forest trails, an easy ridge and tremendous views of Cader Idris) with an attractive valley to end on, this round takes a lot of beating! Half a day is all you really need, so try it on a rain-shortened day or when the tops stay cocooned in mist and look too daunting.

LOWER-LEVEL WALKS/EASIER DAYS
The easiness of the terrain, and the possibility of relatively high starts from Bwlch Oerddrws, render this section almost superfluous. However here are two suggestions.

Waenllefenni walk (DY L1)
Walk from Aberllefenni to Waenllefenni described in DY3.

Cwm Maesglasau (DY L2)
Explore Cwm Maesglasau using DY8 to get started.

INDEX OF PEAKS

Glasgwm	AN	2557	837195	39
Godor	BN	2224	095307	81
Gorllwyn	CR	2011	918591	235
Gwaen Cerrig-llwydion	BB	2450	055203	147
Gwaun y Llwyni	AN	2248	857205	35
Gyrn Wigau	CA	2109	654676	212
Llechwedd Du	AN	2014	894224	36
Llwytmor	CA	2785	689692	210
Maesglasau	DY	2213	823152	248
Moel Fferna	BN	2066	116398	86
Moel Llyfnant	AG	2464	808352	52
Moel Sych	BN	2713	066319	76
Mynydd Llysiau	BS	2173	207279	102
Mynydd Moel	CI	2804	727137	170
Mynydd Tawr	BN	2234	113324	81
Nameless	BN	2037	089369	84
Pen Allt-mawr	BS	2360	207243	100
Pen Cerrig-calch	BS	2300	217223	97
Pen Llithrig-y-wrach	CA	2622	716623	194
Pen Rhos Dirion	BS	2338	212334	111
Pentwynglas	BS	2115	213257	101
Pen-twyn-mawr	BS	2153	242267	108
Pen y Beacon	BS	2219	244366	118
Pen y Bryn-fforchog	AN	2230	818179	41
Pen y Castell	CA	2043	721688	208
Pen y Fan	BB	2906	012215	137
Penygadair	CI	2928	711131	162
Pen y Gadair Fawr	BS	2624	229287	105
Pen yr Allt-uchaf	AN	2034	871196	35
Penyrhelgi-du	CA	2733	698630	191
Pen yr Ole Wen	CA	3211	656619	186
Post Gwyn	BN	2165	049294	82
Red Daren	BS	2003	281308	114
Rhobell Fawr	AG	2408	787257	66
Tal-y-fan	CA	2001	729727	217
Tomle	BN	2431	085336	81
Twmpa	BS	2263	225350	112
Twyn Tal-y-cefn	BS	2303	222324	110
Waen Camddwr	AN	2035	848207	34
Waun Fach	BS	2660	215300	102
Waun-oer	DY	2197	785148	243
Waun-rydd	BB	2522	061208	143
Y Gyrn	BB	2010	989216	133
Yr Elen	CA	3152	673651	199

LIST OF LAKES

Lake	Group	Height (ft)	Map Ref
Anafon	CA	1625	698698
Aran	CI	1580	734139
Arenig Fach	AG	1500	828417
Arenig Fawr	AG	1326	846380
Bach	AN	2500	837196
Carw	CR	1750	856612
Cau	CI	1540	715124
Cerrigllwydion Isaf	CR	1650	844700
Cerrigllwydion Uchaf	CR	1650	840693
Cowlyd	CA	1200	727624
Creiglyn Dyfi	AN	1900	868226
Cwm Llwch	BB	1910	002220
Cyri	CI	1150	657118
Du	CR	1755	800698
Dulyn	CA	1750	700667
Dywarchen	AG	1400	763420
Egnant	CR	1400	793670
Eigiau	CA	1225	720650
Foel-Dinas	DY	1400	850146
Ffynnon Caseg	CA	2460	679650
Ffynnon Lloer	CA	2165	662622
Ffynnon Llugwy	CA	1800	693628
Ffynnon Llyffant	CA	2800	688646
Fyrddon-fach	CR	1755	797701
Fyrddon-fawr	CR	1755	800707
Grwyne Fawr	BS	1634	230308
Gwngu	CR	1450	839729
Gynon	CR	1400	800647
Hesgyn	AG	1400	885443
Hir	CR	1400	789676
Isaf	CR	1600	803758
Lliwbran	AN	1475	876255
Lluncaws	BN	1900	071317
Melynllyn	CA	2100	702657
Nameless	AG	2200	825355
Nameless (2)	AN	2820	866243
Nameless (2)	AN	2820	865241
Nameless (2)	AN	2460	860215
Nameless	AN	2390	873213
Nameless	CR	1850	926603
Nameless	CR	1800	809765
Nameless	CR	1400	789669

Nameless	CR	1350	779678
Nameless	CI	2053	706112
Pen-aran (2)	AN	2750	868247
Serw	AG	1475	780428
Teifi	CR	1350	785675
Uchaf	CR	1625	803762
Y Coryn	CA	1300	731591
Y Fign	AN	2500	837194
Y Figyn	CR	1600	812704
Y Gadair	CI	1820	708136
Y Gafr	CI	1325	711141
Y Gorlan	CR	1400	787669

Printed by CARNMOR PRINT & DESIGN
95-97 LONDON ROAD, PRESTON, LANCASHIRE, UK.